MY LIFE IN FOOTBALL

MY LIFE IN FOOTBALL

Trevor Brooking
with Michael Hart

**SIMON &
SCHUSTER**

London · New York · Sydney · Toronto · New Delhi

A CBS COMPANY

First published in Great Britain by Simon & Schuster UK Ltd, 2014
A CBS COMPANY

1 3 5 7 9 10 8 6 4 2

Simon & Schuster UK Ltd
222 Gray's Inn Road
London
WC1X 8HB

www.simonandschuster.co.uk

Simon & Schuster Australia, Sydney
Simon & Schuster India, New Delhi

A CIP catalogue record for this book
is available from the British Library

ISBN: 978-1-47113-044-1
Ebook ISBN: 978-1-47113-046-5

Typeset in the UK by M Rules
Printed and bound by CPI Group (UK) Ltd, Croydon, CR0 4YY

To Mum and Dad. who believed in me.

And to Ron Greenwood and John Lyall,
who encouraged me to believe in myself.

CONTENTS

CONTENTS

CHAPTER I

WHY I JOINED THE FA

I WAS WONDERING WHAT to do with the rest of my life when the Football Association called me at home one morning in the autumn of 2003. It was a few weeks after my 55th birthday. Alan Pardew had just taken over as manager of West Ham so my caretaker role there had finished. My Sport England commitment was over and although I had a small book-binding business, Colbrook, it ran very successfully without my presence every day. I remained a non-executive director at West Ham but, in truth, that wasn't going to occupy a great deal of my time. 'What are you actually going to do with yourself?' asked David Davies, the FA's executive director.

He told me they were thinking of creating a new position at the FA. They thought that I had the kind of experience that made me an ideal candidate for the job. Apart from my football background, I'd had more than ten years as chairman of the Eastern Region of the Sports Council and a further four years as chairman of Sport England – jobs that gave me a deep insight into the worlds of sports politics, administration and the development of young talent.

This wide range of experience clearly appealed to Mark Palios, the new FA chief executive. 'Mark asked me to call,' David told me on the phone that day. 'He'd like to meet you.' So a few days later I met David Davies and Mark Palios in the quiet conference room of a west London hotel. I'd known David for some years. Sir Bert Millichip, the former FA chairman, had lured him to the FA to oversee media matters. As a former BBC TV correspondent he had a lot of media experience and my own role at the BBC meant I had regular contact with him when England were on the road. The BBC were one of the few organisations usually given access to the England team hotel at home and abroad.

Although I knew Mark Palios had enjoyed a long playing career at Tranmere Rovers and Crewe Alexandra I couldn't remember ever meeting him. His appointment at the FA had been warmly received by most because, since his playing days, he had established himself in the world of finance and, at that time, his kind of expertise was desperately needed in the FA offices in Soho Square. I liked Mark from our first meeting. We got on well. He asked if I could remember when we had played against each other in the seventies. I couldn't. 'Obviously I didn't make much of an impression on you,' he smiled.

He was right, though; we *had* played against each other. In September 1974 West Ham were lucky to survive a League Cup visit to Tranmere. Mark played in their midfield. The game ended goalless thanks largely to the heroics of the young West Ham goalkeeper Mervyn Day. In the replay a week later Mark again wore the number eight shirt in a Tranmere team that included a tricky 19-year-old winger called Steve Coppell. This time West Ham won 6-0 at Upton Park – Bobby Gould scoring a hat-trick – but eventually succumbed to an all-too-familiar defeat at Craven Cottage in the next round. I scored that night but Bobby Moore had the pleasure of leading Fulham to a 2-1 victory, interrupted by a floodlight failure, against his old team-mates.

It was obvious from the outset that if I accepted the FA's offer I would have to get along with Mark. We would need to have a sound working relationship. Although the job title was undecided, they wanted someone to oversee the development of the game from grass-roots level upwards. I was to be given total control of coaching and development at all levels of the game. I would be responsible for putting a coaching structure in place and I would also have a role in identifying future England managers and the development teams below that.

Mark explained that he was looking for someone with a credible reputation in football to work across the board. The 'credibility' factor was important to him because he thought it might be difficult for him to get too deeply involved in some of the issues occupying the senior international team at that time. One of the most contentious episodes that autumn involved Rio Ferdinand. Mark hadn't been in the job long when Rio failed to take a scheduled drugs test. Rio was the world's most expensive defender and his profile with Manchester United and England meant that he was a role model for many children.

Rio said that he had simply forgotten about the drugs test and left United's Carrington training ground that day to go shopping. It was a big story that season, and in the days immediately before England's European Championship qualifier in Turkey there was speculation that David Beckham and the team might actually go on strike in support of Rio! Mark had made it clear when he took the job that he cherished honesty, sportsmanship and high standards of discipline and behaviour, so the Ferdinand case inevitably became one of the first big tests of his leadership.

The FA appointed an independent tribunal that found Rio guilty of misconduct, banned him for eight months and fined him £50,000. Manchester United appealed on Rio's behalf, describing the sentence as 'savage and unprecedented', but the punishment was upheld. The decision generated a lot of ill feeling among senior players, particularly Rio's United team-mates in the England squad. Rio would not appear in the England team again until October 2004.

Mark knew that the fallout from this episode might make some elements of his role difficult, especially those directly involving the players, and he wanted me to be involved with the national teams. He wanted to focus on the financial side of an organisation that clearly required his specialist skills in budget restructuring. He also wanted to raise the stature of the governing body and improve the infrastructure and leadership team at Soho Square. From the football point of view, he wanted me to look at the technical side. Were we doing it right? Could we do it better? Les Reed, an ex-professional with extensive coaching experience, had been acting technical director since the departure of Howard Wilkinson. Mark wanted someone with a wider brief to take an overview of the game from the elite level down to the grass roots.

We knew that my lack of up-to-date coaching qualifications might become an issue. I had taken the FA coaching badges as a player at West Ham years before but these had now been super-seded by the UEFA licensing system. Sure enough, the fact that I didn't have modern qualifications was quickly pounced upon by one or two mischievous individuals in the professional game when the FA announced my appointment. My proposed role didn't actu-ally involve any coaching – either of players or coaches. But some argued that I might have influence over who would be appointed to these roles in the future. So, in a sense, it was rather like a direc-tor of football role at a big club. If you're the director of a club you don't have to be a holder of the full pro licence to appoint a coach, do you? The important thing, surely, was to get in the right people to deliver the right coaching philosophy.

The prospect, as presented by the FA, excited me. It was an

interesting challenge and, of course, very flattering to be offered such an opportunity. When I went home that evening I outlined the plans to my wife Hilkka. A few weeks earlier we had been talking about the prospect of my taking the West Ham management job for the season. She thought it would be very stressful. I wasn't too worried about the pressures on me, but I suspected that it would be stressful for the family. When I finished with Sport England at the end of 2002, Hilkka asked me what I was planning to do with my time. 'I don't want you under my feet all day,' she said. 'Why don't you go and get a proper job?'

It became a source of amusement to us. I had time on my hands, more than at any other stage in my career. I was getting my golf handicap down but, apart from two spells as caretaker manager at West Ham, there had been little to occupy me on a daily basis. The FA job meant going from one extreme to the other. If I accepted I would be based in an office in Soho, central London. I would be expected at my desk most days by around 9am. If I took the job I would become a commuter for the first time in my life.

I still had eight months of my broadcasting contract with the BBC to run and although I hadn't discussed this with the FA I knew it would become an issue. I could hardly be on the FA payroll and sit in a BBC commentary position saying of the England manager: 'Sorry, Sven, but I think you've got this one wrong.' I couldn't offer an impartial assessment if I was on the staff at the FA. People would wonder whether I was voicing a personal opinion or whether my view was perhaps based on inside knowledge or some recent private conversation with the manager.

The other issue I had to address involved my directorship at West Ham. Although at the time the FA had many committeemen involved with clubs – David Dein at Arsenal and Noel White at Liverpool were just two examples – none of those individuals was on the full-time staff at the FA. There could be no conflict of interests, so I knew that my commitments to West Ham and the BBC would both have to be terminated. I talked all this over with my wife and our children, Collette and Warren. The kids felt that it was a fantastic compliment. 'Dad, it's a chance to make an impact, to put something back into the game and leave a legacy,' they said. 'You can't say no.'

Put like that, how could I turn it down? I had a second meeting with the FA, this time at the offices in Soho Square. We discussed details like the contract and my starting date. They had to put this new development in front of the appropriate FA committee for ratification and I suspected that, within a short time of doing this, news would leak out. I wanted to inform the BBC and West Ham of my intentions before this happened.

There was no real agonising over the decision for me. The FA was offering something entirely new. I wanted the challenge the job offered. Yes, I'd always enjoyed broadcasting and, after nearly 20 years with the BBC, they were keen to extend my contract. The punditry role had been important to me as a second career. It meant that I had retained an involvement in football without going into management or coaching. I was lucky to get that option at the time. I was one of the first ex-players to be offered that kind of role at the BBC, but today TV and radio have become something of a cottage industry for footballers at the end of their playing careers.

Hilkka liked the idea of me joining the FA. She was never keen on me going into club management. She liked where we lived and always wanted to stay in the area. A career in club management, she argued, would almost certainly involve uprooting the family at some stage and neither of us would have wanted to interrupt the children's education. They were settled at school.

I talked privately to Gary Lineker about the offer. 'It's a job made for you, Trevor,' he said. 'You must take it.' I knew it was going to be a bit of a wrench leaving the BBC, but I suspected it would be an even bigger wrench leaving West Ham, the club I first joined as a young apprentice in July 1965. It was my club and I felt a commitment. That's why I was happy to help out in a caretaker management role when Glenn Roeder was taken seriously ill with just three matches remaining at the end of season 2002–03. I filled in again when the club sacked him just three matches into the new season. It was going to be a critical year. It had been a traumatic few months for them and I felt very much part of the club and wanted to help them bounce back to the Premiership. I helped identify the new manager, Alan Pardew, who was previously in charge at Reading, and although I was certain he was the right man for the job he had to wait eight games for his first win.

I had a good working relationship with Alan, but I felt that by moving away from the club I would actually help him. I was still travelling to the away games and often fans would come up to me and say: 'We all wanted you to stay in charge, Trev.' This was flattering, of course, but it was also embarrassing. I thought that by distancing myself from the club at that moment I would help Alan emerge as the undisputed boss in his own right. You couldn't hide the fact that I'd already done the job twice with some modest success and that if anything went wrong under Alan I would be the convenient option. The FA approach was timely in as much as it took me out of that equation.

It wasn't easy for Alan in the early weeks. Some supporters were still asking me to help out with the coaching and team selection, but I was trying to detach myself from West Ham. I hoped the fans would accept that and realise that I wouldn't be going back. I had no desire to be manager on a full-time basis. The club chairman, Terry Brown, was very understanding. He knew that from a football point of view it was an offer that I couldn't turn down. He wished me luck, gave me six seats in the directors' box for life and told me that if it didn't work out I would always be welcomed back.

I started at the FA in the first week of January 2004. Collette and Warren, both of whom were used to commuting to London, found it very funny that their dad, at the age of 55, finally had a day job like everyone else. They kept asking me if I found the travelling tiring. I soon realised that the journey from Shenfield in Essex to Soho Square in central London was easier the earlier I left home. I quickly slipped into a routine that got me to the office around 8.30. People who recognised me were always amazed to see me on the train with the commuter crowd. I'd try to bury my head in a book or paper but there was always someone who'd ask: 'What are you doing here?'

For the first couple of months I was in the office practically every day while I tried to get to know people and understand the roles they had at the FA. My personal assistant, Emma Kernan-Staines, was enormously helpful in guiding me through the early basics of office life. She introduced me to the delights of the laptop and something called a BlackBerry. But after several months I still hadn't sent an e-mail. I preferred the telephone – and still do.

I discovered that the FA was an organisation in a period of transition. They'd had a traumatic 12 months of uncertainty and cost-cutting. I sensed that the staff felt a bit battered and lacking in confidence. Everyone was worried about their job. But, without exception, they welcomed me to Soho Square. They were very supportive even though they realised that I had been brought in to change the direction of certain departments. Quite naturally, many wanted to know how my presence would affect them in the long term. The FA hierarchy hoped that I would act as a unifying influence between the traditional amateur-based committee system and the professional game.

The FA is one of the world's great sporting bodies. Founded by 11 clubs in 1863, the fact that the FA is now known around the world as simply *the* Football Association demonstrates the global status and reputation of the football world's oldest ruling organisation. The three lions on the FA badge remain emotive and iconic and still carry weight, especially at grass-roots level in developing countries. As a newcomer, walking through the glass-fronted lobby of the offices in Soho Square, I got an immediate sense of the importance of the place. They gave me an office on the fourth floor. Sven's office was on the same floor. At the time they had a staff of about 250 people, all, in one way or another, guardians of the game of football.

The man with the highest profile on the payroll was, of course, Sven-Goran Eriksson, the England team manager. I'd met him before and found him charming company, knowledgeable and willing to listen. He was very positive about my new role. The FA had sounded him out before approaching me and I found his support encouraging. The good news, from my point of view, was that he had decided to extend his contract for a couple more years. This helped the decision-making process in other areas because it gave some medium-term stability. I was pleased when they eventually announced that he had decided to stay until 2008. It meant that I could sit down with him, get some idea of his plans and see how I could make a significant contribution on the development side.

My title at the FA was Director of Football Development. Mark said that the FA board no longer liked the title of Technical Director. For them, apparently, it suggested an employee who was all-powerful. Initially, my role would largely involve the grass roots of the game and was therefore different. So Director of Football Development was agreed because it reflected a wider role, rather than one involving just the elite teams. The truth was that, for me, the grass-roots participation was the attraction of the job. I had many views on sport at this level and, in my role at the Sports Council, had frequently voiced my opinions about the decline in competitive sport at schools and the loss of playing fields. Football was the nation's biggest and most popular sport and I felt that things had to improve at grass-roots level. I thought that, given time, I could make a difference, not just on the playing field but perhaps off it too. Sport has a part to play in establishing role models and promoting good standards of behaviour, particularly among the young and impressionable.

There were other issues for me to look at in the short term. English football had barely progressed in 20 years. In my opinion the technical quality in many areas of the English game was unacceptable. In the elite section we had several national coaches and a technical director, and one of my first tasks was to assess whether we needed all of them. Did we need national teams at all the age groups from 16 to 21, and was the playing style and structure appropriate?

I was asked to examine the strengths and weaknesses of the 'coaching education' structure but, at the time, was unaware of the sensitivities involved. In reality, elite player development was in the hands of the Premiership and Football League clubs, and Howard Wilkinson, the former FA technical director, had been frustrated by the politics that stalked him throughout his reign. He had put a ten-year plan in place called the 'Charter for Quality'. This allowed professional clubs access to the most talented youngsters aged from nine to 18. The clubs felt schoolboy football had deteriorated significantly and they wanted control of the development of the best young players. I came in after five years of the Charter for Quality and the FA felt it was a timely moment to review it. After all, nothing in the modern game is going to survive ten years.

As a result of my review I came to the conclusion that the overall youth development system was flawed, with no proper quality assurance of work programmes, few decent facilities, no verified coaching qualifications and insufficient financial accountability. There seemed to be little agreement on the development of players, or even on how our teams should play. Howard Wilkinson, for instance, was a coach of huge experience whose Leeds United team had won the League Championship in 1992, the last before the introduction of the Premiership. He favoured an international playing system that involved four at the back and a little triangle in front, with two players wide and one at the top of the triangle. This was very similar to the Dutch system and he believed that was how our youngsters should be taught to play the game.

But Sven, the England manager, was locked into a conventional 4-4-2 system. He believed that was the way to play. Me? I thought, 'Why have a set or rigid system?' Surely it depends on the players available and their individual strengths. But is there any logic in having, say, your senior team playing a set system and your Under-21 team adopting a completely different style? There was a lot to consider, not least the personalities involved. Sven didn't get along with Howard Wilkinson. The Under-21 coach David Platt, the former England captain, wasn't close to Les Reed, the coach responsible for the Under-20s and the younger groups. When I arrived David and Les would barely even speak to each other.

This was what I inherited. So, on my first day, when I sat down in a little Soho café to enjoy my lunchtime tuna baguette and caffè latte, I knew that there would be plenty of challenges ahead.

CHAPTER 2

'PLEASE, SIR,
CAN I TAKE IT?'

As those of a certain vintage will recall I learned the basics of my trade – and indeed the finer points, too – on a large field alongside the main London–Norwich railway line at Chadwell Heath. This was the home of the West Ham training ground. Most of the local boys with dreams of becoming footballers would at some stage pass through this green oasis in the east London suburbs. There are too many to list them all but if I mention Bobby Moore, Martin Peters and Geoff Hurst from my early days at West Ham and players like Rio Ferdinand, Frank Lampard and Michael Carrick from the modern era you get some idea of the quality that has emerged from Chadwell Heath over the years.

Ron Greenwood was the man who turned my dreams into a reality but it was my father, Henry Charles Brooking, who had instilled in me the work ethic and discipline that were to prove so essential in the early years of my career. My parents – 'Harry' and Margaret to everyone who knew them – came from the East End of London. They met in their teens while working in a Co-op store and my father later joined the Metropolitan Police. He served for 26 years, before retiring at the rank of sergeant, and then worked as a school attendance officer for the Greater London Council.

He was, in fact, fortunate to survive the Second World War. One night during the Blitz he was on duty at the police station when a bomb fell on a nearby pub. He rushed to the scene with a fireman but as they approached another bomb fell, killing six people including the fireman. My dad survived but was seriously injured and required several operations to remove fragments of glass from his head. He eventually made a full recovery but it was a slow process. Glass shards were still being removed from his head years later.

I was born in Upney Lane Hospital on 2 October 1948 and at the age of five was sent to Ripple School, a 15-minute walk from our two-up, two-down terrace with an outside toilet in Barking. Each morning, my elder brother Tony, who was to follow Dad into the police force, and I ran to school, kicking a tennis ball against the garden fences as we went. Preventing the rebound from ricocheting off the fence into the road was an early lesson in ball control.

My first teacher, though, was my dad. An aggressive, uncompromising centre-half in the local police team, Dad used to encourage Tony and me to practise with both feet in the back garden or over the park. He would throw the ball at my 'bad' foot – the left – for hours at a time, until I was equally adept with both feet. He did the same with my brother. I was about four when he started doing this. It is so much easier to adopt good habits at an early age. Kicking with one foot only can quickly become a habit, a bad one from the footballer's point of view.

My brother and I used to spend hours playing together, climbing over the spiked railings to use the pitches at the South-East Essex Technical College. We invented competitions in the back garden when we'd use only our weaker foot. We had two drainpipes running down the back wall of the house and we'd 'pass' a tennis ball against the wall between the pipes as many times as we could. We were allowed only one touch each time the ball came off the wall. I could do it easily with my right foot and worked to improve my left until that was just as good.

By the time I was playing professionally I was generally regarded as a left-footed specialist. Nothing could be further from the truth. I am naturally right-footed but it was my father's diligence and patience in the garden that turned me into a player equally proficient with either foot.

I was about eight when a teacher at Ripple School – Mr Clarke – spotted me kicking a tennis ball around in the playground. He asked me if I had any football boots. 'Yes, sir, but they're at home,' I replied. 'Run home and get them,' he said. 'I want you to play in a school trial this afternoon.'

I've never forgotten the role Mr Clarke played in my early development. Many years later, when I'd retired from the professional game, I used to run a couple of soccer schools during the summer holidays in Redbridge and Brentwood. I was absolutely delighted one day when who should turn up but Mr Clarke with his grandson. I hadn't seen him for years but I recognised him immediately.

Although I was a couple of years younger than most of the rest of our school team, I must have made a good impression on Mr Clarke in my first trial game because I was selected for the next match. Happily we won. When we were leading 2-1 the referee awarded us a penalty. Despite being one of the youngest in the team, I said: 'Please, sir, can I take it?' He must have liked my confidence because he let me go ahead. I strolled up to the ball and scored easily. At that age you don't think about it. Years later, when I was about 15, I was asked to take a penalty while playing for Essex Schools against London Schools. It wasn't quite the same this time. The tension was too much for me. I missed it. We lost the match and it was several years before I again took a penalty.

I was ten when my father took me to watch West Ham for the first time. We stood on the North Bank surrounded by other fathers and sons. There was no police presence to speak of and stewarding was minimal. If there was a crush the boys would be handed down to the front over the heads of the adult spectators, and we'd stand there quite happily until our parents picked us up at the end of the match. I can still remember the excitement I felt during my first visit to Upton Park. It was April 1958. Liverpool were the opponents and West Ham were bidding to clinch promotion from the old Second Division and win back a place among the elite of the game after a 26-year absence.

This was the final home game and not surprisingly the crowd of 37,734 was the biggest of the season. Ernie Gregory, Noel Cantwell, Johnny Dick and Vic Keeble were the among the star names, but on the day it was a thunderbolt shot from full-back John Bond that gave West Ham a 1-1 draw. A week later they won 3-1 at Middlesbrough and were promoted to the old First Division, where they stayed until 1978.

After that first visit to Upton Park I regularly attended West Ham's home games until my own football commitments at school and district level took priority. Having passed the eleven-plus, I went to Ilford County High School, a grammar school where John Lyall, later to be my manager at West Ham, had been a pupil. It was a good school with high standards and there was little indiscipline among the students, so the cane was used only rarely. Similarly, in those days there were few instances of hooliganism at football matches.

I played for Ilford County High and, while there, was selected for the district Under-13 team. Although originally chosen as a left-half I played at right-back. This upset my father who used to watch all my matches when he could. He made his feelings known and I was moved into midfield where I was to establish myself. I also played for London Schools and Essex and was called into the England Schoolboy squad.

In 1963–64 I was chosen by England as a right-half. But George Luke, a promising youngster from the North-east who had a brief career with Chelsea before moving to South Africa, was preferred in that position for the season's opening match against West Germany at Wembley. I came into the side for the second game against the Germans at Ayresome Park but my performance was far from distinguished. When they reduced the squad from 16 to 15 for a trip to play Northern Ireland in Belfast I was the unlucky one left behind. I was bitterly disappointed. But it was an early taste of the uncertainties of life in football.

To be honest, football as a career hadn't crossed my mind at this stage. It was simply a game I loved to play. I wanted to become as good as I could simply for the enjoyment I got from it. Mind you, at that time it wasn't the glamour industry it was to become. Players' wages had gone through the £100-a-week barrier a few years earlier and the weekly wage in the old First Division was higher than the average working man's salary. But there were no millionaires and even the highest paid, like Fulham's Johnny Haynes who was the first to earn £100 a week, were unlikely ever to attain that kind of status from simply playing football.

I enjoyed watching West Ham and had you asked me if I would like to play for them one day I would probably have said yes. But I didn't seriously think about it as a career until later in my school-days. Although my dad encouraged me to improve as a player I don't think either of my parents would have wanted me to become a professional footballer because it wasn't considered a proper career in those days.

Most young players at that time left school at 15 and signed a three-year contract with a club as an apprentice but my parents were keen for me to continue at school for another year and take my GCE O levels. I had an idea that I might become an account-ant – but others thought differently.

Dick Walker, the Tottenham scout, had been to see me and so had Jimmy Thompson of Chelsea. I'd trained with both clubs with-out indicating to either whether I was serious about a career in football. Millwall were also interested. West Ham? They seemed indifferent, until the manager Ron Greenwood came to see me play for Ilford against Oxford in the quarter-finals of the English Schools Trophy. Wally St Pier, West Ham's renowned scout, was also at the match. Ilford lost 3-2, but I played well. First thing next morning Wally turned up at our house to see my mum and dad. He said that Mr Greenwood had watched me himself and wanted me to sign for West Ham. My mum was unimpressed and quite blunt with him. 'Why has it taken you until now to come round?' she asked him.

I talked it over with my parents. They had mixed feelings, but they suspected that I would always regret it if I didn't try to make the grade. They agreed that I should join West Ham provided I continued with my education so that I had something to fall back on if I failed to establish myself as a footballer.

Tottenham and Chelsea wanted me to sign apprenticeship forms immediately. Tommy Docherty, the Chelsea manager, sent us four complimentary tickets for the West Ham v Preston FA Cup final of 1964. My father returned them because West Ham had already sent us two, for which he paid.

West Ham's willingness to allow me to continue with my stud-ies, plus my schoolboy allegiance to them, meant there was no real decision about which club I would join. I signed as an apprentice at Upton Park in July 1965. By that time I had seven O levels from Ilford County High. I'd failed English language and when I retook it four months later I achieved an A pass! You can't tell me that I'd improved that much in just four months. I often think about that when I read about the controversies surrounding education these days. The degree of difficulty seems to vary between different exam boards and for that reason I think it's often worth persevering by retaking important subjects.

Encouraged by Mr Greenwood, who was one of football's most innovative coaches, I continued my education at West Ham. I did a day-release course in economics and accountancy, took and passed four more O levels and two A levels, and gained a diploma in business studies. I knew football would be a risky career and I thought it was vital to have some qualifications, as insurance.

I didn't want my parents to feel guilty, at some stage in the future, if I failed to make the grade as a footballer. They gave me the chance of a career that was a schoolboy's dream. But we knew there was an element of risk. If I failed, I didn't want them to feel that it had been time wasted. When I was given the opportunity, I knew that I wanted to be a footballer more than I wanted to be an accountant or anything else. But I also knew that if I continued to study I could always look at accountancy or some other profession in the future. I was happy to be a £7-a-week apprentice at West Ham but my mum and dad had encouraged me to have a plan B. It was sound advice.

I found the first few days at West Ham a bit daunting. It's probably the same for any youngster starting a job for the first time. Dressing rooms are full of banter and mickey-taking but I wasn't going to be intimidated. I was quite tall for my age and the fact that I'd always played football, and other sports, with my older brother and his friends meant that I was used to the kind of verbal sparring that goes on among teenagers. Even so, I was a bit overawed when Ron Greenwood introduced me to the other players. I vividly remember meeting Bobby Moore, who was at his peak at the time. He was not only the West Ham captain, but also the England captain. He shook my hand and wished me well.

It quickly became apparent to anyone who watched me on the training pitch that there was nothing I could do with my right foot that I couldn't also do with my left. Even in those early days at West Ham there was no occasion when I was concerned about controlling the ball when it was on its way to me. Whether it was coming at me from my right side or my left side made no difference. Many years later, when I was studying technique and ability levels as Director of Football Development at the FA, I was alarmed at the number of professional players in the modern game who were not comfortable receiving the ball sideways on. This is a horrendous deficit among our midfield and attacking players. I cannot tell you how many of those we selected for England's international teams who were still not good at receiving the ball on the half-turn.

The only area where my left foot was slightly weaker than my right was when driving the ball. I could summon more power driving the ball with my right boot. Apart from that, I could use the inside or outside of either foot with equal confidence, and I could still hit moving balls powerfully with my left foot. But I tended to strike a dead ball with my right.

The goal that everyone seems to remember is the second of the two that I scored for England against Hungary in Budapest in a World Cup qualifying tie in June 1981. I remember it because it was the day of my wedding anniversary but I think the fans remember it because the ball stuck in the stanchion inside the net. It was a moving ball, a pass from Kevin Keegan, and I struck it from distance with my left foot. It was my most spectacular goal for England and it so surprised my wife Hilkka, watching at home on TV with my parents, that she told me later: 'I had to look at it twice to make sure it was really you!'

I gave my dad all the credit for that goal. He had encouraged Tony and me and had stressed the importance of being able to kick with both feet. I quickly realised the value of all that he had taught me during those first months on the West Ham training ground. Ron Greenwood was a coach who appreciated players who had a complete mastery of the ball. There were many occasions in the years that followed when I had good reason to be thankful to Dad. I'm sure there were moments before he died – in the week before Christmas 1997 – when he must have watched me play and felt a sense of satisfaction. I owe a huge debt of gratitude to him and my mum. She died 11 months after him. They had been married for 56 years.

They provided a happy and stable home for Tony and me, and our success in life – my brother went on to become a chief inspector in the Metropolitan Police – was undoubtedly due to the care and devotion of our parents. We were comfortable in our terraced house in Barking, but never well off. I remember my mum making Christmas crackers to supplement the family income when we were small children. My dad rode a bicycle until he could finally afford a car. It was a bit of a banger that struggled up hills. I think I was seven or eight when our first TV set arrived in the house. Tony and I didn't watch it much because most evenings and weekends we were outside, playing football or cricket.

A couple of years ago, I addressed a group of 14-year-old girls at an FA Centre of Excellence. I explained to them that young people today have so many more distractions in life than I did when I was their age. 'For a start,' I said, 'you've got seventy or eighty TV channels to watch. When I was a kid we had one.'

I continued talking for a few seconds until a girl put up her hand and said: 'Sorry to interrupt, but do you mean there was only *one* television channel?'

'Yes,' I said. 'BBC, black and white!' There was a collective gasp and they all started chattering among themselves. They could not envisage living in a society that had only one TV channel!

If Tony and I were not playing football we'd be indoors doing our homework, reading the adventures of Roy of the Rovers in *Tiger* comic or playing card games like cribbage with mum and dad. Holidays were spent in a holiday camp at Lowestoft or Yarmouth and occasionally we'd have a day out to Southend. When I became a footballer the family invariably travelled to watch me play. We'd all discuss my performance afterwards. We were close and had a lot of fun as a family and I like to think that Hilkka and I enjoyed the same kind of relationship with our children, Warren and Collette, as they grew up.

My parents made sure we maintained certain standards of behaviour. If my brother or I stepped out of line we'd get a clip round the ear. My dad would give me a look and I'd know straight away, 'Hello, I'd better watch out.' You respected that. It seems to me that some parents nowadays defend their children blindly and let them get away with anything. That's not doing them any favours. It's much the same in some schools. Some teachers find it difficult to discipline children and it's often because they know the parents will side with their wrongdoing offspring.

My years with Sport England gave me plenty of opportunities to witness at first hand the decline in standards of behaviour at schools. Good behaviour, bad behaviour . . . it all starts in the home, of course. All my own personal standards are based on what I learned from my mum and dad. I believe what we had as a family all those years ago is achievable in modern life if you treat your children fairly and firmly and make them understand the difference between right and wrong.

It's rather like learning to control a football. You have to do it at a young age. I used to argue with the Government about sport in schools. You can't begin at 11. You've lost them by that age. You've got to start with them at primary school age. Some primary schools do absolutely nothing for their children in the field of sport. It's much the same with teaching them how to behave properly. I see some parents with children who simply don't know how to behave properly. Had my two kids behaved in the way some youngsters do today, I'd have felt hugely embarrassed and ashamed.

Happily, old-fashioned disciplines still apply at most professional football clubs. Young players are reminded of their responsibilities to behave well and set examples. The rewards are huge for those who are successful, but so are the temptations and distractions. A recent survey discovered, for instance, that 98 per cent of all academy players in the Premier League had Twitter accounts. Quite what it is they think they have to tell the world at that age is beyond me, but it gives some idea of their priorities.

As a young apprentice at West Ham in the mid-sixties, a time when all sorts of new opportunities were presenting themselves to the young, I was careful not to take too much for granted. Yes, I could kick with both feet, but I knew I had a long way to go before the dream of making the big time became a reality.

CHAPTER 3

THOSE BOLEYN BOYS

I WAS INTRODUCED TO the vagaries of professional football as a career in my first week of pre-season training at West Ham. I had signed my apprenticeship papers and was full of youthful optimism, and when I turned up for work I was keen to show what I could do.

The mood at the training ground in Chadwell Heath that July in 1965 was buoyant. Just a few weeks earlier West Ham had won the European Cup Winners' Cup, beating the German side TSV Munich 1860 2-0 in a Wembley final that would come to be regarded as a minor classic. A year earlier, of course, West Ham had qualified for the European competition by beating Preston North End 3-2 in the 1964 FA Cup final.

It was a good time to be at West Ham. Johnny Byrne, a record signing from Crystal Palace, was considered one of the most gifted attacking players in the country. John Sissons, who had become the youngest FA Cup final goalscorer in history in 1964, was a winger of huge potential. Bobby Moore, Geoff Hurst and Martin Peters had still to claim their places in World Cup folklore, but were well-established top-quality players clearly benefiting from the innovative coaching of Ron Greenwood.

There was a sense that West Ham, traditionally a family club of modest ambition, were growing in stature. I don't think anyone expected us to be challenging the might of Tottenham Hotspur, Manchester United or Leeds United but there was a noticeable spring in the step as the players prepared for the coming season. As with all clubs in the weeks before the big kick-off, West Ham organised a press day when the newspaper photographers turned up to take a team picture and then individual shots of all the players. These photographs were catalogued and stored and would appear in the newspapers at regular intervals over the following year.

Alan Sealey was of particular interest to the newspapermen that summer because he had emerged as the unlikely hero of that European win over TSV Munich. 'Sammy the Seal', as he was known, had been in and out of the first team for five seasons, sharing the number seven shirt with Peter Brabrook for much of that time. But he had played in six of the eight European ties that season so it was no surprise when Ron Greenwood picked him to play in the ninth – the final at Wembley.

I was lucky enough to be in the 100,000 crowd that night. It was a thrilling game that drew a TV audience of 30 million from across Europe. West Ham had the better chances but Munich's Yugoslav goalkeeper Petar Radenkovic stood defiant until he was suddenly beaten twice in two minutes – by Alan Sealey.

'Sammy' scored his first, firing home a pass from Ronnie Boyce, in the 69th minute. The West Ham fans were still dancing on the terraces when Radenkovic made his one mistake, failing to reach a difficult cross from Bobby Moore. 'Sammy' was in the right place at the right time to make it 2-0 and secure a unique place for himself in the club's history. Greenwood described it as 'West Ham's greatest win' and, years later, when Bobby Moore was asked to select the most memorable game of his illustrious career he picked this match – not the 1966 World Cup final. 'We had all come through the ranks together,' he said. 'It was like winning the FA Cup with your school team.'

For Greenwood it was the reward for three or four years of hard work, patience and faith in the principles that he tried to instil in his players. He believed that football was a game of beauty and intelligence and that night at Wembley his team showed that he was right.

English football at the time was noted chiefly for its power, aggression and commitment but praise for West Ham poured in from across Europe, congratulating the team on the quality of their passing game. A few months later the Hammers were voted Team of the Year at the BBC *Sportsview* annual awards ceremony.

Greenwood was a celebrated tactician but also gave a lot of thought to his preparation for matches. We knew that our opponents in the final would be either TSV Munich or Torino and when they finished level on aggregate after two legs of the semi final the manager decided to send the entire squad to Zurich to watch the play-off. Can you imagine that happening today? It was a priceless move. The players had to watch the game in open seats in a thunderstorm but they all agreed that the information gleaned from seeing the Germans in action had been of significant benefit when the team faced them in the final.

So, a few short weeks after that memorable night at Wembley, I was on the training pitch rubbing shoulders with the players who had made West Ham only the second English club to win a major European trophy. It was clear that no one was looking forward to the new season with more enthusiasm than our Wembley hero Alan Sealey. He had been married about a week before the final – all his team-mates attended the wedding – and after his success at Wembley he believed he had a great chance of finally pinning down a regular first-team place.

As with a lot of West Ham players in that era, Alan was also a keen cricketer. This, of course, was at a time when the overlap between the football and cricket seasons was minimal, allowing some players to pursue both sports. The West Ham goalkeeper Jim Standen, for instance, played regularly for Worcestershire and was once 12th man for England. Geoff Hurst and Eddie Presland both played for Essex and Ronnie Boyce, Brian Dear and Bobby Moore all played a good standard of club cricket.

This enthusiasm for cricket led to frequent knockabout matches during the lunchtime break in pre-season training. It was all light-hearted stuff until the afternoon when, with the press in attendance, Alan's football career was suddenly thrown into serious doubt. He was fielding at long-on during one of our impromptu cricket matches when someone skied one. 'Sammy' started running to make the catch, his eyes firmly on the ball. Two or three seconds before it happened you could see that he was running into trouble. Other players were shouting to warn him, but he couldn't hear them. 'Sammy' collided with one of the long wooden school forms that had been used by the players to sit on for the team photo shoot.

When he crashed into the long, low bench he broke a leg. He was out of action for 18 months and when he finally returned, in December 1966, he made just four more appearances for West Ham before moving briefly to Plymouth Argyle. He finished his playing career with his local club Romford in the old Southern League.

I remember how deflated we all felt that afternoon when 'Sammy' was taken to hospital. It showed me just how risky and fickle football could be as an occupation. We were all delighted when he recovered and returned to training but it was soon obvious that he was never going to be the player he had been before his accident.

It was a good lesson for me and the other seven youngsters who had signed as apprentices that summer. Only two of us – Frank Lampard senior and myself – had long careers at West Ham but most of the rest stayed in the game in one capacity or another. Roger Cross, for instance, was Geoff Hurst's understudy and the reserve team's top scorer for two seasons. But his first-team opportunities were limited. He made just eight appearances before deciding to move across London to Brentford where he was a first-team regular. He later played for Fulham and Millwall before starting a coaching career that eventually took him back to West Ham, where he served four different managers.

Like so many of the club's players at that time, Roger was a local lad from East Ham. He was one of my pals at the club, along with Bob Glozier, a full-back who captained England Schoolboys. He was also captain of the West Ham team that reached the semi-finals of the FA Youth Cup. We were beaten 2-1 on aggregate by Birmingham City, whose centre-forward Bob Latchford would later play with me in the England team. In those days clubs like West Ham had 50 to 60 players on the staff. The majority would have joined the club as youngsters and, in the case of West Ham, almost all of them were either from London or Essex. Foreign players? They were a rarity. This was before mass immigration, and the Football League's rules about residential qualification meant that few foreigners were able to register with Football League clubs.

Clyde Best, for instance, had arrived here from Bermuda as a 17-year-old and met the residential requirements. But Mordechai Spiegler, a technically gifted midfield player and captain of Israel, was told quite bluntly by the Football League secretary, Alan Hardaker, that he was ineligible to play in England. Ron Greenwood had been impressed by him during the 1970 World Cup in Mexico and invited him to train with us. Mordechai had an encyclopaedic knowledge of English football and one day sat with Jimmy Greaves on the bus taking us to a pre-season training run. Sitting next to the great Greaves must have been a wonderful experience for Mordechai, who talked non-stop about English football all the way to training. Now for Jimmy, football was for playing, not for talking about. When he got off the bus he sidled up to Greenwood and said: 'Don't let sit him next to me again – please!'

Sadly, Mordechai wasn't with us long. But West Ham's interest had put him in the shop window and he moved on to Paris St Germain. Clyde Best, on the other hand, played in the first team for six years and became part of the 'family'. West Ham was a real community club. We had our own patch of east London and for many of the locals the club was the focal point of their lives.

The fans identified strongly with the players and would follow closely the progress of the local lads through the youth ranks. As a young player your route forward was mapped out for you and if you worked hard and ticked the right boxes you would make progress. First, there were two youth teams and all the mundane chores that were part of the apprenticeship in those days, such as sweeping the dressing-room floor and cleaning the senior players' boots ready for training the next morning. It was all part of the learning curve for a young player. Once you had graduated from youth level you were promoted to the Metropolitan League side and then the reserve team that played in the Football Combination. Once you reached reserve-team level you could think about challenging for the first team. I progressed through the youth teams, and it was in the Metropolitan League team that I began to blossom.

The Metropolitan League team was coached by a West Ham loyalist with strong club connections – Jimmy Barrett junior. A local West Ham lad, he played for the club for five years before moving to Nottingham Forest, where he played a big part in their rise to the old First Division. He eventually returned to West Ham as player-manager of the Metropolitan League side, where he was to be an influential figure in my own progress.

In 1945–46 Jim had played in the same West Ham A team as his father, 'Big' Jim Barrett, who at the end of a distinguished playing career had returned to the club to take charge of the A team. 'Big' Jim, born in Stratford in 1907, was a legendary figure at Upton Park, having made a total of 467 first-team appearances between the years 1925 and 1939. Few today will know that one of 'Big' Jim's first games for the club was a schoolboy match against Liverpool in the English Shield final in 1921. The then Duke of York (later King George VI) was among a wall-to-wall crowd of 30,600 that established a new attendance record for Upton Park that day.

Although his later life was beset with ill-health – he died in 1970 at the age of 63 – 'Big' Jim was delighted that his son had carried on the family tradition at West Ham. I was delighted, too. Jim junior was a good coach and, like his boss Ron Greenwood, was happy to try new ideas. I started in what was essentially the third team as a wing-half but after a couple of months Jim decided to try me in a more attacking role in central midfield. This turned out to be a really good move for me. It gave me the freedom I wanted. It was the role that suited me best.

Ernie Gregory, another legendary figure at West Ham, soon took notice. He was coach to the reserve team in the Football Combination. Ernie, 14 years the first-team goalkeeper, retired in 1987 after 51 years as either player or coach at West Ham. His funeral in 2012 attracted probably the biggest turn-out of former West Ham players I've ever seen.

When I first joined West Ham my family were still living in Barking and Ernie would sometimes give me a lift home. When the family moved to Gidea Park I travelled to the training ground at Chadwell Heath on the train or bus, but when I was 17 and had passed my driving test I treated myself to my first car – a Ford Anglia. Ernie was a mine of information and advice and I enjoyed playing in the reserves. You knew you were just one step away from the first team. Fortunately for me, I hadn't been in the reserves long before Mr Greenwood called me to one side and asked if I felt ready for first-team duty. It was Jimmy Barrett junior's decision to switch my role that had fast-tracked me to the first team.

There had already been newspaper speculation about my first-team potential. Vic Railton, the affable cockney football correspondent of the old *London Evening News*, had suggested that '18-year-old Trevor Brooking might make his debut at Burnley'. His information was good. Even so, it was still a surprise. I'd been named in the squad to travel to Turf Moor and, just before the pre-match meal, Mr Greenwood told me that he felt it was the ideal game for me to make my first-team debut. I didn't have long to think about it. 'You're ready,' he said. 'The fact it's away from home makes it a bit easier. It takes a bit of the pressure off you.'

Ron Greenwood always enjoyed taking his team to Burnley. He was born on the outskirts of the town and had first watched football with his dad at Turf Moor. He had a lot of respect for the club and was particularly impressed by their youth development system. For such a small town, surrounded by all the big clubs of Lancashire, they had a wonderful reputation for producing their own players. Most, of course, had to be sold to keep the club alive but it was a formula that worked for them.

At the time they were one of the most accomplished teams in the First Division. League champions in 1960, they were runners-up to Alf Ramsey's Ipswich and beaten FA Cup finalists two years later. They had some really talented individuals, such as Jimmy McIlroy, Willie Morgan, Brian O'Neil and Gordon Harris, and the manager warned me what to expect. He told me he thought that it would be an open, attacking match.

West Ham's start to season 1967–68 had not been encouraging although we had beaten Burnley 4-2 at Upton Park in our second home match. Our visit to Turf Moor produced the same number of goals – six – but this time it ended 3-3. Bobby Moore was at the heart of everything, scoring the first goal of the game and then making two goal-line clearances. By now, of course, Moore, Hurst and Peters were global celebrities, having played such major roles in England's 1966 World Cup triumph.

All three scored on the night of my debut and even though we hadn't won I remember my sense of exhilaration at the end. I was brought in to replace Brian Dear and played wide on the right. I avoided any heroics. I didn't want to make mistakes. I was pleased with my performance and the mood in the dressing room at the end was one of satisfaction. Back then you did well to come away from Turf Moor with a draw.

It was an exhausting introduction to the pace and intensity of first-team football. It was different to what I had become used to in the reserves. In my first 90 minutes among the elite of the English game I finally understood why we had to work so long and hard in training day after day. Players at the highest level not only move quicker, but they think quicker too. The thinking part of the equation was never a problem for me. It was the movement, the pace and particularly the acceleration required that could prove challenging. As a youngster I found the fitness programmes tough, especially in pre-season. I think a lot of young players did. In fact, if I'm honest I'd say that I found pre-season training arduous throughout my career. I didn't shirk anything. It's just that I wasn't built for speed!

Some of my contemporaries would report back for training after the summer break more than a stone overweight. Clyde Best was a classic example. He had the build of a heavyweight boxer but he certainly knew how to relax and enjoy himself once the season was over. His optimum playing weight was somewhere around 13½ stone. We all held our breath when he climbed on the scales at the start of pre-season training. He always returned from Bermuda a bit beefy. But this summer he got married and gained more than two stone. The club put him on a strict diet, forcing him to wear sweat suits whenever he trained. He lost weight but felt weaker. Although he had a career-long battle to keep his weight down he was then the highest profile black player in the English game and in 1971–72 had his best season when he was our top scorer with 23 goals.

Clyde was a hugely popular figure and after six seasons in the first team moved on to play in the United States and for the emerging Feyenoord side in Holland. Later he coached his native Bermuda, was awarded an MBE and was for a while a prison officer on the island. He still visits West Ham from time to time and over the years has clearly found controlling his weight no less a burden.

I enjoyed his company, particularly on our training runs all those years ago when super-fit people like Billy Bonds regularly showed us up. Bill, one of my great friends at West Ham, was sickeningly fit and dominated the cross-country running until a young man called Tony Cottee joined the club. He was as fit as a fiddle and a natural runner. Bill suddenly realised there was a young whipper-snapper in our ranks who wasn't going to be caught. To be fair, Bill was in his mid-thirties by this time. Even when I was fully fit I wasn't close to Bill's level. When we reported back for training each summer he needed only a couple of days' work to be fitter than me.

He never actually realised that I spent far longer running than he did simply because it took me a lot longer to finish. This gave me endurance and Bill never appreciated that fact! I acknowledge that speed was always a bit of a problem, though I was 200 metres champion three years running at school. I would like to have been quicker over the first few yards – and I did try!

Nowadays things are different. No club spends ten days on cross-country running in pre-season. We used to run for miles in Hainault Forest. After about three days we'd have blisters the size of half-crowns, as well as tight thigh muscles and calf strains. By about day four everyone was hobbling before we'd even started running. It's far more scientific today. The top players have individual pre-season training programmes designed to get the best out of them. This even extends to things like diet. Years ago I'd have steak and chips before a match. It was generally accepted that red meat gave you the energy you would need. We now know that red meat takes 24 hours to digest, so everyone eats pasta and salad before a match. Modern sports scientists would have palpitations if we tried to reintroduce the pre-match regimes that existed when I was playing.

I also believe that most of today's professional footballers take better care of themselves during the close season. For the top players the summer break is probably shorter because so many have to report back for lucrative pre-season tours to foreign countries weeks before the Premiership season starts. They cannot afford to let themselves deteriorate during the summer. Most monitor their physical condition during their holiday and get enough exercise to keep ticking over. Some actually report to the training ground and barely stop work, apart from two or three weeks in the sun, once the season ends.

What mattered to me in the early weeks of season 1967–68 was that my level of fitness was good enough for Ron Greenwood. Four days after my debut at Burnley I was retained in the squad even though Brian Dear was fit enough to return to face Manchester United at Upton Park. Matt Busby's great team, rebuilt from the ashes of the Munich air disaster in 1958, were the league's defending champions that autumn.

Their team included some of the club's most famous names –

Bobby Charlton, George Best and Paddy Crerand among them – and although we had the best of the first half neither Geoff Hurst nor Brian Dear could put away the chances that fell to them. With Billy Bonds injured, I was summoned from the substitutes' bench when we were two goals behind. I felt I made some positive contributions but we ended up losing 3-1. Of course, later that season United became the first English club to win the European Cup.

Despite the defeat to United, I'd clearly made enough of an impression to stay in the team. I kept my place for the next three games and particularly enjoyed the 5-1 win at Sunderland when, in the space of three minutes, Peters, Hurst and Harry Redknapp all scored. I had to wait until December for my first goal but then, like London buses, they came along in clusters. We were 2-0 down to Leicester City at Upton Park on Boxing Day when Brian Dear rounded Peter Shilton to spark an epic fightback. Brian scored a hat-trick and I got the other one in a 4-2 win.

In those days clubs played each other twice over the holiday period and four days later we met Leicester again. I scored in another 4-2 win – our first at Filbert Street since 1948. Manchester United were our first opponents of 1968. A crowd of 59,516 squeezed into Old Trafford and saw Bobby Charlton celebrate his 400th league game with a goal from 25 yards. Brian Dear created my equalising goal but we lost 3-1.

Early in February I scored twice in a 7-2 win against Fulham. Bobby Robson, later to be England manager, was in charge at Fulham. It was his first big job in management and ended in relegation to the Second Division. I scored again in a bitterly fought 1-1 draw with Arsenal – my former youth team-mate Frank Lampard set up the chance – but it was in the next game that I really made it into the headlines.

On a sunny afternoon, Newcastle – whose striker Bryan 'Pop' Robson would later become a close friend and team-mate – came to Upton Park with ambitions of finishing in the top four or five in the First Division. They had a good team, with players like the prolific goalscorer Robson, the Wales striker Wyn Davies, and the experienced Frank Clark at left-back and Bobby Moncur at centre-back.

Moncur, the Newcastle captain, marked me and, with Geoff Hurst absent, thought he was going to have a comfortable afternoon. Geoff was injured and Ron Greenwood had asked me to play his role at the front of our attack. Bobby thought he had little to fear from a 19-year-old. He was wrong. I scored my first goal from Harry Redknapp's free kick in the 25th minute. I scored my second in the 64th minute and completed my hat-trick with a sweet volley in the 75th minute. Johnny Sissons weighed in with two more goals to give us a 5-0 win.

I was delighted with my first hat-trick. It took my tally for the season to nine goals. There was a lot of back-slapping in the dressing room afterwards. I was allowed to keep the match ball. The rest of the lads signed it for me and I took it home and presented it to my mum and dad. For years it sat on top of the TV in the lounge. These days it's a bit shrivelled but I'm sure if I were to search I'd find it in the loft of my house – a treasured memento of my one and only hat-trick in professional football.

CHAPTER 4

THE TURNING POINT

IN JUNE 1970 THE AMERICANS were bombing the Ho Chi Minh trail, Ted Heath was securing a surprise general election victory for the Conservatives, Tony Jacklin was winning the US Open and Bobby Moore was about to face Brazil in the World Cup in Mexico having just been accused of the theft of a bracelet in Colombia.

Me? I was about to be married. On 6 June, 24 hours before Moore, Hurst and Peters lost 1-0 to Brazil, I walked up the aisle with a pretty blonde Finnish girl called Hilkka and said 'I do!' I was 21. Hilkka was working as an au pair in Golders Green. We'd known each other for two years. I met her at my brother Tony's wedding to Ritva, another Finnish girl.

Ron Greenwood always advised his young players to get married because he felt it gave them a sense of responsibility and kept them out of the pubs and discos. But that wasn't the reason I married Hilkka! I chatted with her at my brother's wedding but it took me three months to pluck up the courage to ask her for a date. She made me suffer for my apparent indifference by replying that she was too busy in the foreseeable future.

Eventually we met and I took her out in my car. Negotiating the busy streets of central London was not easy for someone who had not been driving for long, but I did my best to impress. I drove her to the cinema to watch Stanley Baker in *Robbery*, the story of the Great Train Robbery. I loved the film, and afterwards took Hilkka to the Golden Egg, a restaurant in Oxford Street, for dinner.

It is possible that she wasn't overly taken with my choice of eatery. She certainly hadn't been impressed by my choice of movie. 'Why did we have to see a film like that?' she asked. 'Well,' I replied, 'I didn't know how the evening was going to unfold so I thought that at least I'd enjoy the film!'

It wasn't the most sophisticated of evenings. But something must have made an impression. We started seeing each other regularly and within eight months were engaged. Her mother had died when she was young but most of Hilkka's family came over from Finland for the wedding. My brother was best man and Billy Bonds and Harry Redknapp were among the guests on our very special day. Our children, Collette and Warren, are both grown up of course and our grandchildren, Harry and Amy, are a constant source of joy who will continue to give us much happiness in the future.

Over the years Hilkka grew to appreciate my unassuming nature and generosity of spirit, qualities that I discovered were not always helpful on the football pitch. As my career at West Ham developed it began to occur to me that taking a back seat was not always the best option. It was my nature to sit quietly in the background and as a young player I was always happy to pass the ball to someone else rather than take the initiative and use my talent to express myself as an individual.

My role up until now had been essentially to give the ball to someone more experienced than me and, deep down, I still wondered whether I would make the grade at the highest level. I had been in and out of the first team for two or three seasons and found playing in the reserves in front of a couple of hundred spectators a bleak and frustrating experience.

These are the moments in a fledgling career when you sink or swim as a young player. These are the moments when you discover whether you have the mental strength to overcome problems and disappointments. Obviously I had the support of my family but when you go to take a throw-in and someone in the crowd hurls insults at you, your confidence can dip. I realised, watching players like Billy Bonds and Bobby Moore, that you had to have total confidence in your own ability otherwise you would crumble. Looking back, I would probably have benefited from some help in this area but, in the end, I sorted it out myself.

Years later, when I was deeply involved in the development of young players at the FA, there were times when I recalled my own experiences as a young professional trying to get a foothold in the team. Today the monitoring of young players is far more sophisticated. The Premier League, for instance, called upon the expertise of a Belgian company called Foot Pass, which specialises in auditing football talent development systems. Having done a lot of work for the Bundesliga academies, they were asked to do the same job in England. They produce a quality evaluation based on relevant and objective criteria that demonstrate the strengths and weaknesses of a club's youth training schemes. The four areas they look at are: technical, physiological, social and psychological.

I had recognised, during my time at the Sports Council, that coaching quality varied in different sports but many of the more discerning sports focused on the 'four-corner' model. This was something we strengthened during our expansion of football development at the FA and in recent years the Elite Player Performance Plan was introduced at professional clubs, with a significant increase in the funding of youth development.

Of the four areas we worked at, my own enthusiasm focused initially on improving the technical ability, but I soon came to realise the importance of the other areas. For example, the biggest failing among young English players was found to be in the psychological domain. I was surprised, but the Belgian company's audit discovered that the biggest gap between us and some of the other big European nations was in the confidence factor. You have to be mentally strong to succeed. If you are going to be among the best in football, in any sport in fact, you have to believe in your own ability. I convinced myself that I was good enough to make the grade, but there were plenty of challenges along the way.

When I chipped an ankle bone against Nottingham Forest in December 1969 I lost my place in the first team and, by the time I'd recovered, West Ham had invested £90,000 in Peter Eustace from Sheffield Wednesday. He was similar to me in playing style. He was not a defensive player and I knew there was little prospect of us both being in the team together. He was a creative two-footed midfield player and, as the club had just sold Martin Peters to Tottenham, he clearly felt that he'd been given the opportunity to succeed the World Cup hero as a first-team regular. I was on the sidelines for about two months, during which time Peter established himself in the team.

It was a depressing period for me. I seriously asked myself whether I wanted to continue with my football career. Even when fully fit I seemed to be sharing my first-team role with a handful of other players. Five of us were in a similar situation – me, Harry Redknapp, Bobby Howe, Jimmy Lindsay and Peter Bennett. We were fighting for two places. The other nine seemed to be safe regardless of the results. If we lost, the five of us always knew the outcome. 'One of us will get the blame for this,' we'd tell each other. We were rotated.

Ron Greenwood didn't like confrontation, particularly when it came to his established big-name players. When we lost, he found it easier to leave out the younger players if he wanted to make changes. Peter Bennett would have a run of three or four games, then me, then Harry. Then we'd be out. We wouldn't know we'd been dropped until the day of the game. You wouldn't know until you saw the team sheet pinned on the wall. I thought that was terrible and never forgot it. Years later, when I had two brief spells as caretaker manager at West Ham, I always made sure that the players knew whether they were in the team. Those left out might not agree with the decision but to my way of thinking it was important to be honest and tell them why they hadn't been picked.

I was just drifting along so I went to see the manager to discuss my future. I told him I wasn't happy. In those days when you played in the reserve team it meant your bonuses were smaller. At home, we were struggling financially. Hilkka worked for the first five years of our married life because we were short of money. I remember her telling me one day that she'd had to hide in the bathroom when the window cleaner called for his money because she didn't have enough to pay him.

Ron Greenwood listened sympathetically to my case, offered some advice and some criticism, and suggested that I should be more aggressive on the pitch and get more involved in matches. He pointed out that, for someone of my size, I got knocked off the ball far too easily. I hadn't been conscious of this. He made the same point in training in front of my team-mates one day. 'It's a bad habit that you should get out of your system,' he said. 'You're like the carpet man – you're always on the floor.' Typical of footballers, I was suddenly given a new name – Cyril. This stuck for a while and came about because of a TV advert proclaiming Cyril Lord 'the carpet king'. He made his fortune selling carpets in the sixties.

The only explanation I could offer for this 'habit' of mine was the fact that I had a long stride and was perhaps off balance more than I should have been when running at full tilt. I watched and learned from other players and tried hard to lean into tackles when a challenger came at me. Although I fell a lot I was rarely accused of diving. If I was playing in today's game I would probably be awarded plenty of penalties.

The only time I remember being accused of diving was some years later when Tony Grealish, the Republic of Ireland international, clipped my ankle as I was running into the Luton Town penalty area. I took a couple more strides before falling and we were awarded a penalty. David Pleat, the Luton manager, claimed afterwards that I had dived. I hadn't. Tony's attempt to knock the ball away was just enough to tip me off balance. I don't agree with diving. I don't agree with any attempt to deceive the referee.

I had just grown accustomed to cries of 'Here, Cyril!' when we went on an end-of-season tour to the United States, where I was given a new nickname – once again, it did little to flatter my ego. While based in Baltimore we went to see a really good baseball team called the Baltimore Orioles. They had a big star in their ranks who was a renowned hitter of home runs. His name was 'Boog' Powell.

A bulky individual, 'Boog' could hit the ball for miles, but when he started to run he could barely reach second base. His running speed could best be described as leisurely. Of course, the lads immediately spotted the resemblance. 'He's about as quick as you, Cyril,' they chuckled. From that day I was known as 'Boog'. Even now, when I meet Billy Bonds, he'll greet me with, 'Boog, how are you?'

The baseball aficionados among you will know that John Wesley 'Boog' Powell was a major league first baseman for the Orioles, the

Cleveland Indians and LA Dodgers. These days he runs his own restaurant in Baltimore – Boog's Barbecue. He's 6ft 4in and at his peak weighed nearly 17 stone. Of the many cruelties inflicted on me by team-mates at Upton Park few matched the day they likened my pace to that of 'Boog' Powell!

The other thing I remember in particular from that trip to the States was having my first taste of Scotch. I never touched alcohol. It wasn't a moral thing. I just never liked the taste of anything I tried. I like Coke and still do. During our time away, Peter Bennett's wife had a baby. All the lads met to have a drink and toast the new arrival.

We had an uncompromising Scottish centre-half called John Cushley with us. Ron Greenwood had signed him from Glasgow Celtic for £25,000 to strengthen our defence. John liked a drink and after he'd had a few he wasn't a man you could reason with. He refused to allow me to wet the baby's head with a Coke. I had to have a Scotch and ginger ale.

Because of my aversion to alcohol many people thought I'd been brought up in a teetotal household. That isn't true. My mum and dad both had a drink from time to time. It wasn't taboo in my family. My mum liked a glass of sherry and my dad enjoyed a pint of beer. I tried but discovered early in life that it wasn't for me. I remember some of my young team-mates trying to lace my Coke, but I could always tell. I understand the pleasure drink gives other people; I'm not precious about it – I just prefer a Coke or a cup of tea.

Those summer trips to the States, introduced by Ron Greenwood shortly after he took over as manager in 1961, were an essential part of the team-building process and, in the days before West Ham qualified for European competition, provided vital experience against club sides from Brazil, Mexico, Germany and Italy. The manager believed that the knowledge gained on those trips was priceless. I don't think it was any coincidence that West Ham won the European Cup Winners' Cup at the first attempt. I don't think they would have achieved that without the experience of playing those foreign sides in America.

Apart from the experience of playing against foreign teams, I learned the importance of keeping yourself occupied on long trips away from home. Years later, of course, I had many long foreign trips with the England squad. When West Ham travelled I usually shared a room with Billy Bonds. The club would not allow the players to have single rooms because of the costs involved. Bill and I became friends soon after he joined West Ham from Charlton Athletic for £50,000 in 1967. I've always considered him to be the best signing in the club's history.

We always got on well together, enjoying the good times and sharing our worries. We played cards for days at a time and, if there was an hour to kill, I enjoyed a good novel. If there was ever any disagreement between us it was about what time the light should go out at night. He wanted the lights out, while I wanted to finish the chapter I was reading.

He was a bit like me in that he had a quiet, unassuming nature. Even though he was West Ham's captain for many years, he was not much of a socialiser and rarely enjoyed talking to the media. The instant a match ended he was on his way home. He was invariably first out of the dressing room and first into his car at Upton Park.

Had he pushed himself to the forefront more I believe he would have played for England. He's one of the best players of my generation never to have won an England cap. When Ron Greenwood took over as England manager he called up Bill but he had to withdraw when he suffered a pelvic strain. Then in May 1981 Ron selected him to play against Brazil at Wembley alongside young West Ham centre-half Alvin Martin. Ron had decided to give Alvin his international debut and thought Bill, also uncapped of course, would be a steadying influence. Sadly, two days before joining the squad Bill broke a rib in a collision with Phil Parkes in West Ham's last match of the season and missed out again.

Bill played a record 804 first-team games for West Ham in 21 seasons. When he finally retired as a player in 1988, aged 42, he was appointed the club's youth-team coach by long-serving manager John Lyall. Bill had been an inspirational figure in John's teams over the years and when John was sacked only one name featured on the radar for the majority of West Ham fans. But Bill was overlooked as John's successor and Lou Macari was the board's surprise choice as manager. Lou lasted just seven months and this time the job went to Billy Bonds. He managed the club, with mixed success, for four years, admitting that the demands of modern-day management could never compare with the pleasures of playing the game.

Bill's loyalty to West Ham inspired generations of players – including me – at a time when it wasn't unusual for a footballer to tie himself to one club for the greater part of his playing career. Bill is just one example, but there were many in my time. Bobby Charlton (Manchester United), David O'Leary (Arsenal), Ian Callaghan (Liverpool), Tony Brown (West Bromwich Albion), Steve Perryman (Tottenham), Terry Paine (Southampton), Jack Charlton (Leeds), Mick Mills (Ipswich), Neville Southall (Everton) and Ron Harris (Chelsea) are just a few of the big names that come to mind. In the modern game, players like Ryan Giggs and Paul Scholes, who spent their entire careers with Manchester United, are rare.

There were times when my own loyalty to West Ham was tested. During the period when I was unable to pin down a regular first-team place, I occasionally wondered whether I would be better off, both financially and from a playing point of view, moving to a new club. In February 1971, for example, after a bit of a run in the first team, we were beaten 4-1 by Derby County at Upton Park. There was some dressing-room disarray at the time – Bobby Moore, Brian

Dear, Clyde Best and Jimmy Greaves had all been axed from the starting line-up because of their nightclubbing exploits in Blackpool.

Much as expected, following the Derby County defeat Jimmy Lindsay and I were both dropped from the team by Ron Greenwood. For the next match, at Coventry, Moore and Greaves were reinstated and we won 1-0. I knew that I would have to wait my chance before getting back into the first team. Jimmy Lindsay, substitute against Coventry, was in the same position. He played only one more game for the club before being sold to Watford. I was out of the starting line-up for six months and when I went to see the manager he told me that as the club was in imminent danger of relegation – we finished 20th out of 22 – no player would be released from their contract.

He said that we would review the situation at the end of the season, at which point, we agreed, I would go on the transfer list. In those days this meant that your name was circulated to other clubs, informing them that you were available for transfer. I would like to claim that there was a rush to sign me. But there wasn't. I was never told anything officially at the time but learned later that Luton and Millwall considered making bids. As far as I know nothing materialised between the clubs. Had it done so I may well have been tempted to accept a move to a lower division. Neither club was in the First Division but I would happily have joined either to escape reserve-team football.

As it was I started the new season, 1971–72, where I finished the old season – in the reserves. The future looked bleak, particularly as Greenwood had chosen a centre-half, Tommy Taylor, to play in midfield. Tommy had signed from Leyton Orient for £75,000 the previous October and was given the number ten shirt on the opening day because the manager wanted Bobby Moore and Alan Stephenson as his centre-back partnership. It was also another example of the manager's reluctance to upset his big-name signings. A 1-0 home defeat to West Brom suggested that all was not right with his team selection that day. Four days later he fielded an unchanged team for the visit to Derby County. This time we were beaten 2-0.

Had the experiment with Tommy Taylor come off I may well have had no other option but to walk out of football and find another way to earn a living. But Greenwood recognised that it wasn't working and for the next game, away to Nottingham Forest, dropped Stephenson, moved Taylor back alongside Moore and recalled me in midfield. We lost 1-0 but our general play was more cohesive. The boss kept me in the team. We drew 0-0 with Ipswich and then beat Everton 1-0.

It was the turning point for me, the defining moment in my career at West Ham. In August 1971 I was on the point of walking out of the club. A few weeks later I was back in the team – and would stay there for the next 13 years. I was ever-present for the rest of 1971–72, playing a total of 54 matches, including the four-match League Cup semi-final epic against Stoke. To cap it all, I was voted Hammer of the Year. How fickle football can be!

Within a year I was one of the players Ron Greenwood couldn't be without. I played 44 first-team matches, scoring 11 goals, in 1972–73, unaware that I was being trailed by Brian Clough, the manager of league champions Derby County. He was also trying to sign Bobby Moore and judging by his later remarks about me I suspect I was very much the lightweight in the transaction.

Clough had long admired Bobby. Who didn't? One day in August 1973, right out of the blue, he contacted Ron Greenwood with a huge offer – £400,000 for Bobby Moore and Trevor Brooking. That was big money in those days. What Greenwood didn't know at the time was that Clough had already met Moore for lunch at The Churchill hotel, just off Oxford Street. Bobby said nothing to me but was obviously hooked on the idea of going to play for Derby.

Clough already had two outstanding centre-backs in Roy

McFarland and Colin Todd – both England internationals – and Bobby wanted to know how, if he signed, the manager would fit all three of them into the team. 'I want to play young Todd at full-back so that he can watch and learn from a master,' said Clough.

Greenwood told Clough that neither Bobby nor I were available for sale, but that he would put the bid before West Ham's board of directors with his recommendation that they reject it. 'Call me next Monday evening after the board meeting and I'll tell you their decision,' Ron told Brian. The board would probably have liked to bank that amount of money but they had no hesitation in backing the manager. That, back then, was the way it worked. The manager had the final say. Greenwood waited for Clough's call. And waited. And waited. No call came. Two days later the story, probably leaked by Clough, was all over the newspapers. Bobby accused Ron of denying him a last chance to win a League Championship medal. That may have been true. Who knows? What I do know is that within a month of Clough's extraordinary bid to sign me and Bobby he was sacked by Derby County.

Like everyone else, I followed his career in the newspapers. He was one of the most outspoken figures in any walk of life in the seventies and had millions of fans who all thought he should have been made England manager. I think he was irked when the job went to Ron Greenwood in 1977 and, although Ron offered him the very important role of England Youth coach, Brian showed very little appetite for it. I suspect the job was a testing ground to see whether he could conform in the way the FA would have expected had he got the big job. If it was a test, he failed it.

He was the most opinionated of all the managers of his generation and was never slow to publicise his thoughts. In 1980 he was writing a column in the *Daily Express* and used this platform to criticise me the day West Ham met Arsenal at Wembley in the FA Cup final. Borrowing a famous pre-fight quote used by Muhammad Ali's colourful corner-man Drew 'Bundini' Brown, Clough said of me: 'He floats like a butterfly and stings like one too!' What Brown had said of the great Ali before his 1964 fight with Sonny Liston was: 'Floats like a butterfly, stings like a bee, the hands can't hit what the eye can't see.'

Clough had mangled one of the most memorable sporting quotes of that era to draw attention to the fact that, in his opinion, I wasn't punching my weight. Remember, this is the manager who had tried to sign me seven years earlier. He claimed that people were asking why it was that a team like West Ham could reach cup finals, but not perform as successfully in the league week after week. If people like me, he said, had played consistently well then West Ham would never have been relegated.

We had been relegated in 1978 and had just finished our second season in Division Two. We finished seventh, way off the three promotion places, and Arsenal, the FA Cup holders, were overwhelming favourites to win at Wembley. Happily, we beat the mighty Gunners 1-0 and as most West Ham fans of a certain age will recall I scored the goal. With my head!

I was puzzled by Clough's attack on me. His comments were due to appear in the newspaper on the morning of the match but, luckily for me, I was forewarned by a journalist friend, Peter Watson, who said that the *Express* sports editor, Ken Lawrence, had asked him to tell me of Clough's criticism. I had written some cup final columns with Peter in the *Express* that week and the sports editor didn't want me to think that his paper was being disloyal to me. So I knew what to expect when Clough's column appeared on the Saturday morning. Even so, I was disappointed by the claim that 'his lack of application and that of other players like him meant relegation for West Ham in the past and failure to win promotion this time'.

Years later he suggested in publications that I had asked him why he chose to criticise me in this way on the day of the FA Cup final. I think his memory must have been clouded on this issue because I would never have given him the satisfaction of even raising the subject with him. On matters of this sort I'd never allow my critics to believe that I was annoyed or, indeed, aware of what they had said. It's a personal policy I've always followed, both as a player and in my career since I retired as a player.

From my point of view, not a single word about what he had written was mentioned between us until 11 years later, long after I'd hung up my boots. It was January 1991 and I was working for the BBC as part of their match coverage team. I went to Selhurst Park with Barry Davies to cover Crystal Palace v Nottingham Forest in the third round of the FA Cup.

We were in the corridor outside the dressing rooms when Barry decided to go up to the TV gantry, leaving me alone. A couple of seconds later who should walk out of the Forest dressing room but their manager Brian Clough. He spotted me and quickly looked up and down the corridor. When he had satisfied himself that there was no one else around he walked up to me and said: 'Young man, I owe you an apology. I did you a disservice many years ago before a big cup final. I said something that I shouldn't have said. I was wrong and I apologise.'

He didn't linger for a reply. He turned and walked back to the dressing room. I was amazed that after all that time that he had taken the trouble to say sorry. He was someone I respected for his managerial achievements and it meant something that he had apologised for something that had happened so long ago. It must have been nagging at him for years. At least he had the good grace to admit he was wrong. To be honest, I don't know whether I would have enjoyed playing for Brian Clough had the opportunity come my way. I don't respond to the kind of abrasive treatment he used to hand out to some of his players. He had a reputation for being arrogant and a bully, but he was an outstanding motivator and there is no doubt that his two European Cup triumphs with Nottingham Forest made him one of the all-time great managers.

Another of the managerial giants of my time in football was interested in signing me in 1974. Bill Nicholson, whose Tottenham team were the first in the twentieth century to achieve the fabled league and FA Cup double in 1961, had a reputation for building fine teams that played good football. Spurs, of course, had been serious contenders for my signature when I was still a schoolboy.

I knew, though, that new signings – Terry Venables and Alan Mullery, for instance – sometimes struggled to satisfy the demands of the White Hart Lane fans. I also figured that Bill was coming towards the end of his illustrious career. But he believed he could build one last great team and I was flattered to be in his thoughts. He had heard that I was involved in a contract dispute with West Ham. People knew I was easy-going, so they assumed matters were serious when I dug my heels in and sought the support of the Professional Footballers' Association.

Derek Dougan, the tall, eloquent former Wolves and Northern Ireland striker, who became a very strident and successful PFA chairman, supported my case and proved to be a very useful ally and advisor. In those days most professional footballers were offered a contract with an option – one-year contract with a one-year option, or two years with a two-year option and so on. I was offered a 'two-and-two' by West Ham. This meant that if they chose to exercise the option at the end of the first two years they couldn't offer any less than my existing salary but were not obliged to offer any more. In essence it meant that they could lock me into the same salary for four years.

As I was now a regular first-team player and had just broken into the England team I felt that it would be unwise to commit myself to the same wages for the next four years. I'd happily sign a one-and-one but the club were holding out for a two-and-two.

We reached an impasse. It was an important contract at that stage of my career and I wasn't going to be bullied into agreeing a deal that didn't suit me. The club took the case to an independent tribunal where Derek represented me. He suggested a compromise – a two-and-two with an escape clause after the first two years. Neither the club nor I realised such a clause was permissible, but it was, and so we agreed the terms of my new contract. My old contract had expired in July. It was now October. Like a good trades union negotiator, Derek argued that West Ham should backdate my pay rise to the expiry date of the old contract. West Ham were reluctant, but finally agreed. It was a nice little bonus! Back then the clubs held the upper hand in negotiations of that sort. Today it has switched around completely and the players, and their agents, are in the driving seat.

I always did my own negotiating and at no time in my career did I have anyone representing me in the way that agents do today. But there was one man, Jack Turner, who was very helpful early in my career at West Ham. A former insurance broker, Jack worked with West Ham from 1950 to 1966. Initially he was involved in the administration of the houses owned by the club and rented to players. He became close to many of the players and acted as an agent and advisor to Phil Woosnam and then Bobby Moore. He helped me with financial advice and provided encouragement during the time I was in and out of the first team. He also introduced me to the concept of promotion and marketing and would occasionally get me a paid job, like a shop opening, for which he took 10 per cent of the fee.

By the time my dispute with West Ham had finally been resolved, my chances of joining Spurs had all but gone. The reason? Bill Nicholson, the manager for 16 years, had quit, a sad and disillusioned figure. 'Players have become impossible,' he said. 'I'm abused when they come to see me. There is no longer any respect.'

That autumn when West Ham met Tottenham Terry Neill, the Hull and Northern Ireland manager and former Arsenal captain, was in charge of the Spurs side. It was his first game as manager. I was recalled to the team after missing four matches with a broken nose. Spurs won 2-1 and we slumped to the bottom of the table, having won only one of our first seven games of the 1974–75 season.

The Tottenham–West Ham 'derby' fixture is among the highlights of the season but this one was unusual. For years the two managers in the dugout had been Billy Nicholson and Ron Greenwood. Over the years they had become friends. Now, though, times were changing. Bill had resigned. A few weeks earlier Ron had stood down as manager of West Ham after 13 years, handing over the first-team reins to his assistant John Lyall. Ron stayed on at Upton Park as general manager and later offered Bill a job as chief scout.

It was an extraordinary season that started with the dismissal of two of the game's great names, Kevin Keegan (Liverpool) and Billy Bremner (Leeds), in the FA Charity Shield match at Wembley. The FA handed out unprecedented punishments. Both players were fined £500 and banned for ten games for removing their shirts, throwing them to the ground and thus bringing the game into disrepute.

The Leeds United manager at the time was Brian Clough. He had walked out on Brighton, who immediately issued a writ, a few weeks before the Charity Shield. He lasted just 44 days at Elland Road before they sacked him. The rumour-mongers insisted that he had been forced out by the players. There were plenty of other surprises that autumn. Dave Sexton was sacked after seven years as Chelsea manager and Liverpool's Bill Shankly ended a 15-year reign and was replaced by Bob Paisley, who would lead them through a golden era during his decade at the helm.

Paisley was in charge when several of his players, all England colleagues of mine, began to suggest to me that I might like to move to Anfield. This kind of thing happened often during international get-togethers. It was the spring of 1978 and Liverpool were the defending European champions. Clough was about to win the First Division title with Nottingham Forest and West Ham were about to be relegated.

We had struggled for a couple of seasons and I knew that if we were relegated my England place might be in jeopardy. Ron Greenwood had been England manager for a year and his squad included several Liverpool players, such as Ray Clemence, Phil Neal, Terry McDermott and Ray Kennedy. Two of my closest England pals were Kevin Keegan and Emlyn Hughes. I would spend hours playing cards with them.

Some of them had played in my testimonial match – West Ham v an England XI at the Boleyn Ground in October 1977 (programme 15p). Ron had used the match to help prepare his team for a vital World Cup qualifier against Italy at Wembley a fortnight later. A crowd of 23,220 supported me that night, contributing around £30,000 to my testimonial fund. I was touched that so many had turned up. They watched West Ham win 6-2 – Derek Hales scored a hat-trick in ten minutes – and saw a really outstanding youngster who would later make a big name for himself with England, the Crystal Palace left-back Kenny Sansom.

West Ham had spent most of 1977–78 in the bottom three, the relegation places, and inevitably when a club went down there was speculation about whether they would sell their best players. Everyone accepted this and there was a lot of talk about my future as the season approached a climax. Liverpool's interest was flattering but, to be honest, I was more concerned with keeping West Ham in Division One.

We staged a fantastic late revival, winning six of our last nine matches. The critical one was the final match – against Liverpool at Upton Park. We needed to win to have a chance of staying up. But we lost 2-0, Liverpool scoring through Terry McDermott and David Fairclough. Wolves had two matches to play and if they lost them we would be safe. But they beat Aston Villa on 2 May and we were relegated.

If I needed an excuse to leave Upton Park, relegation was it. But I loved the club and I felt I owed it to the fans to stay. I wasn't sure what was going to happen. I was concerned about my England place but Ron Greenwood reassured me on that score. Even so, there were many other good reasons why it would make sense to go to a club like Liverpool. They were the best side in Europe. They were about to win the European Cup for the second consecutive season.

But I wanted to help West Ham bounce back. I owed a debt of gratitude to the fans. They had always been good to me. I decided that my duty was to stay and help them get back to Division One. Had you told me then that we would spend three years in Division Two I might have felt differently. But I wasn't to know that those three years would produce the most fruitful and rewarding period of my time at the club.

CHAPTER 5

GOOD TIMES

THE LATE DANNY BLANCHFLOWER, an inspirational captain of Tottenham and Northern Ireland in the fifties and sixties, always relished the atmosphere of a big London derby at Upton Park. 'West Ham get twenty-six thousand cockneys turning up every week and they all sing "Bubbles" on good days and bad, and they don't believe any other club exists,' he once said. He was a bit of a romantic, Danny, but I think he was probably right!

Blanchflower explained his personal recollections of the bond between West Ham and the supporters in Charles Korr's excellent 1986 history of the club, *West Ham United: The Making of a Football Club*. As a boy who had played his earliest football around the lamp-posts in the back streets of Belfast he knew how passionately local communities in working-class areas identified with their football teams.

In those days in London's East End, and probably in the Belfast docklands, too, football was an escape from the grim realities of daily life. For a couple of hours on a Saturday afternoon the working man could temporarily put his problems to one side and join his mates in the Chicken Run at Upton Park. At one stage the club directors formally considered a scheme whereby the unemployed would be allowed to attend matches without charge. After much discussion this was finally rejected because it was feared the system might be abused.

Even when I was a child, street football was the only amusement for many of the local kids, who dreamed of one day pulling on the claret and blue shirt. It was an accepted article of faith that West Ham was a club built on the foundation of local talent. We all wanted to be part of that dream, part of the extended family of local lads who progressed through the ranks and eventually had the honour of representing the East End on a Saturday afternoon.

Although this was the case when I was a youngster, it had been very different earlier in the club's history. West Ham supporters relived the thrills of their FA Cup run in 1923 for decades, but the truth is that most of the star names in the team that lost 2-0 to Bolton Wanderers in the first Wembley final were from the provinces. Billy Moore and Billy Henderson were from the North-east, George Kay from Manchester, Jimmy Ruffell from Barnsley, Vic Watson from Cambridgeshire and the goalkeeper Ted Hufton from Nottinghamshire.

The club, formed in 1895 by Arnold F. Hills, owner of Thames Ironworks, was more than half a century old before it made any sustained effort to attract local players to Upton Park. But when they did they tapped into a rich and deep vein of talent. Ted Fenton, who in 1950 became only the third manager in the club's history, immediately recognised the need for a change of direction. He instigated a youth policy that produced rapid results.

In 1957 West Ham reached the final of the FA Youth Cup for the first time, repeating the feat two years later, with London youngsters like Bobby Moore, Eddie Bovington and Jack Burkett, who were to graduate to the 1964 FA Cup-winning team. Inevitably, a sense of unity and team spirit took root among these local lads. The fans loved the fact that here, at last, was some success, achieved with boys from their own streets. The team that beat Preston 3-2 in the 1964 final was made up of players from the London area, or Essex, apart from two – Geoff Hurst, born in Lancashire, and Johnny Byrne, born in West Horsley, Surrey.

In 1964 I discovered that the party atmosphere in the East End when West Ham were involved on Cup final day was wonderful – flags, bunting, parades, street parties, a knees-up in every pub. It was then, and still is, an experience to be treasured. West Ham had waited a long time to go back to Wembley. Generations of fans had suffered the gloating of more successful local rivals like Arsenal and Spurs.

Wembley must have seemed a distant dream on Boxing Day 1963 when West Ham lost 8-2 to Blackburn Rovers at Upton Park. Two days later manager Ron Greenwood made one change for the return holiday fixture at Ewood Park. With Eddie Bovington replacing Martin Peters in the side, West Ham not only gained revenge, winning 3-1, but discovered a cup-winning combination that remained unchanged in the FA Cup for the rest of the season and eliminated Manchester United in the semi-final.

Many in football and the media considered West Ham to be an 'unfashionable' club. But that victory over Preston gave them status. West Ham already had a reputation for playing attractive, attacking football, but now they could entertain – and win. I was a spectator at Wembley in 1964, but 11 years later I was on the pitch when West Ham won the FA Cup for the second time.

Once again West Ham's cup-winning team reflected the close bond with the local community. Only two of the 11 players were not from London or Essex. Graham Paddon came from Manchester and the FA Cup hero that season, Alan Taylor, came from Hinckley,

Leicestershire. Perhaps even more significant is the fact that this West Ham team is the last all-English side to win the FA Cup.

It may be, of course, that an all-English team will never again win the FA Cup. The fact that around 70 per cent of the players currently in the Premier League are foreign obviously means that fewer and fewer English boys have the chance to play in the FA Cup final. Foreign players have been very good for the English game. There's no doubt in my mind that they have raised the quality, but their numbers have increased to a level that is now worrying. In my view a high percentage of them are simply not good enough, but they are blocking the progress of home-grown players. We now have a bloated system that is restricting the development of good English youngsters.

In 1975 all the players in the top division were English, Irish, Scottish or Welsh. Even the occasional foreign-born player, such as Ipswich Town's Colin Viljoen who was born in Johannesburg, qualified to play for England. As it turned out, Viljoen was one of the obstacles we had to overcome that season on our way to Wembley. To be fair, there were plenty of obstacles at the time. The previous season West Ham had just avoided relegation by a single point and Hereford had famously knocked us out of the FA Cup in the third round. Ron Greenwood, manager for 13 years, had stepped aside, and his assistant John Lyall had taken over. It was a period of transition.

Happily for us, Ron stayed at the club in a scouting and consultancy role and recognised the fact that the playing squad needed strengthening. He went about the task with great diligence and persistence. Perhaps the production line in the East End was in decline because Ron found the men we needed outside London. He signed Alan Taylor from Rochdale for £45,000 – a substantial fee for a Fourth Division player – Keith Robson for £60,000 from Newcastle, and Billy Jennings for £115,000 from Watford.

What a difference they made that year. They all chipped in with goals and top-quality performances as we headed towards Wembley. We beat Southampton 2-1 in the third round and then faced Swindon at Upton Park. The last time we'd met in the FA Cup was in 1964 when West Ham won and went on to Wembley. A repeat looked likely when Jennings put us in front but Peter Eastoe equalised with seven minutes to go and earned a replay.

Swindon took the lead in the replay but my diving header – yes, a diving header – and a late winner from Pat Holland secured a fifth-round home tie against Queens Park Rangers. When we played our London rivals, the Rangers goalkeeper Phil Parkes, who joined West Ham four years later, was in outstanding form and we had to be at our best to beat him. Dave Clement, capitalising on a mishit backpass from Keith Robson, gave Rangers the lead but Holland equalised and then Billy Jennings and I set up Robson for the goal that redeemed his earlier mistake and gave us a quarter-final with Arsenal at Highbury.

I must have played well against Rangers because the following morning's newspapers were full of praise. One said that I had 'inspired West Ham to win a superb match much more comprehensively than the score suggests'. I thought Robson was our best player that day. He was a real talent with a terrific left foot. He was capable of scoring magnificent goals and, had it not been for his temperament, would have become one of the game's top players. He was sometimes reckless, though, on and off the field. He liked a drink, too, and could be very, very funny. He could always be relied upon to liven up the dressing room and in that sense reminded me of my old England team-mate Terry McDermott. Sadly, he missed the semi-final and final because he failed to take advice and rest a thigh muscle injury. He was devastated to miss out on the big day at Wembley and was even more upset when told that he would not qualify for a winner's medal because he had not appeared in the final. He'd promised his dad, Thomas, a winner's medal. Ron Greenwood tried to console him by telling him that he would win a European Cup Winners' Cup medal the following season. Although we got to the final and Keith played, and scored a goal, we were beaten – so he was still without a winner's medal ... I saw him not so long ago and he said: 'You won't believe it, Trevor, but I'm a real sensible dad now!'

What gave us an edge in the Arsenal game was the introduction of Alan Taylor. John Lyall decided to give him his first start in the FA Cup because he figured that he could use his speed to exploit the left side of Arsenal's defence, where Bob McNab was nearing the end of a long and distinguished career. John was right. Bob couldn't catch him, nor could Peter Simpson or Terry Mancini. Alan was a lovely bloke and became a big favourite with West Ham fans. Everyone called him 'Sparrow' because he was little more than a bag of bones. There was nothing of him, but he was the fastest player in the club. That's what caught all the opposition out in the second half of that season. We'd clip the ball in behind the defence and he'd chase it. He also worked well with Billy Jennings, who was a good target man and finished the season as our top scorer with 14 goals.

Bill was a confident lad who settled quickly. He was single and a trendy dresser, and he and Keith Robson, who was also single, became good pals. They liked a night out but they were both fully committed on the pitch. Bill's great strength, considering he wasn't that tall for a central striker, was his ability to spring high and then hang in the air. He, Keith and Alan Taylor gave us all sorts of fresh attacking options. Alan came from Rochdale, and there were no airs and graces with him. It's extraordinary to think that within five months of leaving Rochdale, in the Fourth Division, he was scoring two goals in the FA Cup final.

We were fortunate to play Arsenal when we did because there

was some dressing-room discord at the time and their manager Bertie Mee was locked in a dispute with the former World Cup star Alan Ball. It was obvious that Arsenal were not mentally prepared for the match. Even so, no one expected us to win. Alan Taylor gave us the lead after 15 minutes, prodding home a chipped pass from Graham Paddon. Then we had a lucky escape. Frank Lampard under-hit a backpass that stuck in the mud. Arsenal's John Radford slipped it past the oncoming Mervyn Day, only to be bowled over by the goalkeeper as he tried to reach it. Despite Arsenal's appeals, referee Ken Burns waved play on.

Immediately after the restart, 'Sparrow' netted his second goal with a fierce right foot shot from my pass. I remember thinking how fortunate we were that Ron Greenwood had had the foresight to insist that Alan should not be cup-tied before West Ham signed him. Having got such a good return from his first game John Lyall decided to keep Alan in the team. What a good move! He scored in his next two games, and by the time he faced Ipswich at Villa Park in the FA Cup semi-final his confidence was sky high. Ipswich had developed as an accomplished and talented team under Bobby Robson. But they were wracked by injury, having played six matches in the previous 15 days. The situation for them actually worsened during the match when they lost both centre-backs, Kevin Beattie and Allan Hunter, and had to move striker Trevor Whymark into defence.

We couldn't capitalise on this disarray and would have lost had it not been for a goal-line clearance by Billy Jennings in injury time. Even with their problems Ipswich were the better team, but it ended goalless – just about what a poor game deserved. We met again four days later at Stamford Bridge and, once more, Ipswich outplayed us for long periods. They pummelled us. They had two goals disallowed before Alan Taylor's far-post header gave us the lead. Just before the end he scored his second, meeting a John

Wark headed clearance with a drive that skidded on the ice and went in off a post.

In the dressing room afterwards we were all scratching our heads, wondering how we had got to the final. The other semi-finalists, Fulham and Birmingham, were in extra time at Maine Road. We were praying that Fulham from Division Two would get through. Suddenly a steward burst into the room and said: 'Fulham scored fifteen seconds from the final whistle.' Fulham were managed by one of the most respected personalities in the game – Alec Stock. He had gathered a talented and vastly experienced team that included two England captains: our former West Ham colleague Bobby Moore and the former Spurs skipper Alan Mullery. They had already beaten us once that season, 2-1 in the third round of the League Cup at Craven Cottage.

It was only the second all-London final in history – the first was Spurs–Chelsea in 1967, when Mullery had played for Spurs – and sadly it was no classic. We all thought that, once again, the speed of Alan Taylor would be a key element in the tactical battle. Bobby Moore, though still a fine player at 35, had lost some pace and his centre-back partner John Lacy was not the quickest either. Alan was in his element but this time he was gifted his two goals by the Fulham goalkeeper, Peter Mellor. Perhaps the tension of the occasion undermined his confidence, but his mistakes gave us the cup. Mistakes by outfield players are often eclipsed by other incidents whereas mistakes by goalkeepers tend to stick in the memory. The goalkeeper is so exposed. He has little time to redeem his error and the consequences can haunt him for a lifetime.

Sadly, not much about the match itself lingers in the memory apart from the 2-0 scoreline, a couple of fine saves by Mervyn Day from John Mitchell and the fact that a standing ticket cost £1.50. You can't get a cup of tea for that nowadays! I've never forgotten, though, all the details of the day that followed. After the match we had a big party in a west London hotel and the next day we drove in an open-top coach through the streets of the East End. People who knew said it was the best party in east London since VE Day. It took us hours to edge through the crowds thronging the streets from Stratford to East Ham Town Hall where the mayor was holding a reception for us. The noise, colour and carnival atmosphere of the occasion will stay with me forever.

One notable absentee was Ron Greenwood, who had done so much over the years to bring about this success for West Ham. Asked afterwards why he didn't go he said simply: 'It was John Lyall's day.' The win over Fulham qualified West Ham for a place in the 1975–76 Cup Winners' Cup – a first taste of European football for ten years. The 1964 FA Cup winners had won the Cup Winners' Cup the following season and, as defending champions, had reached the semi-finals in 1965–66. A few weeks before the World Cup, Moore, Hurst, Peters and colleagues were beaten 5-2 on aggregate by a very talented Borussia Dortmund of West Germany – the club's last experience of European football.

Ron Greenwood was in charge then but now it was John Lyall's job to prepare us for the challenge of Europe. None of us had experienced European football previously so it was an exciting prospect, providing we didn't allow it to undermine our chances in the First Division and in the domestic cup competitions.

We started well enough in front of 4,587 fans in Helsinki's huge Olympic Stadium. Billy Bonds and I scored to secure a 2-2 draw with Lahden Reipas and a fortnight later we beat them comfortably 3-0 at Upton Park. The second-round draw against Ararat Yerevan of the USSR meant a long plane journey to one of the world's oldest cities. Founded in 782 BC, Ararat is thought by many to be the resting place of Noah's Ark after the Flood. I wasn't particularly interested in the historic significance of the city, or anything else for that matter, because within hours of arriving I'd picked up a bug that produced sickness and diarrhoea on a biblical scale. We drew 1-1 in front of 66,662 fans and although I was well enough to play in the return leg – a 3-1 win – the sickness kept returning over a period of two months.

This meant that I missed the first leg of the quarter-final with the Dutch team Den Haag. We were 4-0 down in 40 minutes. It was a frustrating match, not helped by the bizarre refereeing of the East German, Rudi Glockner. He had refereed the 1970 World Cup final, so he was no slouch with the whistle. But some of his offici-ating was eccentric and one of the strangest moments came when he stopped the match and ordered Kevin Lock to pull up his socks. He wouldn't restart the game until he was sure that Kevin had used tie-ups to keep his socks in place.

I was at home listening to the match on the radio and had to switch it off when the Dutch scored their fourth. I didn't know until later that Billy Jennings had scored twice to make it a 4-2 defeat – a result that ensured the return at Upton Park would be a tense occasion. Indeed, that night we made a great start and were 3-0 up in 38 minutes. But the Dutch drew level on aggregate when Lex Schoenmaker scored with 30 minutes remaining. It was an anxious finish but we hung on to qualify for a semi-final place on the away-goals rule.

We met Eintracht Frankfurt in the semi-final with the first leg in West Germany. We couldn't have made a better start because after just nine minutes Graham Paddon hit one of his 30-yard specials that flew into the net, thus maintaining our record of scoring in every away game. The Germans pulled it back, scoring either side of half time, but they knew they really needed a bigger advantage than 2-1 to overcome us at Upton Park.

The second leg was a truly enthralling match and provided me with one of the best memories of my career. Eintracht were a good side and Mervyn Day was in fine form early on – and needed to be.

More than 39,000 had squeezed into Upton Park and the place was rocking. It was one of the great European nights and I was happy to make a significant contribution to our 3-1 win, having missed important games because of my illness. I scored twice, one a header, and set up Keith Robson, who curled one in. Right at the end Tommy Taylor cleared the ball off the line. A 3-2 win would have seen us go out.

So, a big European final beckoned but we were very conscious of the fact that our domestic form had not matched our success in Europe. Back in November, when we played Ararat in Armenia, we were top of the First Division and firing on all cylinders. But we didn't win one of our final 16 First Division matches and we finished a disappointing 18th in the table.

After our final league match of the season, a 2-0 defeat against Everton, Billy Bonds apologised to the fans on behalf of the team. Nonetheless, thousands of them travelled to Brussels a fortnight later for the European final against Anderlecht. The fact that it was to be played in Anderlecht's Parc Astrid stadium gave our opponents a big advantage. Anderlecht were a class act with far more European experience than us. Their best player was the Dutchman Robbie Rensenbrink but they also had the gifted Belgian international Francois Van der Elst, later signed by John Lyall for West Ham.

We weren't overawed, though, and took the lead through Patsy Holland after 29 minutes. Unfortunately, Frank Lampard mishit a backpass and Rensenbrink pounced to equalise. Frank's studs got caught in the long grass and he had to go off with a groin injury that later required a pelvic operation. Van der Elst put Anderlecht in front and although Keith Robson equalised in the 69th minute, late goals from Rensenbrink and Van der Elst, again, gave the cup to the Belgian side. I thought we had played well in difficult circumstances, but I knew that I had been below my best in the second half. I had a badly bruised leg as the result of a tackle by Ludo Coeck. We collided heavily and he probably came off worse because he had to be substituted. He was a talented player and I've never forgotten him. He later played for Inter but in 1985, at the age of 30, he crashed his BMW and died two days later.

Losing to Anderlecht was one of the biggest disappointments in my career but it was nothing like the despair that engulfed us when we were relegated from Division One. To be fair it had been creeping up on us. We finished 18th in the 22-club First Division in 1976, 17th in 1977 and 20th in 1978. With three going down, we were relegated with Newcastle and Leicester. I had the consolation of being voted Hammer of the Year, but it wasn't much comfort.

After a 20-year run in the top division relegation was a terrible blow to the club, the fans, the players and manager John Lyall. He tried to keep it in perspective. I remember him talking about a telephone call he'd received from the actress Billie Whitelaw, whose young son was a West Ham fan. She was an established star of stage and screen but she told John that she had reached a point in her career where she was no longer examining the qualities of her own performances. She simply took them for granted. She told John that she had decided to move into provincial rep for a while and make herself work a little harder with people perhaps not quite so efficient or professional.

She said it was like moving from the First Division to the Second in football and she found working in smaller theatres a refreshing and stimulating experience. She was able to look at her career in a new light and move forward. John pointed out that she had made the decision consciously while we hadn't, but we might find it had the same effect.

There was little immediate sign of recovery in 1978–79 – Fourth Division Newport County beat us 2-1 in the third round of the FA Cup – but the following season provided the greatest memory of my career. I refer, of course, to my headed goal in the FA Cup final win over Arsenal at Wembley. It was the highlight of my club career. Everyone seems to remember it. I've played in greater games and scored better goals but the occasion made it especially memorable. I have always been a deeply committed supporter of the FA Cup. It is an institution, globally recognised and one of the blue-chip events in the sporting calendar.

In January 1980 when we began our run to the FA Cup final only Frank Lampard, Pat Holland, Billy Bonds and myself remained from the 1975 team. The game was beginning to change – even at West Ham. We had two new defenders – Ray Stewart, a Scottish full-back signed from Dundee United, and centre-half Alvin Martin, who had worked his way through the youth ranks. But he was originally from Bootle, on Merseyside. There were other new additions, none from London. Phil Parkes, who John had bought in a world record-breaking deal for a goalkeeper, came from Sedgley in the West Midlands. Stuart Pearson, the England striker, joined us from Manchester United but was originally from Hull. David Cross, signed from West Brom for £180,000, was from Heywood in Lancashire.

The strong London flavour, once deeply entrenched in the West Ham dressing room, was beginning to fade. Since Ted Fenton's day, Wally St Pier had provided the club with a stream of good young players from the London area. A big man with a smile and a warm handshake, he was one of the best-known figures on the scouting scene in London and the South-east. He'd played briefly for the club but made his name as a scout. One or two slipped past him, including Terry Venables, who went to Chelsea as a youth. 'Wally was like your granddad,' Terry once said. 'When I signed for Chelsea the only thing that bothered me was that Wally would be upset.'

Wally spent 40 years at West Ham and never lost his touch. The supply line simply slowed. Instead of the cockneys dominating, we now had accents from Lancashire, the Midlands and elsewhere in the provinces echoing around the dressing room. Very often the loudest voice was that of the biggest man – Phil Parkes. He was full of himself, and rightly so, after we drew 1-1 with West Brom at the Hawthorns in the third round of the FA Cup.

He was quite magnificent that day and produced one of the best performances of his career. The finest of his many saves came when he pushed a low shot from Derek Statham against a post. Stuart Pearson's header gave us a 33rd-minute lead but Cyrille Regis equalised in the 90th minute. In the replay Geoff Pike was moved from midfield to makeshift striker and played a blinder. He scored our first goal in the 53rd minute and I added another just before the end to give us a 2-1 win.

I missed the fourth-round tie against Leyton Orient at Brisbane Road because of a groin strain. Our physio Rob Jenkins tried desperately to get me fit, even applying a hot potato wrapped in a sock to the damaged muscle! It didn't help. The match against our Second Division neighbours was a potential banana skin but we emerged as 3-2 winners with Ray Stewart claiming two of our goals.

I was back in the side for the fifth round at home to Swansea. Late goals from Paul Allen and David Cross gave us a 2-0 victory and a quarter-final tie against Aston Villa at Upton Park. The drama in this match was confined to the dying seconds, when Villa defender Ken McNaught was penalised for handling my corner. Had I been a Villa player I would not have been happy with the decision to award a penalty. But we were given our chance in the last minute. Ray Stewart didn't miss from the penalty spot. He successfully converted 81 of 86 spot kicks taken during his time with West Ham. Our overall performance said a lot about the way this group of players had evolved and developed as a team. Villa were enjoying a terrific spell and the following season, of course, won the

First Division title and followed that with their European Cup triumph. We more than matched them in the quarter-final and still believe we thoroughly deserved our victory despite the dispute at the time.

It was a narrow 1-0 victory but enough to put us in the semi-final draw with Everton, Liverpool and Arsenal. We were obviously the underdogs and we wanted Everton. That's how the draw worked out. We were also delighted that our tie was to be staged at Villa Park, where we had played our semi-final in 1975. The match itself was a highly charged thriller that tested the referee Colin Seel. I was amazed when he awarded a penalty against Alan Devonshire for a tackle on Andy King. It was a mistake and a costly one for us because Brian Kidd scored from the spot in the 42nd minute. Kidd was later sent off following a fracas with Ray Stewart, and Trevor Ross was fortunate to escape expulsion when he hacked me down. Our one-man advantage eventually told and in the 70th minute Stuart Pearson side-footed home my cross for the equaliser.

The replay, at Elland Road, was just as dramatic. Goalless after 90 minutes, Alan Devonshire scored the opening goal four minutes into extra time. The former England striker Bob Latchford, recalled to replace the suspended Kidd, equalised with a diving header in the 113th minute. A second replay looked imminent until I centred to David Cross, who headed the ball towards the penalty spot. Who should pop up but Frank Lampard, whose header had just enough power to beat Martin Hodge and secure us a place at Wembley.

Frank was so overjoyed that he immediately raced to a corner flag and danced around it – an often repeated piece of newsreel film. In the dressing room afterwards we all wondered how he had managed to be up in attack at the time. 'Parkesy' joked in his booming voice that Frank had got stuck up there simply because he didn't have the energy to return to his position at full-back.

We celebrated our triumph without knowing who we would face

on the big day. Arsenal and Liverpool required four matches to determine which of them would face us at Wembley. Arsenal eventually won the third replay at Highfield Road with a goal from Brian Talbot. It was their third consecutive final and they were the FA Cup holders, having beaten Manchester United 3-2 in a classic final the previous year.

Once again we were the underdogs, up against an Arsenal side that was close to exhaustion. In addition to 42 First Division matches, they had played eight in the European Cup Winners' Cup, seven in the League Cup and ten in getting to the final of the FA Cup. Four days after their date with us they had to play Valencia in Brussels in the final of the Cup Winners' Cup. That season they played 69 first-team matches – but won nothing. Talbot played in all of them.

Our win against Arsenal at Wembley was a tactical triumph for John Lyall. Either he or his scout Eddie Baily had watched three of the four games against Liverpool and come to the conclusion that the best way to unhinge Arsenal's defence was to take one of our strikers out of the front line. This meant that either David O'Leary or Willie Young, Arsenal's two centre-backs, would have no one to mark.

John decided to withdraw Stuart Pearson from our attack and play him in a free role in midfield. Within minutes of the kick-off, O'Leary was complaining to the Arsenal bench that he had no one to mark. David Cross was our lone striker and he did a wonderful job working his way back and forth across the Arsenal back four. They were marking one man while we outnumbered them in midfield.

It was a strategy that worked well for us and although it wasn't a classic game it was a wonderful occasion. It was as if the East End had moved to Wembley. It was lovely to hear the West Ham anthem echoing around the rafters of the old stadium. 'I'm Forever Blowing Bubbles' is one of the most easily recognisable of all the football chants. I've always considered it a strange choice of song for such a tough part of London but, apparently, it was introduced to the club's fans by the former West Ham manager, Charlie Paynter.

It was a popular American music hall song, first published in 1919, and Paynter took a liking to it when he heard his friend Cornelius Beal, a schoolteacher, singing it. Beal ran a schoolboy football team and one of his players, Billy 'Bubbles' Murray, looked like the boy in the famous *Bubbles* painting by Millais that was used in a Pears soap advertisement at the time. Beal used to sing 'Bubbles' every time Murray and his team won a match.

Whatever the origins of the association with West Ham, the song has certainly been around since I was a boy and that day at Wembley it filled us with pride and a sense of belonging. To be honest, I hadn't been too confident about the outcome of the match. When I left home to join the squad the day before, my daughter Collette asked: 'Are you going to score a goal for me, Daddy?'

I said I'd try, but I knew it was a long shot. As it turned out, it was a header after just 13 minutes that took everyone by surprise, me included. I remember the goal as clear as day. We'd won the ball in midfield and got it out to Alan Devonshire on the left, and his acceleration carried him past Talbot and Pat Rice. He got to the by-line and crossed, trying to keep the ball away from Pat Jennings. An outstanding goalkeeper, Pat stretched and just got a touch but the ball fell at the feet of David Cross on the right of the goal. I was moving towards the six-yard box when Dave's shot was blocked by Young. The ball bounced out to Pearson who was at the corner of the 18-yard box on the right of the goal.

At this point I admit that an element of good fortune was involved. Like any striker in that position, Stuart decided to shoot rather than pass to a team-mate. More often than not, of course, they don't hit the target – and Stuart was no exception on this occasion. It was my good luck that his shot was dragged across the penalty box, hurtling in my direction. Instinctively, I knew that if I stood still it would just miss me on the right-hand side, so simply by falling backwards I was able to divert the ball with my head towards the goal. The power of Stuart's shot was such that not even Pat Jennings or the two full-backs on the line could stop it.

I've explained my role in this goal many times over the last 30-odd years. Even today, within minutes of climbing into a London taxi – almost all the cabbies are, it seems, Arsenal fans – I'm asked to confirm that the ball simply hit me on the head and bounced into the net. I always enjoy telling them the true story! Such was the confusion at the time, and the disbelief that I'd actually scored with my head, that even the revered ITV broadcaster Brian Moore got it wrong in his live commentary. He initially gave the goal to Stuart Pearson but told me later that, in the half-time break, he had to voice over his original commentary to correct the error and acknowledge me as the goalscorer.

So, as the ball flew into the net, the goalscorer – me – had a quick look at the referee to make sure he wasn't blowing for some offence and then raced off towards the touchline with arms raised. Billy Bonds grabbed me, demanding: 'What are you doing scoring with your head?'

I was the match winner, but for me the real West Ham hero that day was Paul Allen. At 17 years and 256 days Paul became the youngest ever Wembley finalist, taking the record from Howard Kendall who had played for Preston against West Ham in 1964. One of a large footballing family, Paul worked tirelessly in midfield and shackled Liam Brady so effectively that the little Irishman was unable to repeat the damage he'd inflicted on Manchester United in the previous final. Liam, who later played for West Ham, likes time to pick his passes but Paul denied him that. He very nearly scored a second goal for us with just minutes remaining. He broke free and was bearing down on goal when he was tripped from behind by Willie Young. Referee George Courtney flourished a yellow card for what was generally regarded as a 'professional foul' in those days. In the modern game Willie would have been sent off. Paul? He jumped up and in front of a global TV audience simply shook Willie's hand, securing for himself a special niche in the history of the FA Cup.

Such was my jubilation in the dressing room at the end of the match that I allowed myself a sip of champagne! A few hours later, after the club's official banquet at the Grosvenor House hotel in west London, I was having a late dinner with family and friends at the Inn on the Park when a bottle of champagne arrived with the compliments of some Sunderland fans sitting at a nearby table. They explained that a 'heavy night' might slow me down when West Ham played at Roker Park two days later. As it happened 47,129 fans turned up to watch Sunderland beat us 2-0 and snatch a promotion place from Chelsea by one point.

We were disappointed to finish seventh in the Second Division table but not as disappointed as Arsenal's shattered players who, four days later, were beaten 5-4 on penalties by Valencia of Spain in the European Cup Winners' Cup final, thus finishing a momentous season empty-handed. Our success at Wembley, on the other hand, meant that we were back in European football.

As extraordinary seasons go 1980–81 was right up there with the most memorable. It was a season of triumph and despair and, if you include our FA Charity Shield defeat by Liverpool at Wembley in the first week of August, we played a total of 61 matches. Phil Parkes and Geoff Pike played in all of them. Ray Stewart, Alvin Martin and David Cross each missed only one game. Much of what we achieved as a club around this time can be traced back to the consistent excellence of our defence.

For 17 years I was a regular first-team player at West Ham and for six of those years I had the pleasure of playing with the best defence in the club's history – goalkeeper Phil Parkes behind a back four of Ray Stewart, Billy Bonds, Alvin Martin and Frank Lampard. As a defensive unit they were untouchable. Once Parkes and Stewart were embedded in the side in the 1979–80 season we were no longer a soft touch. Because of the dominance in the seventies of the northern heavyweights, teams like Liverpool, Leeds, Nottingham Forest and Derby County, clubs in the London area were often derided for their supposed lack of physical commitment and the term 'southern softies' was much used in the tabloids.

West Ham, of course, attracted their share of criticism in this respect until opponents began recognising the qualities of our defensive unit. But after the opening three games, we had only two points and were languishing in 17th place in the table. For the fourth game, our strongest defence was back in action and we registered our first win – 4-0 against Notts County. We then remained unbeaten in domestic competitions until mid-November – a run of success spoiled only by our unedifying return to European competition.

Our first-round opponents were Castilla. They were a good side playing in the Spanish Second Division and they acted as a nursery club for the mighty Real Madrid, with whom they shared their spectacular Bernabeu stadium, which has a capacity of 100,000. On the night we played, the crowd numbered 40,000 with about 2,000 of those in the claret and blue of West Ham.

The match itself was a thriller and David Cross put us ahead after 18 minutes. The Spanish were technically excellent, fought back in the second half and won 3-1. But we lost far more than the match. The club's reputation was seriously damaged as a result of disturbances on the terraces. The vast majority of the West Ham fans behaved impeccably but a small minority disgraced the club with their violent anti-social behaviour. What made matters worse were incidents outside the stadium after the match, when a West Ham fan was hit by a motor coach and later died in hospital.

Hooliganism was a growing problem in English football and 'hooligan' headlines filled the newspapers the next day. The unrest on the terraces was considered in those days to be simply a symptom of the times but, whatever the root cause, it's good to know that the problem has been pretty much eradicated from the modern domestic game. The introduction of all-seater stadia played a big role in improving control and behaviour within football grounds. Later investigations established that there had been two arrests (both away from the ground) in Madrid that night and five supporters detained during the match itself. It took the football authorities many years to find a long-term solution to the hooligan menace but the immediate response by UEFA, European football's governing body, was to fine West Ham £7,700 and order the second leg to be played 300 kilometres away from Upton Park. They further ordered that if we beat Castilla on aggregate, our home leg in the second round would also have to be played away from Upton Park.

UEFA gave the club 48 hours to appeal and three days in which to find an alternative venue for the second leg against Castilla. The club's board sent manager John Lyall, commercial manager Brian Blower and two directors, Jack Petchey and Brian Cearns, to the appeal. They presented a dossier of facts, the results of the club's own exhaustive enquiries. UEFA listened sympathetically and at the end of the hearing announced that they were lifting the fine imposed on the club and allowing us to play the second leg behind closed doors at Upton Park. Furthermore, if we progressed to the second round we would be allowed to stage the home leg at Upton Park.

This was good news but the sense of relief began to evaporate as we puzzled over how to prepare for a big European game, which we needed to win, remember, in an empty stadium. A wall-to-wall crowd at Upton Park generates a terrific atmosphere and plays a big role in lifting the players. This time there would be only the sound of silence interrupted by the echo of the referee's whistle.

John Lyall organised two full-scale practice matches at our Chadwell Heath training ground and asked the reserve lads to tackle and chase as if it was a competitive match. At least we got some idea of playing competitively without an audience. The match itself was a unique occasion in the history of West Ham. The official attendance that night is recorded as 262 – players, coaches, match officials, admin staff and media.

As the match progressed the voices of the radio commentators drifted across the pitch and you could also hear what the coaches were saying among themselves in the dugouts. But the voice I remember best was that of the West Ham scout Eddie Baily. Born and raised in Clapton, the former Spurs and England midfield player never lost his common touch. I'm sure his cries of 'Get stuck in!' could be heard a couple of miles away in Barking!

Anyway, we got stuck in and led 3-0 at half time with goals from Pike, Cross and Paul Goddard, who had signed for us from QPR for £800,000 at the start of the season. The Castilla captain, Miguel Bernal, then scored with a superb long-range shot to take the game into extra time. By now even the ball boys, chasing around deserted terraces to retrieve the ball, were exhausted. But not David Cross. Tall and sparely built, he seemed to have energy to burn. He scored twice more to complete his hat-trick and give us a 5-1win on the night, 6-4 on aggregate.

Happily, there was no crowd trouble on our next foray into Europe for the simple reason that only a handful of our fans wanted to go to the match. We were drawn to play Politehnica Timisoara of Romania, and back then a trip behind the Iron Curtain was something very few looked forward to with any relish. Timisoara had drawn 2-2 with Celtic in the previous round, qualifying on the away-goals rule, and Celtic manager Billy McNeill, a friend of John Lyall, gave him lots of information about the Romanians. Furthermore, Eddie Baily, John's assistant, occasionally accompanied Ron Greenwood, then

England manager, on scouting trips and was invited by the FA to travel with the England party to a World Cup qualifying tie in Bucharest. He watched England's 2-1 defeat, and the night before had also seen the Under-21 side lose 4-0 to the Romanians. A number of Timisoara players had been involved in both games, and the big bonus for us was that he stayed on and watched the Romanians lose 2-1 in a friendly match against OFK Belgrade.

John Lyall had more information about the opposition than he could have hoped for and we knew what to expect from a talented side. We also knew their weaknesses. We took a 4-0 lead into the second leg and were confident we would finish the job. Our hotel in Timisoara was dimly lit and barely functional – we even took our own food – but the people were hospitable. At the stadium the crowd sang 'Poli, Poli' to the tune of The Beatles' 'Yellow Submarine' but they had little chance of overhauling a four-goal deficit. They kicked lumps out of us and scored in the 54th minute but we held on and progressed to the quarter-finals.

The Timisoara experience underlined the value of arming yourself with sound information about opposing teams, but in the next round we learned just how costly it can be to play against unknown opponents. Dinamo Tbilisi of Soviet Georgia fell into this category – but we weren't due to play them until March. First, though, we had a protracted FA Cup third-round marathon with Wrexham, also of the Second Division. We drew 1-1 at Upton Park, then 0-0 at Wrexham three days later. John Lyall spun the coin for the choice of venue for the second replay and Wrexham manager Arfon Griffiths called correctly. The second replay at the Racecourse Ground was twice postponed because of the weather. On the first occasion we travelled all the way to Wrexham by coach, returning almost immediately after a pitch inspection. Eventually a Dixie McNeil goal after 104 minutes of the second replay forced us to relinquish our grip on the FA Cup.

Then we had a classic League Cup quarter-final win over the Tottenham all-stars of Glenn Hoddle, Ossie Ardiles and Ricky Villa. A David Cross goal gave us a semi-final date with Coventry. We squandered a 2-0 lead in the first leg at Highfield Road, losing 3-2, but redeemed ourselves at Upton Park with a 2-0 victory that secured another Wembley final, this time against Liverpool. Before that, though, we had to resume our European adventures and, of course, ensure that our promotion challenge maintained momentum. We had been top of the Second Division since November and people were now talking about us breaking the 65-point record set by Jack Charlton's Middlesbrough in 1973–74. Promotion was beginning to look like a formality but John Lyall knew that things would not be so straightforward in Europe.

Tbilisi were an outstanding team and the fact that the Russian domestic season had only just resumed after their winter break meant that we had not seen them play. We had to settle for some film clips of their epic 4-2 aggregate triumph against Liverpool in the European Cup the previous season and their 5-0 aggregate win over Waterford in the Cup Winners' Cup a few months earlier.

Technically they were a wonderful side and in the first leg at Upton Park attacked us with breathtaking pace. It was an education to watch them and I was hugely impressed by the movement and individual skills of players such as Aleksandr Chivadze, Vitali Daraselia, David Kipiani and Ramaz Schengeliya. They remain one of the finest European teams I've seen and it was a shame that a broken leg ended Kipiani's career prematurely. But even greater tragedy was to strike. Daraselia died in a car crash on a mountain road a year later at the age of 25, and Schengeliya died of a brain haemorrhage in Tbilisi in June 2012. He was 55.

But on the night they met us at Upton Park they were practically unplayable. They were irresistible from the moment Chivadze burst through to score from 25 yards in the 23rd minute. They beat us 4-1 but they could have scored six or seven. At the final whistle our crowd gave them a standing ovation.

Having seen what they had to offer we were far better prepared for the second leg. Our chances of winning on aggregate were slim and not helped by the exhausting 4,000-mile journey to Tbilisi. We had to fly via Moscow, where a stony-faced official in the transit lounge refused to accept that Bobby Barnes, with his new crinkly haircut, was the same person as the fresh-faced youth in his passport photograph. But the biggest problem at Moscow was the snow. The de-icing machine was working overtime spraying the wings of aircraft when, after a three-hour wait, they closed the airport. We were stuck in the transit lounge again, until the club finally persuaded the officials to take us by bus to an airport hotel. We waded through snow drifts and checked in at midnight for five hours' sleep. At 6am we were back in the airport, but had to wait a further six hours before taking off to Tbilisi.

Considering the travel ordeal, we played well in front of 80,000 fans. Tactically, we were well prepared this time and Stuart Pearson, making a rare first-team appearance following a lengthy lay-off, scored the only goal of the game. The match was played in a wonderful spirit and at the end we exchanged shirts and were applauded off the field.

We flew home through the night and, once again, had to land at Moscow. The customs officials there asked me to explain why I was leaving the country with more money than I'd had when I arrived. In those days when you entered the USSR you had to fill in a form detailing all the cash and valuables you were carrying. On leaving you had to fill in another form. 'I won the cash playing cards with Billy Bonds!' I explained.

We were a tired bunch when we eventually arrived at Stansted at seven in the morning, and our fatigue showed three days later when we drew 1-1 with Oldham at Upton Park. But Paul Goddard's goal was enough to give us a ten-point lead at the top of the table. We were already guaranteed promotion when we met Liverpool in the League Cup final. They were en route to another European Cup triumph and were the best-equipped team in the First Division, with players like Ray Clemence, Kenny Dalglish, Graeme Souness, Alan Hansen and Ray Kennedy. We played a possession game, not easy against the masters of the art, but it worked to a degree. It was scoreless after 90 minutes. Then Alan Kennedy scored a questionable goal for Liverpool after 117 minutes, but in the last seconds of extra time Ray Stewart equalised from the penalty spot. Emotions were running high as the players left the pitch because we felt that Kennedy's goal should not have been allowed to stand.

When he struck the ball his team-mate Sammy Lee was crouching on the ground near the penalty spot in an offside position in front of our goalkeeper Phil Parkes. The linesman flagged. Sammy ducked dramatically to avoid being hit by the ball and clearly blocked Phil's view of the travelling shot. He *had* to be interfering with play. That was blatantly obvious. The referee Clive Thomas moved towards the linesman but then decided to overrule him and pointed to the centre circle. In the mayhem on the pitch, John Lyall told Clive that 'we feel cheated'. He didn't accuse him of cheating but the tabloid headlines the next day suggested that he had. John was cautioned, faced a charge of bringing the game into disrepute and risked a touchline ban for the replay at Villa Park.

To be fair to Clive he accepted his share of the responsibility at the FA hearing and John was cleared and allowed to take his place in the dugout for the replay. At the end of the hearing he and Clive had lunch around the corner from the FA offices in Lancaster Gate. Clive was again the referee for the replay and handled the game impeccably. We started encouragingly, Goddard scoring with a near-post header from Jimmy Neighbour's cross. Dalglish equalised with a stunning goal in the 25th minute and three minutes later Alan Hansen scored their second. We nagged away at them in the second half but couldn't break them down or disturb their rhythm.

Three days later we shrugged aside the Liverpool defeat and beat Bristol Rovers 2-0 in front of 23,544. The place was rocking and 'Bubbles' reverberated around the ground. With 55 points, promotion was guaranteed – and we still had six matches to play. We remained unbeaten and our 1-0 win over Jack Charlton's Sheffield Wednesday at Hillsborough on the final day of a long season gave us the 66 points (in the days of two points for a win) that meant we had beaten the record set by Charlton's Middlesbrough. We were back in the big time. It felt good to be a Hammer!

CHAPTER 6

NIGHTMARE IN NEWPORT, MAYHEM IN MANSFIELD!

N<small>O HONEST ACCOUNT OF LIFE</small> at West Ham in the seventies and eighties can disguise the fact that for long periods of time my team-mates and I were regarded as a bit of a pushover in the big domestic cup competitions. All clubs claiming a place among the elite of the game stumble occasionally but West Ham's catalogue of disasters cast a long shadow over our three FA Cup final triumphs in 1964, 1975 and 1980. We had world-class players in Bobby Moore, Geoff Hurst and Martin Peters but still suffered more than ten embarrassing defeats to clubs from lower divisions during my 17 years of first-team service. Some were narrow defeats, just about acceptable, to Second Division teams like Middlesbrough, Fulham and Hull, but others were truly humbling. How do you explain losing to Fourth Division clubs like Stockport County and Newport County, who both enjoyed historic giant-killing victories over West Ham in my time at Upton Park?

I played in both of those defeats and the soul searching after-wards went on for weeks. Ron Greenwood was the manager in 1972–73 when we lost 2-1 to Stockport in the third round of the League Cup, and John Lyall was in charge when Newport's 2-1 win knocked us out of the FA Cup in 1978–79. The fact that we were in Division Two at the time was no excuse. As a youngster in my early days at Upton Park it was an honour and privilege to be play-ing alongside our three World Cup heroes, but I soon realised that their presence in the side often lifted inferior opposition in cup matches. In those days the scalps of Moore, Hurst and Peters were highly valued. Everyone wanted to test themselves against England's three big stars and, in fairness, the way West Ham played encouraged them to do just that.

Ron Greenwood's coaching gospel was based on attacking foot-ball, forward runs, good passing, creating space and maintaining an offensive momentum. We worked hard on the training ground to devise new ways of making space and in my opinion there were few better passing teams than us at that time. Our one-touch game was built on confidence and when we were passing the ball well we were a match for anyone. It was an exciting way to play and I was delighted to be a part of it. The players loved the simplicity of it, but there was a downside. When we lost possession of the ball the space we had created for ourselves was suddenly exploited by the opposition.

To be honest, our style of play wasn't suited to the kind of one-goal victories and grinding draws away from home that under-pinned so many successful league title-winning campaigns. Our game was about entertainment and five-goal thrillers. We loved it, and so did our fans. The trouble was, rival teams loved it too! They knew that if they stopped us playing, we could be muscled out of games. I'm sure there were occasions when we could have demon-strated greater resilience but we always went out on to the field determined to play our way. That is what the manager wanted, and he had the full support of a benevolent and patient board of directors.

Just occasionally there would be some unedifying episode that suggested some fans were losing patience. I remember West Ham's first FA Cup tie a few months after England's World Cup victory in 1966. I was still to make my senior debut and wasn't involved but can recall a thrilling Hurst hat-trick in a 3-3 draw with Swindon at Upton Park in the third round. Swindon were then in Division Three and had a promising young winger called Don Rogers. He scored two and made the other to ensure a replay at Swindon.

Yes, you've guessed it! Swindon won the replay 3-1 and the next morning Bobby Moore discovered that the windows of his sports shop opposite Upton Park had fallen victim to discontented fans. I dare say these were the same fans who only weeks earlier had been singing and dancing as West Ham beat Spurs (1-0), Arsenal (3-1) and Leeds (7-0) in the League Cup en route to the semi-finals. The seven-goal defeat of Don Revie's mighty Leeds, First Division runners-up the previous season, was an extraordinary result and demonstrated just how good we could be when our confidence was high. There were no weakened teams in those days. Leeds fielded all their stars – Bremner, Charlton, Hunter, Madeley and Giles among them. I heard later that Revie kept his players up until the early hours of the morning discussing the biggest defeat of his managerial career. Leeds didn't lose many games in those days – and certainly not by seven goals.

How inexplicable, then, that the following season we should play so pathetically in losing 2-1 in the FA Cup to Sheffield United at Upton Park. Ron Greenwood was so angry with us that he left his usual seat in the directors' box and sat in the dugout in the hope that he might influence the way we were playing. His mood wouldn't have improved at the end when John Harris, the United manager, chortled: 'We love playing West Ham.' Happily we beat them 2-1 at Bramall Lane in May – a defeat that more or less condemned them to relegation to Division Two. Sadly, Frank Lampard broke his right leg four minutes before the end of the match.

By this time I was established in the first team, though I had yet to sample the bitter frustration that comes when you finish on the wrong end of a giant-killing act. That all changed in February 1969 when we were drawn to play Third Division Mansfield in the fifth round of the FA Cup.

We cruised past Bristol City – the day Upton Park's new East Terrace opened to replace the old Chicken Run – and Huddersfield and were due to meet Mansfield on 8 February. But the winter weather was so severe that the entire FA Cup programme was postponed, plus all but four league matches. The tie was rearranged for 19 February, but this too was postponed. After one further postponement we finally played the match on 26 February.

A crowd of more than 21,000 squeezed into their Field Mill ground to see the big shots from London. Moore, Hurst and Peters played along with recent acquisitions like Bobby Ferguson, then the world's most expensive goalkeeper, Billy Bonds and Alan Stephenson. Just to underline Ron's commitment to attacking football we also had two wingers in the line-up – John Sissons and Harry Redknapp.

With that team we could have beaten anyone – except Mansfield! They chased and tackled and knocked us out of our stride. As the pitch iced up – they did every mid-winter in those days – our passing game suffered and our confidence dipped. Dudley Roberts gave them the lead after 23 minutes. Ray Keeley added a second just before half time. By the time Dominic Sharkey scored, the little coal-mining town on the flank of the Pennines was rocking. A 3-0 victory provided the greatest night in the club's history.

We were well beaten. Although an embarrassing setback for us it was, on reflection, what made the FA Cup such an iconic sporting competition. Despite some recent observations to the contrary, I think the FA Cup is a jewel in our sporting heritage and well worth preserving. The fact that the little team can overcome the odds and beat the bigger team is what gives the FA Cup its appeal and explains why there have been so many imitators since the inauguration of the competition in 1871–72. West Ham may have suffered more than some at the hands of giant-killers, but in Mansfield, for instance, that memorable win all those years ago is still fondly recalled. It is part of football's folklore and, as such, makes the FA Cup a vital and much-loved part of the football calendar. I have to admit that on the night they thoroughly deserved their epic victory.

There were plenty of other moments of disappointment and recrimination in the cup competitions, many coming against teams from Yorkshire and Lancashire. In the circumstances it was inevitable, I suppose, that we should be considered 'southern softies'. The big battalions in the north – Leeds, Liverpool, Manchester United – were always a challenge and they enjoyed picking holes in our style of play. It always made me chuckle to hear the legendary Liverpool manager Bill Shankly ask: 'D'you know of a defender slower than Bobby Moore?'

The big northern clubs ruled the roost for nearly three decades between Ipswich's League Championship win of 1962 and Arsenal's triumph of 1989, although Arsenal did also break the domination in 1971. For us, though, it was the smaller clubs that caused so much anguish. In the space of about three months in 1973, for instance, we suffered the considerable embarrassment of losing to Fourth Division Stockport County in the League Cup and Second Division Hull in the FA Cup.

The following season the 'cup curse' followed us out to the West Country. In the FA Cup third round we were drawn to visit

Hereford, a team we had played two seasons before when they were still in the Southern League. On that occasion they held us to a goalless draw before we beat them 3-1 in a replay at Upton Park, and afterwards the West Ham chairman, Reg Pratt, pledged his support for their application to join the Football League. In the previous round, of course, they had secured the famous 2-1 win over Newcastle United that earned them a place in the FA Cup history books and enhanced their claim to Football League status.

When we met them in 1973–74 they were in the Third Division. Their line-up had changed considerably but Dudley Tyler was still on the wing. He'd created such a good impression when he played for Hereford against us in 1971–72 that Ron Greenwood decided he was worth a £25,000 investment. A talented young winger who had survived a hole-in-the-heart operation, he quickly became a popular figure at Upton Park. But after just 35 first-team matches Ron decided that he wasn't quite good enough. He went back to Edgar Street and must have been absolutely thrilled when he learned that he would be returning to Upton Park to play against West Ham in the FA Cup.

It was a day that started badly for us – and then got worse. Hereford scored first through Eric Redrobe and after just 30 minutes Bobby Moore limped off with an ankle injury. He didn't know it at the time, but it was to be his last game for West Ham after a magnificent 17-year reign in the first team. Thirty minutes later John McDowell left the field with an injury and, these being the days when teams were allowed only one substitute, we had to finish the match with ten men. Another humiliating defeat was beckoning when Patsy Holland saved the day with a fine solo goal two minutes from time.

I missed the match with a groin injury and although I hoped to be fit for the replay I failed a fitness test. It's not an excuse but we had a lot of injury problems at the time. Our team for the replay had a makeshift look about it, with Alan Wooler replacing Moore and Bertie Lutton coming in for Bobby Gould. We still had enough class to win the match and when Clyde Best put us in front after 35 minutes it looked as though we would. But Tommy Naylor equalised from the penalty spot two minutes later and Alan Jones lashed in the winner for Hereford 15 minutes from time. Watching from my seat in the stands as my defeated colleagues trooped off at the end, I wondered whether the chairman regretted voting for Hereford's admission to the Football League!

Despite our patchy record in the cup competitions Ron Greenwood remained faithful to his playing style. I admired him for that. He wanted a team that entertained the public. Obviously he also wanted to win, but he wanted to win with a bit of style and panache. So many teams back in the seventies were happy to rely on physical commitment and defensive discipline. The professional game was full of players who were not as quick or technically proficient as they are today. But they could tackle. The laws of the game still allowed tackling from behind in the early seventies. This encouraged defenders to win the ball in a way they couldn't today. Changes to the laws of the game have eradicated many of the questionable practices that were common in my time.

Most successful teams had at least one or two hard-edged individuals whose chief function was to prevent the opposition from playing. As a creative figure in West Ham's midfield, I was often singled out for this kind of specialist treatment. I played in plenty of games in which we had lumps kicked out of us in the opening 15 minutes. Ron would have none of it. He deplored those who employed rough-house tactics and wanted no part in them. Only once can I remember him signing a player principally for the aggression that he would give us. That was when he paid Celtic £25,000 for John Cushley, an uncompromising centre-half who was as tough as old boots. He gave us a fearsome presence in the heart of defence but little else. Ron later admitted that John wasn't one of his best signings. He stayed with us for three years and in that time played just 46 matches.

Deep down, Ron's aim was always to create rather than destroy. He brought up his players to share that philosophy. He wanted us to open up the game while the majority of teams tried to close it down. He taught us that there were finer values than simply winning for the sake of winning. For the most part he carried the players with him but there were occasions when he felt badly let down. Probably the most spectacular betrayal of the boss came in the winter of 1971 when West Ham were drawn to play Blackpool at Bloomfield Road in the third round of the FA Cup. Blackpool were struggling at the foot of the old First Division and hadn't long before appointed a new manager – Bob Stokoe, who would later lead Sunderland to their memorable FA Cup triumph in 1973.

In all honesty, we weren't doing much better than Blackpool but had already beaten them 2-1 in the First Division, and Ron Greenwood was justified in believing that we were good enough to beat them again and have a bit of a run in the FA Cup. He was probably right to feel confident but what he hadn't taken into consideration was that four of his star players would spend the night before the match drinking on the Blackpool sea front.

That Friday evening – New Year's Day – the players enjoyed a relaxed dinner at the hotel, after which we were free to do whatever we wanted, within reason. There were no restrictions, Ron said, because he had complete faith in his players. I wasn't in the chosen 11 for the game next day and spent the evening in my hotel room watching TV. Four of my team-mates decided to go out – Bobby Moore, Jimmy Greaves, Clyde Best and Brian Dear. They were joined by the club physiotherapist Rob Jenkins and all headed off to the 007 Club, a Blackpool night spot owned by the former heavyweight boxer, Brian London.

I understand that the alcohol consumption was modest. Clyde didn't drink anything. In the broader catalogue of football indiscretions this one didn't really rank very high. The party was back at the hotel by 1am, ordering coffee and sandwiches. This would probably have been the end of the matter except for the fact that Blackpool beat us 4-0. We played poorly on a bone-hard, icy pitch and had great difficulty containing Blackpool's Tony Green, who scored the first two goals.

The Sunday morning newspaper reports made dire reading for West Ham fans but it wasn't until he returned to his office on Monday morning that Ron Greenwood heard that four of his players had gone out drinking the night before the match. The man who told him was the club chairman, Reg Pratt, who had been accosted by irate fans complaining that a lack of club discipline had led to our defeat at Blackpool. Initially, Ron refused to believe the story. So he made some enquiries. While he was doing this the club started receiving telephone calls from Fleet Street newspapers, who had been told what had happened by fans. The manager talked to the players involved. They all apologised but insisted that they had done nothing wrong, apart from have a quiet drink. Being a man of principle Ron decided that his only course of action was to recommend to the board the sacking of all five including, of course, the England captain.

The board did some hard thinking. They declined to sack Moore, Greaves, Best and Jenkins, but decided to dismiss Dear. Ron felt it would be unfair to sack only Brian, but the board pointed out that having left the club two years earlier he had then been rescued from the dole after playing a few games for Brighton, Fulham and Millwall. The punishment for the others was a two-week suspension plus a fine of a week's wages. Best, an impressionable 19-year-old, was treated more leniently and stayed at the club for a further five years, making more than 200 first-team appearances.

Greaves played only a handful more games for the club before drifting into premature retirement. Dear simply ran out of clubs. Moore's golden boy reputation was tarnished – unfairly, he thought – and, although he played for the club for another three seasons before moving to Fulham, his relationship with Ron Greenwood was never the same. Ron had taken great satisfaction in Bobby's development – he worked with him initially in the England Youth team – and would never have a word said against him. You can imagine how he must have felt when he learned his captain had taken team-mates drinking the night before a big FA Cup tie.

Greenwood remained faithful to his belief that football is a game of joy, wit, muscle and character, and when he handed over the first-team reins in August 1974 he knew that the man succeeding him, John Lyall, was ready and equipped for the job and shared most of his views. John's playing career at West Ham had been abruptly curtailed by a knee injury and since quitting he'd had 11 years coaching alongside Ron.

The son of a policeman, John was from sturdy Scottish stock. He embraced Greenwood's philosophies but added a little more steel and discipline. He had his own ideas and many of them were good and positive but, for some reason, we remained vulnerable to the cup predators in the game.

In 1977–78, the season we were relegated to the Second Division, Queens Park Rangers hammered us 6-1 in an FA Cup fourth-round replay. This was just a hint of what was to come. The following year Swindon, from Division Three, beat us 2-1 in a League Cup second-round tie at Upton Park. I missed the match, having been injured in a 3-0 win over Newcastle, but I can't hide from the fact that I was very much involved later that season when we faced Newport County in the FA Cup. Newport were 12th in Division Four, had lost 5-0 to Swansea in the first round of the

League Cup and had only once reached the fifth round of the FA Cup, in 1948–49. Such matters were irrelevant on the day, when a crowd of 14,124 packed Somerton Park, paying record receipts of £14,904. They got their money's worth!

Howard Goddard gave Newport the lead with a glancing header after 14 minutes, but seven minutes later Bryan Robson equalised with a thudding drive from 30 yards. It was a great goal and provided us with the momentum that I thought would drive us on to victory. But it was not to be. Our goalkeeper Mervyn Day failed to cut out a cross, leaving Eddie Woods to score a simple headed goal with just nine minutes remaining. Beaten 2-1, we headed home with our tails between our legs. The newspapers made a meal of our latest FA Cup humiliation and, understandably, Newport County enjoyed their day in the sun. It was brief. They were knocked out in the next round by Colchester.

It was a significant defeat for Mervyn Day, who had made such a spectacular entrance as a 17-year-old. Ron Greenwood predicted that he would be West Ham's first-choice goalkeeper for the next ten years. Sadly, Mervyn couldn't live up to the hype. When the crowd at Upton Park began to get on his back, John Lyall knew he had to make a change. Mervyn played only two more games for West Ham after that Newport defeat, the last being a 3-3 draw against Sunderland. The Upton Park fans jeered him as he left the pitch.

John Lyall's response was to sign Phil Parkes from Queens Park Rangers for a world record fee for a goalkeeper of £565,000. He was outstanding on his debut, a 3-0 win over Oldham. The Upton Park crowd gave him a huge reception. The following season, with Phil Parkes in goal, West Ham reached the quarter-finals of the League Cup and beat Arsenal in the FA Cup final.

CHAPTER 7

ENGLAND EXPECTS

BOBBY MOORE TOLD ME what to expect. Alf Ramsey, he insisted, would be welcoming, encouraging and supportive. He was right. To those who knew him well, Alf wasn't much like his public image. After almost a decade as England manager, surely one of the toughest jobs in football, he was still regarded as a cold, distant figure by most people. Much of this, of course, stemmed from his relationship with the media. The newspapers didn't like him. And he didn't like them. They painted a picture of a methodical, arrogant man who had taken elocution lessons to disguise any trace of his Dagenham upbringing. Why this was relevant to anything to do with managing the England football team, heaven only knew!

He was a man who kept tight control of his emotions, but those within his circle knew that he was often deeply hurt by the critics. Any criticism of his team was taken as a personal affront. The devotion of the manager to his players, and the players to the manager, had provided the emotional platform upon which England built their successful World Cup bid in 1966. Even in his finest hour, he allowed himself only a wry smile as he held aloft the Jules Rimet Trophy at Wembley. Repeating such an achievement was always going to be an awesome challenge, and when we first met in the early seventies time was running out for him. He had remained fiercely loyal to those players who had won the World Cup and this was a source of much criticism when England failed in their defence of the title in Mexico in 1970.

When he called me into the Under-23 squad in 1971 he was beginning to look at some of the younger players who might feature in England's bid to qualify for the 1974 World Cup. At that time my international experience had been limited to schoolboy football and a handful of caps for the England Youth team. I played in the European Youth Championship in Turkey in 1967 alongside several other youngsters who would later graduate to the senior side.

Inaugurated by FIFA in 1948, and originally known as the 'Little World Cup', the tournament has been run by UEFA since 1955. England are one of the most successful nations at this level and were champions in 1963 and 1964. We had great hopes of winning it again in 1967. We beat Italy, Spain and France and drew with Yugoslavia to qualify for the final against the USSR. We lost 1-0 in a close match in front of 50,000 in Istanbul. Sadly, I missed the final because of a toe injury.

The England team that day was: Shilton (Leicester City), Craggs (Newcastle), Mills (Ipswich), Reeves (Charlton), Went (Leyton Orient), Kember (Crystal Palace), Want (Tottenham), Evans (Wolves), Todd (Sunderland), Lloyd (Chelsea), Kidd (Manchester United). Other players in the squad included my West Ham team-mate Frank Lampard and Everton's Joe Royle. In all, seven of the squad progressed to the senior England team, which is an out-standing return from a 16-strong group of 18-year-olds.

There was a bit of a reunion four years later when I made my

Under-23 debut at Ipswich, the unfashionable Suffolk club that Alf so stealthily led to the Second and First Division titles in consecutive seasons just before becoming England manager. England met Switzerland at Portman Road on a cool November evening in 1971. The England team included Peter Shilton, Frank Lampard, Steve Kember and Joe Royle, who had all played with me in the Under-18 championship.

According to the official Football Association report of the match it was 'a frustrating game in which Switzerland were content to slow the tempo by retaining possession of the ball'. Apparently, 'England failed to impress and the midfield players were only rarely able to provide their forwards with openings.'

That may explain why I never played for the Under-23 side again. It remains a source of pride, though, that I supplied our goal in a 1-1 draw at Ipswich that night. Only 12 minutes of the match remained when I ran to meet a cross from Mick Channon. I dived full length to head us in front. Five minutes later, according to the FA report, 'Muller, though surrounded by defenders, managed to squeeze the ball past Shilton although there was reason to believe that he had handled the ball before scoring.'

Although the Under-23 results that season were poor – just two wins from seven matches – a significant number of those selected to play at this level began to demonstrate the qualities that would eventually earn them senior call-ups. Among those who would graduate from Under-23 to senior level were Channon, Royle, Todd, Mills, Malcolm Macdonald, Tony Currie, Kevin Keegan, Ray Kennedy, Frank Worthington, John Richards and Phil Parkes. By this time, Shilton had already played for the senior side four times.

Alf must have thought he had the raw materials to build a squad good enough to challenge for the 1974 World Cup in Germany. At that time England had never failed to qualify and, with so many good young players emerging in the First Division, a significant number of people in football shared Alf's belief that England would be strong enough to regain the World Cup. Others, though, were beginning to question Alf's optimism. Some of his tactical decisions during the 1970 finals in Mexico had sown the first seeds of doubt. It was the quarter-final in Leon against the old foe, West Germany, that highlighted the problems. England's cause wasn't helped when Ramsey's loyal goalkeeper Gordon Banks was laid low by a stomach bug. His understudy, Peter Bonetti, an agile, talented goal-keeper, was unproven in big internationals.

Nonetheless, England were 2-0 up inside 50 minutes and heading to the semi-finals when both managers embarked on a crucial deployment of substitutes. Germany's Helmut Schoen introduced the winger Jurgen Grabowski to test England full-back Terry Cooper, who was wilting in the heat. After Franz Beckenbauer had pulled a goal back, capitalising on a misjudgement by Bonetti, Ramsey made what many considered the biggest mistake of his managerial career by taking off Bobby Charlton and Martin Peters. He replaced them with Norman Hunter and Colin Bell and explained afterwards that he wanted to rest Charlton and Peters for the semi-final. One of the consequences of removing Charlton was that Beckenbauer was suddenly given the freedom to exert his considerable influence further forward. Eventually, England cracked. Eight minutes from time Uwe Seeler equalised with a back header that left Bonetti stranded in no-man's-land. Then, in extra time, Grabowski flew past Cooper and created the winning goal for Gerd Muller.

For months, no years, Ramsey's accusers dissected and analysed his tactics. The charge sheet was long: why had Bonetti not played in more big matches prior to the tournament? Why didn't he play Peter Osgood, who was in the best form of his life? Why was Francis Lee played on the right when he was better on the left? Why did he persist with the exhausted Cooper? Why did he make those fateful substitutions against the Germans?

The questions remained unanswered. Alf shouldered the blame and, typically, said little, although he did insist with a tinge of defiance that he would pick the same players again. It was that kind of loyalty that made him so popular with his players. But by the time England began the qualification programme for the 1974 World Cup only Bobby Moore remained from Ramsey's earliest days as England manager.

To qualify England had to beat Wales and Poland, and the first match, against Wales at Ninian Park, was Ramsey's 100th in charge. A few weeks earlier Gordon Banks had been involved in a car crash that cost him the sight of his right eye and ended his career. Ray Clemence made his debut against the Welsh, along with his Liverpool team-mate Kevin Keegan. It was an undistinguished 1-0 win for England, lacking creative power in midfield, but far worse was to come in the return leg at Wembley. The Welsh battled to a 1-1 draw in January 1973 – a dropped qualifying point that was to prove costly to England.

Five months later, with pressure mounting on Alf, England lost 2-0 in Poland in a bad-tempered match in which Alan Ball was dismissed – becoming only the second England player to be sent off. The second leg at Wembley was four months away – time enough for everyone to reflect on the reality of England's World Cup chances. Put simply, we had to beat Poland to qualify.

I was called into the senior squad for the first time in September 1973 – three weeks before the fateful match with the Poles. England played a friendly against Austria at Wembley. I wasn't selected to play so sat in the stands and watched England cruise to a 7-0 victory, with Tony Currie pulling the strings in midfield and Channon and Allan Clarke scoring two goals apiece.

Hopes were high of a victory against the Poles. Once again I sat in the stands, watching with disbelief as the Polish goalkeeper Jan Tomaszewski – Brian Clough's 'clown' – produced a string of

remarkable saves. Once again Alf was uncertain about his substitutions and was widely criticised for waiting until the 88th minute
before sending on the Derby County winger Kevin Hector for his
debut. Bobby Moore, who had been replaced by Hunter and
watched the match from the England dugout, kept urging Alf to
make a substitution. Bobby said that Alf was insistent that the men
on the pitch could do the job.

Alf was wrong. The Poles held out, drew 1-1 and qualified for
the World Cup ahead of England. The next match, a 1-0 defeat
against Italy at Wembley, was Bobby's 108th and last for his country. The match after that, a friendly against Portugal in Lisbon in
April 1974, was my first and Alf's last. But he didn't know that at
the time.

Sensing that it was time to introduce fresh blood into his squad,
Alf called up a clutch of debutants, six in all – Phil Parkes, Mike
Pejic, Martin Dobson, Dave Watson, Stan Bowles and me. Only
Dave and I would claim to have enjoyed long international careers.
A resourceful, uncompromising centre-half, Dave made 65 appear-
ances for England between 1974 and 1982. I made 47 in the same
time. Dobson and Bowles played five games each, Pejic four games
and my old West Ham team-mate Parkes never pulled on an
England shirt again after his debut in Portugal.

Alf always went out of his way to make newcomers feel welcome. This time was no different. He was obviously under
pressure, having failed to qualify for the World Cup, but didn't
show it. His priority was his players. I was impressed with the way
he fussed over us. He could have spent time with the FA
International Committee hierarchy who were debating his future.
Instead he devoted all his time and energy to his players.

I remember him telling me: 'Enjoy yourself with us. We have a
good spirit here. The other lads will make you feel at home.' The
public image of a dull, uncommunicative man did not tally with my

early impressions of him. Nothing happened to change my opinion. When he sent us out to play, the emphasis was always on attacking football. He liked his teams to have a sound tactical structure but he was also passionate about passing. He used to say: 'Treat the ball like a precious jewel.'

In that sense he reminded me very much of my club manager, Ron Greenwood. They were contemporaries as players. An intelligent full-back, Ramsey had the more distinguished playing career. He won a League Championship title with Tottenham in 1951, and his 32 games for England included the infamous 1-0 defeat to the USA in the Brazil World Cup of 1950.

Another thoughtful, defensive player, Ron won a League Championship medal with Chelsea in 1955. He also played for the England B team before coaching Arsenal and joining West Ham as manager. Like Alf, he treated his players with respect and, again like Alf, expected his players to return the courtesy. Alf had experienced no serious problems with any of his players but, towards the end of his reign, there was growing unrest among big clubs who were beginning to pressurise their players to withdraw from international squads when the games were unimportant.

Paul Madeley, a Rolls-Royce of a player who wore every shirt for Leeds except the goalkeeper's jersey, had declined Alf's invitation to join the 1970 World Cup squad when his club-mate Paul Reaney withdrew because of injury. Paul explained that he wanted to rest and, as an understudy, felt he was unlikely to play anyway. Paul and his Leeds team-mate Norman Hunter both withdrew from the squad for the match against Portugal – no doubt hastening the arrival of some of the debutants. Alf was getting irritated by a development that was to bedevil all his successors as England manager. He declared at the time: 'Selected players who fail to appear for matches or training sessions should not be permitted to play for their clubs the following Saturday.'

It was rare in those days for players to say no to England. It's more common now. Before the 2012 European Championship the England manager Roy Hodgson named his squad to travel and decided to have a six-strong stand-by squad. Three of the six he originally selected refused to be stand-by players. Those three haven't played for England since. Roy goes out of his way to be fair to clubs and players. He will always discuss availability with club managers and tries to ensure that the top players are not over-worked. The fact is that most England players in recent years have come from just eight clubs – the most successful. The net was spread a bit wider when I was playing. Timing is also a factor. March, for instance, is a really difficult month from an international point of view because it's when the Champions League and the domestic competitions are approaching their climax. It's the time of year when clubs want to keep their players as fresh as possible.

Madeley and Hunter both insisted they were genuinely injured. 'Sir Alf once told me that unless I was one hundred per cent fit I should drop out of the England squad,' said Madeley. 'Who would be foolish enough to pass up the hundred-pound appearance fee?' Paul had a point. Players were well paid in those days but salaries were nothing like as generous as they are today. Few could afford to give up £100. The money was useful, but to a newcomer like me the real thrill was in pulling on an England shirt and playing for my country in a full international for the first time. My former West Ham team-mate Martin Peters, who had moved to Tottenham, was captain in the absence of Bobby Moore. Sadly, it was an indifferent sort of game that ended goalless.

But for me it was a significant moment in my career. I had achieved a boyhood dream of playing football for my country and now, at the age of 25, knew that I had to make the most of the opportunity. I had no reason to believe that Alf was anything less than satisfied with my debut and assumed that I had a good chance of figuring in his squad for a busy programme of matches in May and June. A fortnight after the Portugal game Alf named what would be his final squad – a 20-man party for the Home International Series, a prestige friendly against Argentina at Wembley and a three-match tour of Eastern Europe. It was the sort of end-of-season schedule that the modern Premiership manager would simply refuse to support.

In the last days of that April in 1974, Bishop's Stortford beat Ilford 4-1 at Wembley in the last FA Amateur Cup final, Arsenal goalkeeper Bob Wilson announced his intention to retire as a player and work for the BBC, Manchester United were relegated after 36 years in Division One and ... Sir Alf Ramsey was sacked as England manager.

The news broke in the *Daily Mirror*, having leaked out at Coventry City. Their general manager, Joe Mercer, had already been lined up by the FA to succeed Alf on a short-term basis. The full FA statement, explaining the sacking of the only coach to lead England to World Cup success, read:

> The committees of the FA who have been considering the future of England football have examined some aspects in detail and progress has been made. At a meeting on 14 February the executive committee set up a sub-committee with the following terms of reference: To consider our future policy in respect of the promotion of international football.
>
> Following meetings, a unanimous recommendation was submitted to the executive committee that Sir Alf Ramsey should be replaced as England team manager. This recommendation was accepted unanimously by the executive committee. He has been informed of this decision. For practical reasons his duties will cease with effect from 30 April. A new manager will be appointed in due course, but it has not been possible to take any positive

action on this matter until this announcement has been made. In view of the forthcoming international matches it was decided that a caretaker manager should be appointed.

With the approval of Coventry City Mr Joe Mercer has agreed to undertake this task. It should be stated that he does not wish to be considered for the job of permanent manager so immediate steps will be taken to appoint a new England team manager as soon as possible. The FA wishes at this time to record its deep appreciation for all that Sir Alf has accomplished and the debt owed to him by English football for his unbending loyalty and dedication and the high level of integrity he has brought to world football.

The reign of the only England manager to win anything worth winning was over. Of the 113 international matches played during his time in charge, England won 69 and lost 17. Typically, Alf refused to speak to the media. He packed a suitcase and took Lady Ramsey away on holiday. The following day six Tory MPs put down a motion in the Commons inviting MPs to record their appreciation of Sir Alf Ramsey. Several other prominent figures, including former FA secretary Denis Follows, attacked the FA for the timing of his dismissal. Five days after his sacking the FA announced that he would be given a 'golden handshake' reputed to be worth £15,000.

I was sorry to see him go, and not just because he had opened the door to an international career for me. He had helped take English football, a sport run by amateurs for almost a century, into the modern era. The game would never be the same again. He had broken down barriers and transformed England's approach to international football. He refused to accept the long-established doctrine of the amateur selection committee, insisting instead that professional players should be controlled by a professional coach.

Every decision involving the England team had to be, in Alf's own words, 'rubber-stamped' by him. He argued that nothing was too good for the England team. He had established a real bond with his players. Most of those who had been with him for a long time really loved him. I know, for example, that long after he'd retired he used to receive a regular visit from Martin Peters for a cup of tea and a chat. I didn't get to know him as well as the 1966 squad but I thought he did a great job for English football.

His future had been debated for months, but the swiftness of his departure was a shock. I think, for someone who had done so much for the nation's prestige, he deserved better. Perhaps it was time for a change. Perhaps we should have done better against Wales at Wembley. Certainly we'd created enough to beat the Poles at Wembley. But they weren't pushovers. People forget that a few weeks after Alf's dismissal Poland beat Argentina, Haiti and the great Italian team of Zoff, Facchetti, Causio, Mazzola, Chinaglia et al to reach the final stages of the World Cup. They finished in third place after beating Brazil 1-0 in Munich. Pushovers? I don't think so. Based on the number of chances England created against them at Wembley, my own feeling at the time was that had England qualified they would have done well in Germany. They would certainly have been competitive and difficult to beat.

But by the time the defending champions Brazil opened the 1974 World Cup with a goalless draw against Yugoslavia in Frankfurt, me and the rest of the England squad had returned home from an exhausting programme of matches and were heading off on holiday. Failure to qualify for the World Cup had diminished the nation's football reputation and the players probably felt the disappointment more keenly than anyone else. At least I was given the chance to stake a claim to a place in the England side by Alf's short-term successor, Joe Mercer.

When I was a young player 'genial Joe' was one of the father figures of the English game. He was 60 in 1974, a former England wing-half whose international career was cut short by the outbreak of the Second World War. He had won League Championship titles as a player with Everton and Arsenal and managed Manchester City with distinction from 1965 to 1972, winning the title in 1968.

He'd been helping Coventry team manager Gordon Milne for two years when the FA approached him with their request to fill in as England boss for a few weeks until they could find a permanent replacement for Alf Ramsey. I remember him telling the players at our first get-together: 'We're going to have a laugh and a joke.' He did add, though, that for those serious about playing for England the next seven games would provide a wonderful opportunity to impress the new manager. 'Let's enjoy ourselves and get some good results,' he said. 'But more than anything else, stake a claim to a place in the 1978 World Cup squad.'

Was he talking to me? I wasn't sure. I wasn't in the squad because *he* had selected me. None of us was. Bizarrely, the FA had allowed Alf to announce *his* squad for the seven summer matches before sacking him and declaring that his selections would play under another manager. Although Alf had included me in his squad for the Home Internationals I wasn't in Joe's line-up for the first game against Wales in Cardiff. Instead, he gave a debut to Keith Weller, a talented attacking midfield player who joined Leicester City from Chelsea, where he'd played in the 1971 Cup Winners' Cup-winning team. Keith liked to run at defenders with the ball and was good at it. I wondered whether his arrival meant goodbye to me after just one game.

Perhaps I was worrying too much. Keith had a good career but he played only four games for England – all during Joe's reign. He was a lively individual with a cockney sense of humour. I was really impressed some time later when he walked out on to the pitch for a First Division match wearing tights! It was winter, but it took a bit of 'bottle' to do that in those days. Keith shared Joe's love of a joke. Team talks were a laugh a minute. 'I haven't had time to do much homework,' Joe said before the start of the Home Championship series. He was right of course. 'I don't know much about this lot,' he used to say. 'Let's not worry about them. We'll let them worry about us.'

Although it was light-hearted it wasn't frivolous. Joe Mercer was a professional football man and he wanted to get the best from his players. He had his way of doing it. Alf had his. Alf had been schoolmasterly. He was clear and concise when explaining your role in the team. There was not a lot of flexibility with him. Joe was far more relaxed. He wasn't planning for the long term. His main priority, he said, was to get us playing together as a unit.

We started well enough with a 2-0 win over Wales in Cardiff. Stan Bowles and Kevin Keegan scored the goals, and Liverpool's Emlyn Hughes, making his 30th England appearance, was given the captain's armband for the first time. There was still no room for me in the team four days later when a Keith Weller goal produced a 1-0 win over Northern Ireland at Wembley. Naturally, Keith retained his place for the big one three days later – Scotland at Hampden Park.

This, of course, is the oldest international football fixture, dating back to 1872, and it's a shame that it had to be abandoned largely because of the growing concerns about crowd misbehaviour. For those fortunate enough to have played in this fixture, particularly in Glasgow, the atmosphere and the intensity of the rivalry remain a lifelong memory.

Once again Joe left me out of the starting line-up, but I remember the chaotic coach journey through throngs of Scottish fans to and from the airport. I remember, too, sitting in the stands and being offered cans of beer by deliriously happy Scotland fans. On this occasion they won – a well-deserved 2-0 victory that gave them the Home International title and sent a 93,000 crowd home fully expecting the Scots to take the World Cup by storm that summer. It was a good Scotland team with class players like Danny McGrain, Billy Bremner, Peter Lorimer, Joe Jordan and Kenny Dalglish. A month later, having beaten Zaire and drawn with Yugoslavia and Brazil, the Scots, unbeaten, experienced the disappointment of going out of the World Cup on goal difference.

England, meantime, were preparing for a Wembley date with Argentina, who were, like Scotland, in the middle of their World Cup warm-up programme. Unhappily, Stan Bowles, a real talent on the field if unpredictable off it, had walked out of Joe's squad having been dropped from the team for the Scotland game and replaced by Frank Worthington. With him missing, and Roy McFarland ruled out for six months with an Achilles injury picked up against the Irish, there were suddenly vacancies in the team. At last Joe picked me to play on the left side in midfield alongside Weller and Colin Bell.

It was Argentina's first visit to Wembley since Alf described them as 'animals'. This was after Antonio Rattin had been sent off in England's 1-0 win in 1966. Some of the lads in the dressing room mulled over the timing of Alf's sacking. There could have been some embarrassment had he still been in charge of the team. As it turned out, cheerful Joe ensured there were no diplomatic incidents. Free of the cares of long-term responsibility, he was enjoying his time as England boss and wanted his players to enjoy it too. He made four changes to the side beaten by the Scots, bringing in Dave Watson, Alec Lindsay, Kevin Keegan and me. It was the first time Kevin and I had played together. The Argentines were typically South American. They were good in possession, passed well, had a resilient defence and, as always, real flair at the front. Mario Kempes provided the flair in this team. It ended 2-2, with Channon and Worthington scoring England's goals and Kempes getting both for Argentina, one a late penalty. Despite losing 3-2 to Poland in Stuttgart, Argentina reached the second group stage of the World Cup but finished bottom of the table after defeats to Brazil and Holland and a 1-1 draw with East Germany.

With Joe in ebullient mood, the England squad embarked on a three-match European tour, originally planned as a warm-up programme for the World Cup. As England had already been knocked out it served no real purpose, particularly as an incoming England manager might have ideas completely at odds with those of Joe Mercer. It could so easily have been a depressing fortnight, especially given that the venues didn't rank very highly on any player's list of places to visit. We started against East Germany in Leipzig, then went to play Bulgaria in Sofia and finished up facing Yugoslavia in Belgrade. These were the days when the Iron Curtain was still a very real barrier between the affluent West and the Communist bloc of Eastern Europe.

All three nations had qualified for the World Cup and, for them, playing against England was a useful yardstick. I'd done enough against Argentina to keep my place and I played in all three matches – a 1-1 draw with East Germany, a 1-0 win over Bulgaria and a 2-2 draw with Yugoslavia. Joe kept the mood relaxed throughout, though he did have to extricate Kevin Keegan from an ugly incident at Belgrade airport when we arrived to play Yugoslavia.

Kevin was among a group of players around the luggage carousel when he was singled out by airport police, marched off and roughed up. He had been sitting on the conveyor belt when it was suddenly switched on. The police thought he was fooling around. We were so angry when we realised that he was being detained that we all told Joe we wanted to fly home immediately.

'No problem,' said Joe. 'But Kevin won't be able to come with us. He'll have to stay here to answer charges.' Joe calmed the players down and with the help of FA officials and team captain Emlyn

Hughes assured the Yugoslavs that the game would go ahead. The FA lodged a formal complaint about Kevin's treatment. He was soon released and, fittingly, headed the equaliser in the 2-2 draw.

Kevin and I played in four of the seven England games that summer. He wasn't a world star in those days. We played well together from the start but we had a long way still to go before we could claim to have a real understanding on the field. He had enormous enthusiasm for the game. His work rate was an inspiration to me. I couldn't do the running he did, but I knew that his movement on the field meant that more often than not he was the best option when a midfield player such as me was looking to make a forward pass. Like me, he was still in the process of establishing himself at international level. Others were doing the same – Channon, Todd, Hughes and Watson among them.

When we got back to Heathrow after that European tour we all said thanks to Joe and wished him well for the future. If nothing else, he had lifted the gloom that had descended following our World Cup failure and the sacking of Alf. The FA had said nothing to the players about a new manager. We were told that we were not due to meet again until October when England faced Czechoslovakia in the first match of the European Championship qualifying programme. No one knew who would be in charge. I went home and watched the World Cup on TV.

Joe, awarded an OBE for his services to football in 1976, slipped quietly into retirement. He remained a hugely popular figure in the game and was a director of Coventry City until 1981. He died in 1990, on his 76th birthday, sitting in his favourite armchair. When the City of Manchester Stadium was built, one of the approach roads, Joe Mercer Way, was named in his honour.

CHAPTER 8

THE DON

IN JULY 1974, FOUR DAYS before West Germany beat Holland 2-1 in the World Cup final in Munich, the Football Association appointed Don Revie as England manager. Most people felt he was the natural choice. His Leeds United team had just won the League Championship, finishing five points clear of Liverpool, and he was widely regarded as the most successful manager in the old First Division.

The original deep-lying England centre-forward – four goals in six international appearances in the fifties – Don was a football theorist and strategist who had lifted a rudderless Yorkshire club out of the Second Division and transformed them into one of the most feared teams in Europe. Unlike Alf Ramsey's Ipswich, Leeds had maintained their position at the top. They were both bruising and brilliant and some blamed their 'professionalism' for the development of a new cynical attitude in football in the seventies.

Leeds had started the 1973–74 season under a cloud, with a suspended £3,000 fine hanging over them. This was imposed by the

FA because it was deemed that their total number of dismissals and cautions was 'unacceptable'. The fine was never implemented because Don made an effort to improve Leeds United's disciplinary record.

This probably helped his case when he sought out the new FA secretary Ted Croker to tell him how much he would like to be England manager. 'I fancied the job,' he told the media at the time. The England players greeted his appointment with enthusiasm. There was an acknowledgement in the professional game that his Leeds team, at their best, had few rivals. Even so, they had suffered an irritating number of near-misses. During his 13 years at Elland Road they had finished runners-up in the league title race five times. They were beaten FA Cup finalists on three occasions.

But the FA were convinced that he was the right man to succeed Ramsey. The game, indeed the nation, needed a lift and he was the man to provide it. These were the days, remember, of power and fuel shortages, three-day weeks and the floodlight bans that led to the first Football League match on a Sunday, between Millwall and Fulham.

A fortnight after Revie's appointment a furious row broke out when his former employer, Leeds United, lured the championship-winning manager of Derby County, Brian Clough, from Third Division Brighton to Elland Road. The outspoken Clough famously lasted just 44 days at Leeds – an extraordinary episode in one of the most turbulent years I can remember in football. Within the space of a couple of months that summer football was rocked by a series of unexpected managerial changes – Bill Shankly quit after 15 years as manager of Liverpool, Bill Nicholson resigned after 16 years as manager at Tottenham, Ron Greenwood stood down after 13 years at West Ham and Dave Sexton was sacked as manager of Chelsea.

This upheaval, involving some of the nation's most distinguished coaches, suddenly threw the spotlight on to the mounting pressures that managers faced as they sought to satisfy the increasing demands of players and fans. Shankly cited 'stress' as his reason for retirement and Nicholson quite bluntly claimed that 'players have become impossible'. His decision came just weeks after he had used the public address system in Feyenoord's Rotterdam stadium to plead with Tottenham fans to stop fighting. More than 200 people were injured at the UEFA Cup final in May 1974 and Nicholson was ashamed of the behaviour of some of the Spurs fans. He wasn't alone among those in the game seriously concerned by the growing cases of hooliganism that blighted football in the seventies and would lead to such harrowing tragedies a decade later.

There were clear signs that the game was about to undergo profound changes. For decades the clubs had been all-powerful, paying a maximum of £20 a week in the winter and £17 a week in the summer with players unable to move to a club of their choice when their contracts expired. In 1960 Jimmy Hill, the PFA chairman, and the Newcastle player George Eastham, who wanted to move to Arsenal, challenged both the rate of pay and the contractual terms. After a protracted battle that reached the High Court they won freedom of contract for professional players.

England's World Cup victory in 1966 further enhanced the social status and earning potential of players and, by the seventies, footballers' agents were starting to have an influence. The media, particularly TV, was increasingly powerful and intrusive, and many of the sport's more gentlemanly aspects were disappearing. Football was becoming more competitive, and in the business of winning and losing the balance sheet quickly assumed as much importance as the team sheet.

Previously, the clubs held all the cards. Players' salaries when I started were essentially about bonuses and incentives. But by the time I finished the basic salary was what mattered and was many, many times the average working wage. Managers like Bill

Nicholson, who had been in charge at Tottenham since 1958, remembered what it was like in the old days. But those long-established values, on and off the pitch, were fading away.

Player behaviour on the field was also a cause for concern. Revie was ensconced among the FA hierarchy at Wembley when his former Leeds team faced Liverpool in the traditional curtain raiser to the season. The FA Charity Shield match – now known as the Community Shield – between the champions and the FA Cup winners was supposed to be a showpiece event. Live on TV for the first time, the match developed into an ill-tempered brawl. The animosity came to a head when Kevin Keegan and Billy Bremner were both sent off for trading punches. As they left the pitch they petulantly tore off their shirts and threw them on the pitch. The players were each fined £500 and handed a ten-match ban. Ted Croker defended what critics claimed was a harsh penalty by saying: 'We are trying to make football more acceptable to a wider range of people.' He knew that the lack of discipline on the field was becoming an issue of mounting concern.

On the afternoon in the autumn when Keegan and Bremner returned from suspension eight players – including Steve Kember (Chelsea), Asa Hartford (Manchester City) and Phil Beal (Tottenham) – were sent off. This was the highest number ever dismissed in one day. Revie carried Croker's message about discipline to his England team when he met the players for the first time. His Leeds team had been among the worst offenders in the First Division but now, in his FA blazer, he was on the side of the righteous. Wisely, one of his first decisions as England manager was to invite 81 players, all of whom qualified for England, to a meeting in a Manchester hotel. These were the people upon whom he would be depending as he attempted to restore England's reputation. Obviously, all the well-established internationals were there, players like Alan Ball, Peter Shilton, Mick

Channon, Emlyn Hughes, Colin Bell and Roy McFarland. Quite
understandably there were a few from Elland Road – Norman
Hunter, Paul Madeley, Terry Cooper and Allan Clarke among
them. There were also a few uncapped surprises on the invitation
list, such as Peter Taylor from Third Division Crystal Palace and
my West Ham team-mates Graham Paddon and Billy Bonds.
Obviously I was particularly interested to see who would be challenging for midfield places under the new manager. Among others
he picked were two I rated highly – Gerry Francis of Queens Park
Rangers and Alan Hudson of Stoke City.

I thought that getting the players together was a clever move by
the new manager. He was letting the fringe players know that they
were in his thoughts and he was telling the established players not
to take too much for granted. Looking back, it's extraordinary that
he could summon 81 players, all of whom he considered to have a
realistic chance of playing for England. Could it happen today? I
don't think so. You certainly couldn't find 81 English players of
international quality – even international potential – in today's
Premier League and Championship.

At the meeting in a five-star hotel, with the Manchester rain
washing down the windows of the evocatively named Peacock
Suite, he told us that he wanted to stimulate competition for places.
He expected exemplary behaviour on and off the field. He found
time to talk to each of us individually. He said that he wanted us to
be one big family. He said England had slipped in the global ratings
and he wanted to see us back near the top of the ladder before the
1978 World Cup. We were going to do it, he said, for the fans and
the country and he then announced that he'd adopted 'Land of
Hope and Glory' as England's anthem.

He appealed to our sense of patriotism but there were other
more basic elements in the Revie package. He said, for instance,
that he was going to negotiate a better financial deal for the players

with the FA. At the time we received £100 as an appearance fee every time we played for England but he later secured an additional £100 for a draw and £200 for a win. He also tossed in the fact that he thought winning the 1978 World Cup should be worth as much as £10,000 a man. We later learned that the FA's International Committee had agreed to the new manager's request to pay £2,000 a man for qualifying for the 1976 European Championship, £1,000 for winning the quarter-final, £1,000 for winning the semi-final and a further £1,000 for winning the title. This was naturally well received by the players. Win bonuses were common at most clubs. But, to be honest, no one was going to play any harder because of the extra money.

Others were not so sure about Revie or his motives. A long-time adversary, Alan Hardaker, the hard-nosed secretary of the Football League, was convinced that Revie was 'money mad'. This perception grew during Revie's reign until it was not uncommon to see newspaper headlines referring to him as 'Don Readies'. I'm not sure that this was entirely fair. The professional game was changing and, like it or loathe it, the FA had a duty to keep pace. Don was criticised for involving the England squad in commercial deals, including the new shirt contract with Admiral, but people forget that most of the revenue filtered back into the game and helped improve standards and facilities at all levels.

The commercial aspect was becoming increasingly important, but for me and the majority of my team-mates the honour of simply playing for England was enough motivation. Even so, the manager said he would test our loyalty and commitment by insisting we report for duty whenever we were selected for an international match. If a player was genuinely injured, he said, he would be sent home after he had been examined by the England team doctor. Most players were desperate to wear the England shirt but some clubs would pull them out of international duty at the first sign of a tweaked muscle. Revie, of course, was well aware of this. As the manager of Leeds he hadn't needed much of an excuse to withdraw his players from international duty.

He hadn't left much to chance as a club manager and he was just as diligent and organised at international level. He was methodical, forthright and liked to ensure the players were kept busy when they were on international duty. The Ramsey regime had been more relaxed. Don introduced games like bingo and carpet bowls and a 10pm curfew. He made it clear when we all gathered for the first time on that Saturday evening in Manchester that any player not in his room by ten that night would not be invited again.

Les Cocker, his assistant, used to tour the corridors when we were in hotels, ensuring that all the players were in their rooms. If you couldn't sleep you were given a sleeping pill. I never had trouble sleeping before a game. I always filled my time reading, listening to music or playing cards with Kevin Keegan and Emlyn Hughes.

Don tried to recreate with England what he had at Leeds. He wanted the kind of unity and camaraderie he had fostered at Elland Road. He loved getting the players together. He loved team meetings. His preparation for matches was thorough. He told you what he expected from you. He loved dossiers. Before a match each player would receive a written breakdown of the opposition. We were expected to study this so that we were prepared for whatever our opponents served up. There were some useful bits of information about how the opposing team took their free kicks and defended at corners. But reading that your opponent 'has a great left foot' isn't good for confidence! In those days, of course, foreign teams and players could be a real mystery package. Today, because of extensive TV coverage, most Premiership players know everything about their rivals worldwide and in many cases play with or against them on a regular basis.

Forty years ago I suppose Don was simply trying to familiarise his team with the opposition. In that sense he was a thoroughly modern manager. Unlike Ramsey, he courted the media. He also renewed hostilities with Hardaker, with whom he had crossed swords many times as manager of Leeds. He wanted the First Division fixtures postponed on the Saturday before international matches so that his players would be well-rested and injury-free – a debate that was to rage on for years.

He wanted to spend more time with the players to work on tactics and team shape. He believed in a rigid structure. I found that strange. I was used to Ron Greenwood at West Ham. He encouraged you to do the unexpected. He liked a good degree of flexibility in his team. But Don wanted us to keep our shape. He was essentially a 4-4-2 man, though he occasionally played with three in midfield, and if you did anything to unbalance the structure you were in trouble.

I played 17 times for England during the three years of Revie's reign and I started most of those games wide on the left. You didn't always see a lot of the ball in the wide positions and if I wasn't getting involved I tended to float inside to look for the ball. But, when I did that, I got a rollicking for unbalancing the team. At West Ham Ron Greenwood had taught me the value of creating and using space. I had been encouraged to search for space. It was almost the essence of the game as West Ham played it. But at half time in the European Championship tie with Portugal at Wembley in November 1974 Don took me to one side and said: 'For God's sake stay wide – you're unbalancing the team.'

A crowd of 84,461 jeered and booed as we left the pitch at the end of the goalless draw with Portugal. We didn't deserve much better, to be fair. But it hadn't been like that three weeks earlier when Don led the team out for his first game in charge. It was against Czechoslovakia, the opening fixture in the qualifying programme for

Euro 1976. We looked good in our new Admiral kit, with red and white stripes down the arms, and the crowd, given song sheets before the kick-off, captured the mood of optimism by singing 'Land of Hope and Glory'. Gerry Francis, then just 22, made his debut in what was quite a young side. Only Emlyn Hughes and Colin Bell had played more than 30 times for England.

I started on the bench which more or less confirmed my suspicions that Revie had a more defensive outlook than Ramsey. As an attacking player I suspected that my England opportunities might be limited under Revie. My chance came in the 65th minute with the game deadlocked at 0-0. I was sent on to replace Martin Dobson and, at the same time, QPR winger Dave Thomas, making his debut, replaced Frank Worthington.

Dave was one of the best wingers in the game at the time and, two minutes after his introduction, he supplied the cross from which Mick Channon scored the opening goal. That was the breakthrough. Suddenly the game changed and we swamped them, scoring twice more through Colin Bell in the space of nine minutes. In the end it was a comfortable victory and the crowd cheered and sang as we left the pitch. I remember the big smile on Don's face. He couldn't have asked for a better start. His decision to introduce twin substitutes was interpreted as a tactical masterstroke. It was obvious that his attitude towards substitutions was very different to Ramsey's.

I thought Dave Thomas and I had made a good impression and, three weeks later, we were in the starting line-up for the game against Portugal. The manager played me wide on the right but, with my tendency to drift out of position, he wasn't very happy with my contribution. How else could you explain the fact that I had to wait a full 12 months for my next England cap? By that time, the Czechs had thrashed Cyprus 4-0, Portugal 5-0 and beaten England 2-1 in Bratislava in a match that was initially abandoned after the first 17 minutes because of fog. Those results more or less secured the Czechs a place in the 1976 European finals. They finished one point ahead of England in the qualifying group and – what most people forget – went on to win the European title, beating West Germany on penalties after a 2-2 draw that went to extra time in Belgrade.

During the year I was on the sidelines as Revie chopped and changed his personnel, giving chances to players like Stoke's Alan Hudson, Leicester's Steve Whitworth, QPR's Ian Gillard, Ipswich's Kevin Beattie, David Johnson and Colin Viljoen, Manchester City's Dennis Tueart and Brian Little of Aston Villa. If the football was sometimes of indifferent quality, the fact was that England remained unbeaten in Revie's first nine games. This run of results included a 2-0 win over West Germany, their first defeat since winning the World Cup the previous year. Revie reinstated 1966 hero Alan Ball as captain for this game and gave a debut to Hudson, who had all the qualities needed, on the field at least, to be an international midfield player.

He played well against the Germans and was retained in midfield for the next game – a Euro qualifier against Cyprus at Wembley. Newcastle's Malcolm Macdonald, who had scored against the Germans, set a post-war record by scoring all of England's goals in the 5-0 rout of Cyprus. Hudson, too, was an influential figure once more but, inexplicably, Revie discarded him and he never played for England again. Looking back, two England caps seems a pitifully small return for a player of Hudson's talent.

While Revie talked a lot about recreating the harmonious atmosphere he'd had at Leeds he was beginning to mystify the players by dropping some without warning and for no obvious reason. He so upset Kevin Keegan when he left him out of the team, without explanation, for a Home Championship clash with Wales that he packed his bags and stormed off. When Revie finally got the chance to explain, he told Kevin that he wanted to rest him so that he was fresh for the big Home Championship clash against Scotland at Wembley. He could have told him that in the first place.

Sure enough, Kevin was in the line-up against the Scots. I was by now beginning to wonder whether I'd ever get back in the side, especially as England thrashed Scotland 5-1, with Gerry Francis, one of my midfield rivals, scoring twice. Gerry had good all-round skills, though he was often troubled by injury. Nonetheless he looked as though he would be an England fixture for years when Revie decided to make him captain.

This decision came out of the blue and no one was more surprised than the 1966 hero Alan Ball, who had been captain in the previous six matches. Alan knew nothing about it until a journalist called his wife, asking for a reaction to his being dropped. 'Bally' was furious. 'I cherished the captaincy,' he said at the time. He wondered whether it was Revie's response to a rare indiscretion when Alan and some other players broke the evening curfew and went out for a drink during a three-day get-together at West Lodge Park hotel near Cockfosters, north London. Whatever the reason, the match against Scotland was the 72nd and last time Alan played for England. He was just 30.

Although no one realised it then, the 5-1 thrashing of the Scots was one of the few highlights of the Revie managerial reign. The defeat in Czechoslovakia put our European Championship hopes in jeopardy and meant that we had to win our final game in Portugal to have any chance of qualifying. I was delighted to be recalled after a year's absence for such an important game, but we performed indifferently. Rui Rodrigues gave Portugal the lead with a spectacular free kick after 16 minutes in the old Estadio Jose Alvalade and although Mick Channon got a goal back it wasn't enough. A week later the Czechs beat Cyprus 3-0, eliminating England and securing their place in the final.

It was the beginning of the end for Don. Bitterly disappointed to fall at the first hurdle as England manager, he embarked on a team-rebuilding programme. I hoped I would be part of this and, despite my long absence, had some reason for optimism. He had called 30 players together at West Lodge Park and I had been one of them. During a private chat he told me that he thought I could be a regular member of his team if I could adopt a more aggressive attitude and dictate the pattern of play. 'You've got a tendency to drift out of the game,' he said. 'You drift along instead of shaping the way you want the game to go.'

It was well-meaning advice and I accepted much of it. I knew I could be more assertive and I vowed then to try to add a little more aggression to my game if and when I was next picked. Sure enough, I was called into the team for the first fixture of 1976 – the Welsh FA Centenary game in Wrexham. With the European failure still raw, Revie gave starting places to six new caps – Trevor Cherry (Leeds), Phil Neal (Liverpool), Phil Thompson (Liverpool), Mike Doyle (Manchester City), Phil Boyer (Norwich City) and Ray Kennedy (Liverpool). He also gave debuts to two of the substitutes – Dave Clement (QPR) and Peter Taylor (Crystal Palace).

Maybe the manager's encouraging words had an effect, but whatever the reason I played well. It was possibly my best game for England during Don Revie's reign. Terry Yorath, the Wales captain who had played under Revie for Leeds, was my immediate opponent. He was a hard ball-winner in midfield and was also a good long-passer. I think he had a hard time that night. I played in central midfield because Ray Kennedy was given the wide role on the left. Ray scored our first goal and Peter Taylor, brought on to replace Channon, scored the second. Pete was the first Third Division player to appear in an England shirt since 1962 when another Palace player, Johnny Byrne, made his debut.

Pete, who later worked with me as a youth coach at the FA

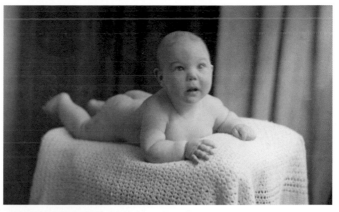

Already a bit chunky –
me at six months.

Father Christmas
eyeing me
suspiciously!

Mum and dad and elder
brother Tony with me
sitting at the front.

The Ilford County High School football team. That's me with the ball at my feet in 1962–63.

I was playing for Ilford Boys against Oxford when the West Ham manager Ron Greenwood came to watch me. I'm in the front row with my England cap on my knee.

Practising our smiles in the summer of 1968. We grew up together on the training ground at Chadwell Heath and were all after the same thing – a first-team place. (Trevor Brooking, Frank Lampard, Harry Redknapp, Peter Bennett, Bobby Howe)

My Finnish wife Hilkka. I met her at my brother Tony's wedding to her friend Ritva.

Warren, aged three, already showing a little of dad's balance and poise!

Collette, aged ten, on her favourite pony Misty.

Buckingham Palace, July 1981. With Hilkka and the children after I received the MBE from the Queen.

Surrounded by two World Cup winners, with Martin Peters to my right and Geoff Hurst to my left during West Ham's match against Southampton in November 1969.
(Getty Images)

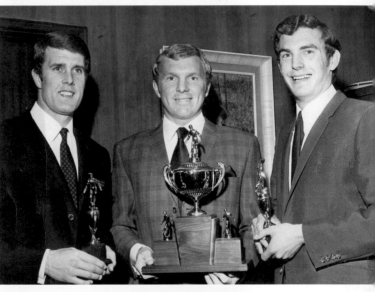

Not bad, finishing third behind Bobby Moore and Geoff Hurst in the voting for Hammer of the Year in 1969–70.

Frank Lampard looks on as I take the attack to Manchester United.
(Getty Images)

Taking on former Hammer Bobby Moore during the 1975 FA Cup final. In truth, it wasn't a particularly great game. *(Mirrorpix)*

Goalscorer Alan Taylor, Billy Bonds and I celebrate winning the trophy at Newham Town Hall. *(Mirrorpix)*

Pat Holland pours me a glass of champagne after I scored two goals against Eintracht Frankfurt to help put us through to the final of the European Cup Winners' Cup in 1976. *(Getty Images)*

David Cross was one of the funniest men to play for West Ham but had no idea how to steer a bicycle. Me and Ray Stewart hang on grimly!

A rare moment indeed. I stoop low to head home the winner in the 1980 FA Cup final against Arsenal.
(Getty Images)

Usually a front-runner, Stuart Pearson (left) was given a withdrawn role behind David Cross in the final. It was a tactical move that disrupted Arsenal's defensive strategy. Here he backs me up as I ride a tackle from Graham Rix.

Paul Allen was 17 years and 256 days old when he became the youngest player to appear in a Wembley FA Cup final, in 1980. He was my man of the match and in this picture is about to embark on a well-deserved lap of honour with the FA Cup and Geoff Pike.

In the olden days we always used to hear news of our next cup opponents on the radio. Here the West Ham manager John Lyall and I wait to hear who we play next in the European Cup Winners' Cup in 1980–81. It was Dinamo Tbilisi, an outstanding team from the USSR, who beat us 4-2 on aggregate.

We still had two games to play but, such was our lead, we were presented with the old Second Division trophy after beating Wrexham 1-0 at Upton Park in May 1981. We finished with a record 66 points.

This was an emotional day for me in May 1984. It was West Ham's last home match of the season and the last of my professional career. An angry John Lyall locked my team-mates in the dressing room after a 1-0 defeat to Everton, while I picked up scarves on my farewell lap of honour.

and, of course, managed England for one match following the departure of Kevin Keegan, was an outstandingly talented winger who never quite fulfilled his promise. Revie, and all the players for that matter, enjoyed his company because he was a funny guy in the dressing room and his Norman Wisdom act used to have us rolling about on the floor with laughter. When looked at in the context of the modern game, it is astonishing to think that Revie unearthed Peter Taylor from the third tier of the English League. He kept him in the side for the next match – against Wales again, but this time in the Home Championship at Ninian Park – and Pete responded with the only goal of the game. Three new players appeared in an England shirt that day – Manchester United's Brian Greenhoff and Stuart Pearson and Tony Towers of Sunderland.

That meant that in consecutive games Revie had handed out 11 new caps. It was becoming increasingly obvious that while he had initially sought to replicate the cosy family atmosphere he'd created among a close-knit bunch of players at Leeds, he was now chopping and changing to an unrealistic extent. Players were mystified when he made seven changes for one match and another seven for the next match. For my part I never felt a permanent member of the squad. I never had the feeling that I was an integral part of his plans. I wasn't the only one who felt that way. There was no stability and no established pattern of play. He was ruthless enough to make wholesale changes but not far-seeing enough to realise that he needed a settled team to be successful.

Revie introduced more new players for the US Bicentennial Tournament at the end of the 1975–76 season. He brought in the Aston Villa goalkeeper Jimmy Rimmer, the Manchester City goalkeeper Joe Corrigan, Ray Wilkins, the 19-year-old Chelsea midfield player and Gordon Hill, the Manchester United winger. It was a good trip designed, I thought at least in part, to help us prepare for the opening World Cup qualifying fixture in Finland in June. We played well but lost 1-0 to Brazil in Los Angeles where I witnessed probably the best pass I'd ever seen – a 60-yarder from the left foot of Roberto Rivelino.

Five days later we faced Italy in New York – a significant game because the Italians were in our World Cup qualifying group. I played again, but Revie decided to make changes rather than field his strongest team. He didn't want to give away too much to the Italians so Ray Clemence, Colin Todd, Trevor Cherry and Kevin Keegan were all left on the sidelines. Revie was always looking for ways to gain a small tactical advantage. Once, in a friendly match against Switzerland in Basle at the start of the season, he tried to confuse watching rival managers by mixing up all our shirt numbers!

We were the ones in a state of confusion in New York, though, when Torino's young striker Francesco Graziani scored twice for Italy in the first half. I thought we might be overrun but we pulled ourselves together in the second half. Young Wilkins played brilliantly on his debut in the centre of midfield and had a significant role in our revival. We scored three goals in seven minutes – Mick Channon, captain for the day, providing two and Phil Thompson scoring the other. It was a good confidence boost, considering what was coming up a few months later. After that 3-2 win we flew to Philadelphia for our final tour match against a North American select team that included Bobby Moore, Tommy Smith, Mike England and Pele. Because 'Team America' wasn't recognised as an official US team the match didn't have full international status, but it was useful. I played again in midfield with Trevor Cherry and Gerry Francis and we won 3-1. Kevin Keegan scored twice for us and the former Watford winger Stewart Scullion scored for the Americans.

A week after returning from the United States we faced Finland in Helsinki. This was the start of a World Cup adventure that we hoped would lead to Argentina in 1978. We were buoyant as we

flew out, with Elton John among the guests on the England charter plane. We couldn't have made a more encouraging start and, for
once, the manager seemed to have something like a settled team
in a 4-3-3 formation. Pearson, Channon and Keegan played at the
front, as they had done in three of the previous four games, and the
midfield of Francis, Cherry and Brooking had played together in
America.

All three front players scored on a bumpy pitch, Kevin netting
two, in a 4-1 win. It was perhaps the highlight of Revie's reign
though, in all honesty, the score did little more than reflect the vast
gulf in football status between the two countries. We started the
1976–77 season with a disappointing 1-1 draw against the Republic
of Ireland at Wembley – Derby County's Charlie George playing 77
minutes of his only England game – and a month later met the
Finns again in the second leg of the World Cup qualifier at
Wembley. This time the gulf in class wasn't so apparent. I retained
my position in midfield, until I was replaced by substitute Mick
Mills in the 75th minute. I was about to take a corner on the far side
of the pitch when the referee halted play so that England could
make the substitution. You're never happy to be substituted but it's
a particularly bleak experience if you have to trot across the width
of the pitch as I did that day. It was a much-changed England team
this time and we struggled to win 2-1. At the end we knew that,
from a goal difference point of view, we had missed a big opportunity. We left the field to growls of disapproval. There was a sense
of foreboding and discontent as we prepared for the big one – the
heavyweight clash with Italy in Rome.

Revie's team selection for this match was partly determined by
long-term injuries to Colin Bell and Gerry Francis but was also
influenced by his own self-doubts and uncertainties. He bowed to
public pressure by recalling the QPR striker Stan Bowles, who had
talent but was so unpredictable. He'd walked out when Joe Mercer

dropped him from the line-up to face the Scots but his inclusion, and that of team-mate Dave Clement at right-back, reflected the emergence of QPR under Dave Sexton in the mid-seventies. Unfortunately, the back four of Clement, Hughes, McFarland and Mills had never played together before. What's more, I was the only attacking player in midfield. Trevor Cherry and Brian Greenhoff were essentially defensive players. It was a team designed to contain the Italians, who Revie had watched seven times. His dossiers were inches thick!

The Italians, who had beaten England for the first time in 40 years of trying in 1973, chose seven players from Juventus and, inevitably, looked far more of a team than we did. But for the first 30 minutes Enzo Bearzot's young side struggled to make any headway. Then, ten minutes before half time, Giancarlo Antognoni's free kick took a wicked deflection on its way past Ray Clemence into the net. Our response was indifferent. We hardly had a sight of the Italian goal. Stan Bowles was isolated at the front and there was a sense that a single-goal defeat might not be the end of the world. We could beat them by a greater margin in the return at Wembley and still qualify. That theory came to an abrupt end 12 minutes from time when Roberto Bettega, the 'White Feather' from Juventus, scored with a flying header. We knew then that we had almost certainly blown our chances of qualifying for Argentina. Bettega was a gifted technical player, a great stylist with many admirers. Years later Liam Brady recalled that when he left Arsenal to join Juventus he shared a room with Bettega, because he spoke English. Liam got an early taste of the Bettega 'style' on their first trip. While he was lounging around their room in his Y-fronts Bettega was resplendent in Givenchy dressing gown and Gucci slippers.

The Italians had a good team that was particularly ruthless and efficient when it came to defending a lead. They had some really strong and devious players, such as Marco Tardelli and Claudio

Gentile. They didn't miss a trick. When Emlyn Hughes lost his boot one of the Italian players kicked it straight into the crowd. Emlyn had to hobble about while the England staff in the dugout searched for another boot. 'The bastards!' said Revie grimly to his colleagues on the bench. 'You don't like it but you have to admire it!' My immediate opponent that day was Romeo Benetti, who was a chunkier version of Peter Storey. He went in hard and wasn't too bothered if he was a bit late with his tackle. His stare alone would stop a buffalo in its tracks!

Morale was low when we flew home from Rome and had not improved much when we faced Holland three months later in a prestigious friendly match. Holland at that time meant Johan Cruyff, the maestro of the Total Football strategy with which the Dutch enthralled the world in the seventies. Their starting line-up that night at Wembley included seven of the team that had been beaten by the Germans in the 1974 World Cup final – Suurbier, Rijsbergen, Krol, Neeskens, Rep, Cruyff, Rensenbrink.

I retained my place in England's midfield and Revie gave a debut to 22-year-old Trevor Francis, who had just scored six goals in five matches for Birmingham City, including a hat-trick against Arsenal. In all, Revie made five changes to the side beaten by the Italians but it made little difference. He had repeated the mistake he made in Rome by fielding two ball-winners in midfield – Brian Greenhoff and Paul Madeley. It was a disaster. The Dutch were all over us. Their concept of Total Football, of creating space and running off the ball, couldn't have been further from Revie's rigid team structure.

We were given a lesson in how to play the game. After 30 minutes, Cruyff and Neeskens split our defence, allowing Jan Peters to run through and shoot past Clemence. Nine minutes later Peters took a pass from Hovenkamp, sidestepped Beattie and drove his second goal past Clemence. It was the first time the Dutch had beaten England in six attempts. For me, the match had been a great educational experience. Watching Cruyff and Johan Neeskens – who were both at Barcelona at the time – was a pleasure. I think the Dutch team of the seventies was the best international side I played against in my career. When they were moving into space and passing the ball well they were untouchable. I'm reminded of them when I watch the current Barcelona in action.

The way they played in the seventies almost defies description. They had a flowing, fluid, rotational style with the emphasis very much on attack. Practically every player was encouraged to go forward and take risks. Cruyff could turn up at right-back or left-wing. It didn't seem to make any difference to the efficiency of the team. It was very different from the structural style of play employed by most English teams. When I was at Lilleshall studying for my coaching badge the FA coaching guru Allen Wade organised a session based on the Total Football concept. In the match, I played at right-back. Everyone played out of their natural position so that they could appreciate the things an opponent would be thinking and doing in a real match situation. It was an interesting exercise but I think the coaching purist would have considered it a disaster.

For five or six years Cruyff was easily the best player in the world. He was two-footed, beat defenders with ease, scored goals, and his decision-making was brilliant. I loved watching him. He won six league titles with Ajax and three European Cups, and was European Footballer of the Year three times. Strangely, he refused to play for his country in the 1978 World Cup in Argentina. Many Dutchmen still feel today that with Cruyff in the team Holland would have won the title instead of losing 3-1 after extra time to the host nation in the final.

I think the nature of the Dutch defeat confirmed the suspicions of several senior figures in the dressing room: while we had good-quality individual players we were not performing well enough as a team. In many ways it was a landmark moment for England, but not as significant as the first Wembley defeat against foreign opposition – beaten 6-3 by Hungary in 1953. After all, we had only *just* failed to qualify for the 1978 World Cup finals. We had the same number of points as the group winners, Italy, and had conceded the same number of goals (four). But they had scored three more goals than us and so qualified on goal difference.

I don't think Don's obsession with tinkering with the team line-ups helped our cause. We had good players but he often used them in unfamiliar positions. He'd often play me wide on the left when I was playing well for West Ham in a central midfield role. I think one of the problems all England managers have faced is the shortage of preparation time. Don had a fabulous team at Leeds – great individuals who played well together – but they had benefited from years of work as a group on the training pitch. A good coach can reap huge rewards from long hours spent working on organisation and team play on the training pitch. Look at what Brian Clough achieved at Nottingham Forest. Even his most ardent fans wouldn't claim that his sides were packed with international superstars. Yet, with players like Ian Bowyer, Frank Clark, John O'Hare, Garry Birtles, Larry Lloyd, Gary Mills and Bryn Gunn he led Forest to consecutive European Cup triumphs. He may not have had the best individuals in Europe but he did have the best team.

Several senior players, Mick Channon among them, were voicing their opinions about England's decline at this time. Mick was the most capped player under Revie, but he thought that the manager was placing too much emphasis on tactics. Others mocked his intensity or his passion for parlour games and dossiers. Don must have sensed the discontent among the players. I was one of seven dropped a month later when we met Luxembourg in a World Cup qualifier at Wembley. More than 81,000 turned up to watch England win 5-0. Ray Kennedy took my place on the left and

Revie handed more debuts, to John Gidman, the Aston Villa right-back, and Paul Mariner, the Ipswich Town striker.

I was back in the team two months later for the Home Championship clash with Northern Ireland in Belfast, not the most relaxed place to visit in those times. On this occasion Revie made eight changes and gave a debut to Ipswich's Brian Talbot, who came on as a substitute and set up the winner for Dennis Tueart in England's 2-1 victory. Then it really started to go wrong for Revie. We met Wales at Wembley three days after the Irish match. It was an unusual England side, with Ray Kennedy and me both in the team that showed another five changes. There was only one goal – and the Welsh scored it. Peter Shilton fouled Leighton James after Emlyn Hughes slipped up and the Welsh winger scored from the penalty spot. It was the first time the Welsh had won at Wembley in peacetime.

Worse was to follow. Four days later, on 4 June 1977, the 'old enemy' visited Wembley for the decisive Home International match. I was picked in the team originally but had to drop out with a training-ground injury. I sat in the stands with the squad members who were not involved in the match. In those days you had to wear your FA blazer, so we were easily identifiable to the Scots sitting around us. We became the focus of their attention as the Scots first dismantled the England team and then the Wembley goalposts. The Scots needed only a point to share the title with Wales but a win would give it to them outright. It had been ten years since they'd last won at Wembley. The Scots delighted their thousands of fans in the stadium by taking the lead two minutes before half time, Gordon McQueen rising above the England defence to head a free kick past Ray Clemence. Kenny Dalglish scored a second in the 59th minute and although Mick Channon scored from the penalty spot in the 87th minute it was too little too late to save England.

It was the first time England had lost successive games at Wembley. The Scots were deliriously happy and their fans invaded the pitch at the end, snapping both crossbars and ripping up the netting and large areas of turf. The TV pictures from Wembley that day made unedifying viewing and strengthened the growing calls for fences, travel bans, identity cards – in fact, anything that might halt the descent into anarchy on England's football terraces.

Three Wembley defeats in the space of three months represented a unique blip in England's long and distinguished record. Those results against Holland, Wales and Scotland plus the almost inevitable failure to qualify for the 1978 World Cup – the Scots, meanwhile, were on their way to Argentina – heightened Revie's disillusionment. I think he believed there was a conspiracy to oust him and so he began quietly plotting an escape route. The players knew nothing of this as they prepared for a summer tour to South America, originally arranged as part of England's rehearsals for the World Cup in Argentina the following year. The press had slaughtered Revie, and when his assistant Les Cocker addressed the touring party before our departure he said: 'The boss has had a bit of stick so I've told him to take a rest for a few days.'

Cocker, a former Stockport County striker who had coached both Leeds United and England since 1962, added that Revie would be flying to Helsinki to watch World Cup rivals Italy play Finland and would join the touring party for England's second match against Argentina. But, secretly, Revie went first to Dubai where he agreed a contract to become the national manager of the United Arab Emirates for a reputed £340,000 over four years, a small fortune in those days. He then went to watch Italy in Finland before flying to Buenos Aires.

The players still knew nothing. The opening tour match was against Brazil and the likes of Zico, Rivelino and Paulo Cesar. It ended goalless in Rio. I had hoped to play but pulled up with a recurrence of my hamstring strain in training and was sent home along with Manchester United's injured Gordon Hill. By the time Revie arrived in Argentina a couple of days later Italy had beaten Finland 3-0 and virtually clinched World Cup qualification. His first appointment in Buenos Aires was with Dick Wragg, the chairman of the FA's International Committee. He told him that he wanted the FA to pay up the remaining two years of his contract, together with that of Les Cocker. He said that he was convinced the FA was about to sack him. Wragg was astonished. When FA secretary Ted Croker heard the news he said: 'To say he was leaving England in the lurch and wanted paying off for the privilege was laughable.'

Revie resumed control of the team for the remaining two matches. A 1-1 draw with World Cup hosts Argentina – Passarella, Ardiles, Tarantini et al – was memorable only for the dismissal of Trevor Cherry, who had his two front teeth knocked out by Daniel Bertoni. The final match was a goalless draw with Uruguay in Montevideo, notable only for the fact that it was Revie's last in charge. But no one knew that at the time.

It wasn't until early July that the *Daily Mail* broke the story of Revie's defection to the UAE. He'd actually been approached by the FA about renewing his contract, but his mind was made up. Like everyone else, the FA learned about Revie's exit from the newspaper. There was a sense of outrage, particularly when rumours emerged that he had been paid £20,000 by the *Daily Mail* for his exclusive story.

I wasn't entirely surprised that he'd gone. Nor were most of the other players. He'd won only two of his last nine games. He'd failed to qualify for the European finals and was about to fail again in the World Cup. He hadn't been able to replicate his success at club level. He hated criticism. As the pressure mounted he became increasingly frustrated. It wasn't the fact that he'd deserted that upset people as much as the way he did it. It was impossible to defend the manner of his departure.

But defend it he did. A messy legal wrangle ensued. Revie was accused by the FA of bringing the game into disrepute on four counts and was banned from involvement in football for ten years. He eventually had the ban lifted in the High Court but the judge's claim that he was deceitful and greedy further harmed his reputation. His deal with the Arabs made him rich, of course, but little else. He worked as national manager of the UAE, then coached two club sides, Al-Nassr and Al-Ahly, from 1977 to 1985. When he returned to the UK he retired to Scotland and died in Edinburgh of motor neurone disease at the age of 61. The FA had no representative at his funeral but all of his old Leeds United players attended.

Sadly, his England reign coincided with one of the darkest periods in the national game. But many of his problems were of his own making. He used an incredible number of players – 52 – during his 29 matches, whereas Ramsey had used 95 players in 113 matches. Ironically, the only unchanged team he fielded was in his last game against Uruguay in Montevideo.

Looking back now, I think his failures to qualify for the European Championship finals in 1976 and the World Cup in 1978 lie behind his inability to build a settled team and find a successful playing style. It was not the failures themselves, but the fact that England's absence from tournament football meant he never had the players together for any significant period. During my time at the FA it became clear how highly coaches value a few weeks of tournament football. These are the only occasions when international coaches can spend quality time getting their ideas across to individuals and the squad as a whole. Don Revie created a successful formula at Leeds United but, naturally, had the benefit of working with his players regularly over an extended period. As

England manager he was never going to enjoy the same advantages as a club manager, but he did have two opportunities to have his squad together for significant periods of time at major tournaments. He squandered both in the qualifying campaigns and this failure, I think, helps explain why he struggled as England manager.

CHAPTER 9

'CAN YOU HEAR ME,
MAGGIE THATCHER?'

IN HIS AUTOBIOGRAPHY, *Yours Sincerely*, Ron Greenwood recalled once being asked to whom he was answerable as team manager of England. Ron replied: 'Nobody – except the nation.' The man who offered me a chance as a youngster at West Ham became manager of England, initially on a caretaker basis, in August 1977. He accepted the FA's invitation to act as team manager for three matches while they searched for a permanent replacement for Don Revie.

His desertion had left a sour taste and the then FA chairman, Professor Sir Harold Thompson, told the media that England needed a steady hand to restore faith and dignity. Ron was the right man for the job at the right time. He had become increasingly disenchanted with the game since handing over the first-team reins at West Ham to John Lyall in 1974, but had never lost his enthusiasm for working with players. He needed to be on the training pitch, and his decision to become general manager at West Ham robbed him of the one aspect of the game that mattered most to him.

The FA's invitation to take over gave him the chance to pull on a tracksuit again and get out on the pitch. It was what he was good at. He was the most imaginative and thoughtful coach I worked with in my career. Technically there was no one to touch him. He was acknowledged globally as one of football's most innovative coaches. Even today, England players of that era will tell you how much they thought of him. The Liverpool lads of the time were playing for the best, most successful club in Europe and they thought he was terrific to work with. It was a great shame that he was lost to the game after his five-year reign as England manager.

In the summer of 1977 he, along with former England manager Walter Winterbottom, was part of the FIFA technical committee at the first World Youth Championship in Tunisia. It was while he was in Tunisia that the FA approached West Ham and asked for permission to speak to Ron. When he returned home the first call he received was from the West Ham chairman, Reg Pratt. He told Ron that the FA wanted to speak to him urgently. 'I think they're in trouble after the Revie business,' he explained.

Many years earlier, when Ron was coaching at Arsenal, he had been appointed manager of the England Under-23 team. Walter Winterbottom was the senior team manager and had hopes of succeeding Sir Stanley Rous as secretary of the Football Association. Walter asked Ron how he'd feel about becoming England manager if he got the FA job as secretary. As it turned out Walter didn't get the job – Denis Follows did – and Alf Ramsey eventually took over as manager.

Ramsey proved to be the right man at the time. Fourteen years later, when Ron was finally appointed as manager, he acknowledged that he simply would not have had the experience for the job in 1963. Looking back, I have no doubt that he had all the necessary qualities when he succeeded Revie. There is a big difference between managing a club and managing a national team but Ron had the knowledge to bridge the gap. The weight of responsibility on the shoulders of the national team manager is huge. Triumph and despair at club level are largely a matter of local interest but, as Ron pointed out, the England manager answers to the country.

Ron was under no illusions. Revie's departure had been sudden. Ron knew that he was probably the only suitable candidate available to take the job at short notice. He also knew that there was a widely held view in the game that he was a 'purist', more concerned about the finer values of the sport than winning for the sake of winning. He knew the FA were advertising for a long-term successor to Revie. He also knew that his ideas about the way the game should be played were better suited to the international game. He wanted to put his ideas into practice but did he have the time to get his thoughts across to the players? Time is always the enemy of the England manager.

Initially, he decided to go on a nationwide tour, visiting every dressing room in the Football League where an England player was in residence. There was only one place to start – Liverpool. They had more England players than anyone else – Ray Clemence, Phil Neal, Phil Thompson, Ray Kennedy, Emlyn Hughes, Ian Callaghan and Terry McDermott, who was to become the first new cap of the Greenwood reign. The biggest name at Liverpool was Kevin Keegan but between his appearances in the 1977 FA Cup final and the European Cup final four days later he had negotiated his £500,000 transfer to SV Hamburg.

Ron listened to what Liverpool's England players – minus Keegan of course – had to say. Emlyn Hughes gave him the impression that they half-expected the latest England manager to walk into the Anfield dressing room wearing a mortarboard and gown. They thought that Ron was a bit of an egghead. He had a mild, schoolmasterly nature and it was true that he had emerged as a coach at a time when footballing academics like Walter Winterbottom and Allen Wade were significant figures in the professional game. But it was unfair to describe him as scholastic. There was far more to the man who was born in a little Lancashire pit village where the kids wore shoes only to go to church and Sunday school.

Ron did nothing to disguise the fact that he had been seriously impressed by the Liverpool players. They had just won the European Cup and were all cult heroes on Merseyside, but there was nothing pretentious about them. That initial meeting was very important in convincing him that he was right to go round the clubs addressing the England men. He took notes wherever he went and, apparently, when he returned to West Ham I told him that the England squad were taking full advantage of the wonderful range of food available at the West Lodge Park hotel!

Some players felt a need for better liaison between the dressing room and the manager. From that suggestion came the appointment of my former West Ham team-mate Geoff Hurst to work on the backroom staff alongside the Scottish-born Fulham and Manchester City coach, Bill Taylor. At the time Geoff was the player-manager of Telford in the Southern League. Only a decade before he'd been a World Cup winner so he had a status that made him ideal for the part-time job with England.

Ron used him to demonstrate ideas he was trying to put across on the training pitch and to sound out the players about things like hotels, travel arrangements and match preparation. It quickly became clear that few had appreciated Revie's strict regime. They had often been pushed into unfamiliar routines. Ron didn't like that. He wanted the players to relax and enjoy their time with England. He told us that, within reason, we could do exactly as we did with our clubs. If we wanted tea in bed in the morning it was okay. If we wanted to go to the cinema in the evening that was okay too. Ron believed that self-discipline was the best kind of discipline. When newcomers joined the squad they were told by the established players: 'Don't mess anything up because you'll be letting us all down.'

Ron's temporary appointment spanned three matches – a friendly against Switzerland at Wembley and two World Cup qualifiers, away to Luxembourg and at home to Italy. As we had already lost the crucial qualifier in Italy a year earlier our chances of getting to Argentina in 1978 were already slim.

The first game against the Swiss, just four weeks after Ron's appointment, followed a winless run of five games. Confidence was low. Not surprisingly, Ron chose a team with six Liverpool players including that new cap for McDermott – and Kevin Keegan. Ian Callaghan's last cap had been 11 years earlier, against France in the 1966 World Cup. Me? I was in the squad, but not in the team. Any hopes I had that Ron's presence might be beneficial to me quickly evaporated.

England didn't play well. The Swiss defended in depth and earned a goalless draw, a result that gave Ron plenty to think about. Five of the Liverpool team retained their places for the next match, including the 35-year-old Callaghan. Goal difference might have been important but we failed to do ourselves justice in Luxembourg, winning the World Cup qualifier 2-0.

Then, in November 1977, we faced Italy at Wembley in our last World Cup tie. Qualification for the Italians, who had still to play Luxembourg, was almost a formality. Ron made changes. He called me into midfield alongside Ray Wilkins and gave new caps to two wingers, Steve Coppell and Peter Barnes, and striker Bob Latchford. We used the width of the pitch well and passed them to death. We could have scored four or five but in the end settled for 2-0, with Kevin and me scoring the goals.

Kevin played just behind Bob Latchford that day in what was

essentially a 4-2-4 line-up. I'd played with him a few times in the past but on this occasion we really hit it off. I supplied the pass for him to score the opening goal and he returned the compliment, creating my first goal for England. It was the start of something special for the two of us. Kevin was brilliant that day. He showed what he was made of. He kept going and never complained despite the attentions of the two Juventus enforcers Romeo Benetti and Marco Tardelli. He was immensely powerful for a little guy and one of the bravest men I played with.

The whole team played with conviction and confidence and Ron was beaming at the end. I was happy too. It was one of my best games for England. But, in real terms, it didn't count for much. The Italians beat Luxembourg in the final qualifying tie, sending England once again into the World Cup wilderness. The style of the England win over Italy did Ron's chances of getting the job on a full-time basis no harm at all. He was interviewed by the FA International Committee, as were Lawrie McMenemy, Bobby Robson, Allen Wade and, the 'people's choice', Brian Clough. On the day the official announcement was made Ron was having lunch with his wife Lucy near Brighton. They heard the news on the car radio.

The next day Ron faced the media, told them how delighted he was and spelled out his plans for the future. These included adopting the Continental idea of establishing a team of coaches to run England's international sides at all levels. Ron believed it would ensure continuity, so that when he left the job the FA would have in place a pool of coaches from whom to select his successor. The system had been in place for years in Germany where it worked very well indeed. The FA agreed and Ron appointed, on a part-time basis, Bobby Robson and Don Howe to run the B team and Terry Venables, Dave Sexton and Howard Wilkinson to run the Under-21 team.

His choice for the Youth side was bold – Brian Clough and Peter Taylor, the management duo who would lead Nottingham Forest to successive European Cup wins. It was a brave move by Ron, but it didn't last. They argued that their commitment to Forest meant they had little time to work with the Youth team so they stood down and Ron appointed one of the game's brightest young coaches, John Cartwright, a former West Ham player, on a full-time basis. Ron believed that the Youth-team coach was one of the most important jobs in the new set-up.

I think it was a shame that this idea, designed to promote continuity, failed to survive because, in the short term at least, the principle was sound. Three of the coaches Ron appointed went on to manage the senior team: Robson, Venables and Wilkinson, though Howard had only two matches in charge on a caretaker basis.

The two games that followed Ron's confirmation as manager were the toughest you could imagine. Both were against world champions – West Germany in Munich and Brazil at Wembley. I played in Munich, a city in the grip of winter. A foot of snow had been removed from the Olympic Stadium pitch and, to be fair, it played well. Kevin was again outstanding in a head-to-head battle with Rainer Bonhof. A Stuart Pearson header gave us the lead but the German substitute Ronnie Worm pinched an equaliser. The previous night Ronnie had played as a substitute against the England B team on a snowy pitch at Augsburg and scored, though we eventually won 2-1.

A 1-1 draw looked the inevitable outcome in the senior match in Munich until the final seconds when the Germans were awarded a free kick on the edge of our area. Bonhof, a dead-ball specialist, spotted a gap in our wall and curled in the German winner. It was Ron's first defeat as England manager.

I missed the game against Brazil at Wembley because I was

injured. Strangely, it was a bit of a kicking match and five of the Brazilians were booked. Their coach at the time, Claudio Coutinho, insisted that Brazil would never recapture their past glories until they learned to be as physical as the Europeans. The match finished 1-1 but I suspect that Ron was really disappointed to see the way the Brazilians played. They were not being true to themselves. In his book there was no greater sin.

We won our next three games, beating Wales, Northern Ireland and Scotland in the British Championship, and then faced World Cup qualifiers Hungary at Wembley. England won 4-1 with a team that I think Ron considered his strongest: Shilton; Neal, Watson, Hughes, Mills; Wilkins, Brooking; Coppell, Francis, Keegan, Barnes.

It was a team without the traditional English-style centre-forward but Ron believed that Francis and Keegan gave us pace and mobility at the front, with Coppell and Barnes providing width and me and Wilkins supplying the ideas and patience to keep the whole thing ticking over. It certainly worked well against the Hungarians, who were in Argentina a couple of weeks later for the 1978 World Cup.

There was a sense that the new England squad was shaping up nicely. England had won six of the nine matches since Ron took over. The Germans had been the only team to beat us. We were, quite naturally, upbeat as we set out to qualify for the 1980 European Championship in Italy. We had some jittery moments – a 4-3 thriller in Denmark and a tough 1-1 draw against a very good Republic of Ireland side in Dublin – but put qualification beyond reasonable doubt with a resounding 3-0 win in Bulgaria.

Ron was also encouraged by the new faces pushing for places in the squad. Glenn Hoddle made his debut in the 2-0 win over Bulgaria on a foggy night at Wembley. Bryan Robson's debut came against the Republic of Ireland. Kenny Sansom was capped for the first time in the British Championship clash with Wales and Viv Anderson secured his place in history when he became the first black player to appear in the senior side against Czechoslovakia in November 1978. Black players are now such an integral part of the game that, looking back, I find it amazing that we didn't have a black player in the England team until 1978. At the time I didn't give it a great deal of thought because I was used to playing along-side black players at West Ham.

Viv was a talented full-back and his introduction was a huge plus for the England side. He had an attacking instinct and long legs that helped him execute some really clinical tackles. Three matches after his debut, Ron brought in West Brom's Laurie Cunningham. He was followed by Cyrille Regis, Luther Blissett, Mark Chamberlain and John Barnes. Then Paul Ince became England's first black captain. Black players are now as much a part of the football landscape as white players. I never experienced any racial issues in the dressing room or on the pitch at any level I played. Footballers judge players on their ability. Nothing else matters.

Anderson, who had just won the European Cup with Nottingham Forest for the second time, was named in the squad for the European finals in Italy. There was some justified optimism in the England camp. In the build-up to the tournament we beat Spain 2-0 in Barcelona, world champions Argentina and Diego Maradona 3-1 at Wembley, and Scotland 2-0 at a boisterous Hampden Park. Steve Coppell and I scored the goals against the Scots. How I used to love those games! They were blue-chip occasions in the football calendar, made extra special by the atmosphere at Hampden Park and the greetings we used to receive from the Scottish fans, tartan kilts raised above their heads, as we drove from the airport to the stadium.

Before we set off for Italy that summer we were invited to a send-off party by Prime Minister Margaret Thatcher in Downing Street. It was a wonderful occasion enjoyed by all the players and coaching staff. Afterwards, we posed for photographs on the steps of No. 10 with the prime minister. One of the Fleet Street photographers produced a football and handed it to Mrs Thatcher. Ron said to her: 'Be careful, Prime Minister, or you'll be heading that ball down the street.' She replied: 'If I'm not mistaken, Trevor Brooking does the heading round here, doesn't he?' I was impressed by her knowledge. A week or so earlier I'd headed the only goal in West Ham's FA Cup final win over Arsenal.

The European Championship in 1980 wasn't a memorable tournament and Ron made no excuses for England's poor showing. England's opening game with Belgium in Turin's old Stadio Communale is remembered chiefly for fighting spectators, interruptions to play and clouds of police tear gas. At one point the fumes from the gas were spilling down the terraces on to the pitch. Ray Clemence, standing on the edge of the penalty area as far from his goal as he could safely go, was wiping his eyes and signalling to the bench that he was in trouble. Ron urged the UEFA match adjudicator to ask the West German referee Heinz Aldinger to halt the game. By the time the match was suspended, several players had streaming eyes. The stoppage lasted five minutes but broke our concentration, and it didn't help knowing that once again it was our supporters who had caused the problem.

We took the lead when Ray Wilkins scored with a wonderful lobbed goal, outwitting their offside trap, after 26 minutes. But we couldn't hold on to our advantage and an equaliser by Jan Ceulemans three minutes later triggered the trouble on the terraces. We had a perfectly good goal by Tony Woodcock disallowed and, of course, we didn't know then how critical that was to prove. A 1-1 draw meant that we would probably have to beat Italy to progress and Ron surprised many by choosing a team with Forest striker Garry Birtles alongside his club-mate Woodcock at the front. Sadly, Trevor Francis missed the tournament because of injury and although Keegan captained the England side throughout the tournament his pace had been blunted by ligament trouble picked up with Hamburg.

The inclusion of Birtles was not the only shock. When Ron stood in the middle of our training pitch at Asti to announce the team to face Italy he had another surprise up his sleeve. Well, at least for me it was a surprise! He decided to leave me out and instead play Liverpool's Ray Kennedy. He explained to me that it was essential that we keep our shape in midfield, particularly on our left where Franco Causio would be Italy's main threat. He felt Ray would be a more solid presence. My tendency to drift would leave young Kenny Sansom too exposed at left-back.

Ray had a good game and struck a post but, in the end, the Italians won 1-0 with a goal from Marco Tardelli. Our hopes of winning the tournament were over. In our final game we beat Spain 2-1. I was recalled and scored but it was all academic by then. That evening we sat in our cliff-top hotel and watched Italy and Belgium play out a goalless draw. Belgium went on to the final – where they were narrowly beaten by West Germany – and Italy to the third-place play-off. We headed home and, for the first time, Ron found himself the target of criticism. The inquests droned on for weeks.

Ron was bitterly disappointed that we hadn't performed as well as we should have done in Italy. He felt there was nothing seriously wrong with the squad or the way we played. It could all have been so different had Woodcock's goal been allowed against Belgium. Of his 29 games before the championship started, England had won 20 and drawn six. That was title-winning form. Perhaps the experience would set us up nicely for the 1982 World Cup. Remember, England had failed to qualify for the previous two World Cups. You had to go back to Mexico 1970 and the days of Hurst, Moore and Peters to find an England team competing among the elite of the world game.

We had good reasons to be optimistic when the World Cup qualifying draw put us in a group with Norway, Romania, Switzerland and Hungary. Two nations would qualify for the finals in Spain. I'd never played in the finals and as I'd be 34 in 1982 I knew that this would be my last chance. I realised that I could no longer assume an automatic place in the England team because of my age and the fact that I was playing in the old Second Division with West Ham. This actually made me more determined than ever to retain my place in the squad. I wanted to be in Spain with England. So, clearly, did a lot of other players.

I wasn't picked for the opening qualifier against Norway at Wembley. Ron gave new caps to Arsenal's Graham Rix and Ipswich's Eric Gates, who was to fill in for the injured Keegan. Bryan Robson, winning his third cap, was beginning to look as though he belonged in the England midfield. We won 4-0 without being entirely convincing.

A groin injury kept me out of the next game – a 2-1 defeat to Romania in Bucharest – but I was fit to face Switzerland at Wembley. Ron restored me in midfield, my 40th cap, but we were still without Keegan. This time we won 2-1, with Robson in the role of 'libero' alongside Dave Watson in the heart of our defence. With 58 caps Dave was the only player in the team who had made more England appearances than me. We had made our debuts together against Portugal in 1974. A newcomer, though, was catching the eye. It was becoming increasingly obvious that the talented and versatile Robson was in the side to stay. He had pace, intelligence, good technique, a crisp tackle and could score goals – a future captain, I thought.

Ron discussed the value of the 'libero' style of defence with the players and found that they weren't in favour. It was an alien concept to most English players. He shelved it and, for the next match against Spain at Wembley, played a flat back four with the Ipswich pair, Terry Butcher and Russell Osman, in the heart of the defence. They were caught out once or twice by the pace and ingenuity of the Spanish, who won 2-1 – Ron's first defeat at Wembley since becoming manager.

Fortunately, our defeat to Spain was a friendly match but, unfortunately, it was a taste of things to come. England's fortunes suddenly dipped miserably. We endured six matches without a win – the Spain defeat followed by more home defeats to Brazil (0-1) and Scotland (0-1) and a goalless draw with Wales at Wembley. Crucially, we dropped World Cup qualifying points against Romania and Switzerland.

I played in the goalless draw with Romania, who returned home delighted by the fact that their dour defensive performance meant they had taken three of the possible four qualifying points in their two games against England. When Hungary beat Romania in Budapest a fortnight later our prospects of qualifying looked increasingly slim. We had taken a total of five points from our four games, so the two qualifiers at the end of the season, against Switzerland and Hungary, were now critical.

When we faced the Swiss in Basle I was not even on the bench. As I had not featured in the games against Brazil, Wales or Scotland either I was beginning to suspect that my international career might be over. Perhaps Ron had decided that it was time for me to go but simply couldn't bring himself to tell me. The newspapers were suggesting that my absence was because I was tired after a long season. It had been an arduous few months, with games coming thick and fast. West Ham had finished the 1980–81 season as Second Division champions. We'd also met Liverpool in the League Cup final and played six matches in the European Cup Winners' Cup, but I still wanted to play for my country. I wasn't too tired. I knew I could still do it at the highest level.

Three days before the Swiss match Liverpool beat Real Madrid

1-0 in Paris in the European Cup final. Ron described this victory as a 'great boost' to English soccer and hoped that it would give the players and fans a big lift. Liverpool were the flag-bearers for the English game at the time and the side that beat Real was all-English apart from three Scots – Kenny Dalglish, Alan Hansen and Graeme Souness. How times change! The Real team was all-Spanish apart from England's Laurie Cunningham and Germany's Uli Stielike.

But of Liverpool's European Cup winners only goalkeeper Clemence was in the starting line-up to face Switzerland. Ron rested the others, although Terry McDermott came on as a substitute and scored England's goal in a 2-1 defeat. The hooligan fringe shamed us again in the squares of Basle and the newspapers began to batter Ron. Unbeknown to us, retirement was beginning to beckon the manager.

It was not a happy time. I suspected the atmosphere in the England dressing room would be depressing after the Swiss defeat so I didn't go in. I had already asked Ron for permission to go into town for a meal with Hilkka, who was over for a few days. It was good to talk to her about family matters and forget England's problems for a few hours. World Cup qualification seemed a long way off. We had six days to prepare for a qualifying match that was now critical. Defeat would almost certainly mean failure to qualify. At least this time Ron had the Liverpool players with him during the build-up period.

What none of us knew was that Ron had made up his mind to retire. He had told Ted Croker and Dick Wragg that he would announce his retirement after the Hungary match. They both tried to talk him out of it but he was insistent. England's poor results were his responsibility and he felt it was time to go. Others agreed. One tabloid headline back in the UK read: 'For God's Sake Go Ron!'

We trained with real intensity for a couple of days outside Zurich and then a disgruntled party of players, officials and journalists boarded the FA charter flight to Budapest. Ron kept himself tucked away in the vast Inter-Continental hotel beside the Danube, alone with his thoughts except when we were training. Usually players pick up a few hints about the make-up of the team during the training sessions but on this occasion no one had a clue.

Ron delayed the team announcement by 24 hours and when he finally revealed his hand there were some surprises. Young Kenny Sansom and Ray Wilkins were among four players dropped. Ron recalled the Liverpool men who had missed the Swiss defeat – and me. 'You'll need some practice pulling your boots on,' Keegan said. 'You've been in cobwebs that long!' There was much sarcastic humming of the *Dad's Army* signature tune by my team-mates as we prepared for the big match. Ron had chosen a well-balanced side with lots of experience and he gave the job of marking Hungary's most influential player, Tibor Nyilasi, to Bryan Robson.

When we arrived in the huge Nep Stadium there was a veterans' match already in progress watched by a packed house of 68,000. They had come to see the Hungarian legend Ferenc Puskas. He was then a portly 54-year-old but he still brought the house down with a hat-trick reminiscent of his great European Cup-winning days with Real Madrid. It was good to see him but I wondered how the warm-up match would affect the pitch. Like all players, I always enjoyed playing on a perfect surface. In truth the pitch in the Nep Stadium was perfect – the best I ever played on. What's more, it was big. I always liked big pitches because small, narrow pitches tended to produce negative, tight, defensive games.

Ron warned us in the dressing room to expect the Hungarians to storm at us in the opening 30 minutes. When they didn't we took the initiative. In the 18th minute Terry McDermott carried the ball to the by-line and pulled it back towards me. The ball clipped a defender on its way to me and was spinning when I connected. I caught the ball on my instep and for a split second it looked as though my shot might curl outside the post. But it swerved just inside the post.

Seconds before the interval Imre Garaba scored an equaliser for the Hungarians and, as we filed off at half time disappointed to have thrown away the lead, I felt a nagging pain in my groin. The Hungarians would have been delighted had they known that during the half-time break Dr Vernon Edwards and England's long-serving physiotherapist, Fred Street, were working hard on the treatment tables with me and Mick Mills.

A versatile defender guaranteed always to give 100 per cent, Mills had a calf muscle strain. Ron asked both of us if we could continue. Mick said he was okay and I asked Ron to give me the first five minutes of the second half to see how the groin reacted to the treatment. As we went back out, Ray Wilkins was warming up just in case I had to be replaced.

The injury nagged away at me a bit but it didn't limit my movement. Looking back, I'm so pleased I stuck at it because in the second half I struck the finest goal I scored in my entire career. It was the 60th minute and the match was finely balanced. Phil Neal, advancing from his right-back position, passed to Kevin, who had his back to goal and saw me coming forward. Kevin laid the ball into my path as I ran towards the penalty area and I struck it first time with my left foot. As I looked up I saw the ball was on target for the angle of post and bar. One worry flashed through my mind – the Continental balls tended to swerve and for a second I thought this might happen. Fortunately the ball didn't deviate an inch. It hit the stanchion and lodged there. I could hardly believe it. Some of our players thought I'd missed the target altogether because the ball didn't bounce down. Many in the crowd, too, must have wondered what had happened to the ball because, initially, it wasn't obvious that it had stuck in the top of the net. 'That was amazing,' beamed Kevin.

At home in Essex, Hilkka and my parents were watching on TV, as were millions of others. She said later that she had to look twice to confirm that it was me that hit the ball. That's how much faith she had in me! It was our 11th wedding anniversary. What a way to celebrate! Two goals, and one a real cracker! To be honest I'd never powered home a goal like that before. It remains one of the great moments of my career. Ten minutes after scoring I was caught by a late tackle that aggravated my groin. I indicated to the bench that I couldn't continue. But before I left the field, to be replaced by Ray Wilkins, Keegan was brought down in the Hungarian area by Garaba. As the referee blew for a penalty Kevin picked up the ball, put it on the spot and drove it into the net, putting the match beyond Hungary's reach.

At the final whistle the TV men grabbed Kevin and me for interviews before the line to London went down. We were late getting back into the dressing room. Ron had thanked the players individually as they filed in, exhausted but elated. 'Where's Kevin and Trevor?' he asked. Doc Edwards explained that we had been snaffled by the TV people. This irritated Ron because no one had asked his permission and he felt the players should have been together at that moment.

A 3-1 victory put us right back in the frame for the World Cup. Ron was absolutely delighted. The great Hungarian side of Puskas and Hidegkuti – 6-3 winners at Wembley in 1953 – had been a huge influence on his career. He had also promised Dick Wragg and Ted Croker that we would win in the Nep Stadium and he had kept his promise. What was unknown to us, of course, was that this was his last match as manager. Finishing with a win in Hungary was, for him, the perfect final curtain.

He kept his after-match press conference short because, as he told me later, he was quite emotional and didn't want to give any-thing away. 'Thanks for all your support,' he said to the journalists. 'It was a good win, well deserved and it has given me great pleas-ure to win in Hungary. I'm sorry, but I don't want to answer questions.'

With that he was gone, climbing into the team bus that rocked and rolled all the way back to the hotel on the banks of the Danube. In the restaurant that night my team-mates broke into their version of 'I'm Forever Blowing Bubbles'. Next morning, as we boarded the plane home, airline staff were handing out the first editions of the Sunday papers from London. The papers hadn't carried the late news from the previous day of England's victory. Instead, the early editions were still mulling over the aftermath of the Swiss defeat. There was a photo of me with a big 'X' over my face. My time was up, the paper claimed. I wasn't the only victim either. In short, the Sunday papers had slaughtered us for the defeat against the Swiss. It amused us all. As we gathered at the air-port, the media were back-slapping and full of congratulations. When we saw the papers we realised what the same people had thought of us just 24 hours earlier!

Still, there was a party atmosphere on the plane home. I remem-ber the pilot announcing: 'Ladies and gentlemen, we are now travelling at 550 miles an hour – faster than Trevor's first goal, but slower than his second!' As we flew home that day only two people knew of Ron's decision to quit and one of them, Dick Wragg, was already back in London. He was waiting at Luton airport for the plane to arrive. Then he would officially announce that Ron had decided to retire.

About half an hour before we were due to land Ron got up and pulled across the dividing curtain at the front of the plane to give him and the players some privacy. He thanked us all, said he was convinced we would now qualify for the finals and then said that he thought it was the right moment to retire. He added: 'It's my decision and Mr Wragg is waiting in Luton to announce the news.' The players were shocked. There was a moment's silence and then suddenly an outbreak of heated chattering and exchanges between us. The players huddled around Ron, all talking at once, all urging him to reconsider. Kevin told him he was out of order. It was noisy and emotional and Ron was a little surprised by the strength of the players' reaction.

We kept at him, even as we walked off the plane. Finally Ron buckled. He had a good relationship with the players and was clearly swayed by the force of our argument. As we waited for our luggage, he came over to us and said: 'Okay, I'll tell Mr Wragg I'm not retiring. I'll give it till after the World Cup.' The players agreed unanimously that they wanted Ron Greenwood to continue but it was the older ones, Kevin, Ray Wilkins, Mick Mills and me who worked hardest to get him to change his mind. Would such a thing happen today? I don't think so. Nor would it be possible to keep such drama out of the headlines. It says much for the character and loyalty of the players involved that not a word of what happened on the plane that day crept out into the public domain until Ron finally retired a year later.

For me, it was a wonderful end to a wonderful season. West Ham had stormed back into the old First Division, I'd scored twice in a victory that set England on the road to the World Cup and I got home from Budapest to learn that I had been awarded an MBE in the Queen's Birthday Honours List.

It was a high point for me. What I didn't realise was that there would be no more of them in my playing career. My groin injury continued to trouble me and I missed the start of the new season. West Ham made a great start to their return to Division One, unbeaten in the first nine matches, but I was on the sidelines. Inevitably, this meant that I wasn't considered for our World Cup qualifier against Norway in Oslo. Ron would later say that while the win in Hungary provided some of the finest memories in his career, the defeat in Oslo three months later provided some of the worst.

England's wildly erratic qualifying campaign began with the fixtures meeting involving the five competing nations. Each national manager wants the best for his team on these occasions and negotiations can be fraught. The Norwegians, for instance, would only agree to be England's first opponents at Wembley if they could play the return leg in Oslo in September 1981. No England manager relishes a September international because the domestic season has only just started and most players are still to hit their best form.

This was Norway's biggest game in the qualifying programme and their manager, Tor Fossen, argued that his team would be at their strongest around September. He thought a match in September would give them their best chance of beating England. How right he was! From Ron's point of view, Norway were the weakest team in the group and if we had to play someone in September it might as well be them.

Our win in Hungary had restored the feel-good mood. We had seven points from six games and wins in Norway and against Hungary at Wembley two months later would clinch one of the two qualifying places. Ron made changes to the team that had beaten Hungary. Glenn Hoddle replaced me, Trevor Francis came in for Steve Coppell and Russell Osman for Dave Watson, now 35 and approaching the end of a distinguished 65-cap England career.

It was a team easily good enough to have beaten the part-timers of Norway nine times out of ten and that looked the likely outcome in the 15th minute when Bryan Robson, running on to a flicked header from Kevin Keegan, bundled his way into the six-yard box and turned the ball into the net as he stumbled over their goalkeeper.

There were no excuses for what happened next. We missed

chances and made silly mistakes. A tight pitch in the Ullevaal Stadium didn't suit us and a wall-to-wall crowd of 28,000 lifted the Norwegians. But we still should have won. Instead, Roger Albertsen touched a cross from Tommy Lund past Ray Clemence at the near post in the 35th minute. Six minutes later Terry McDermott mistakenly turned a cross into the path of Hallvar Thoresen, who spun round and drove a low shot past our keeper.

We battered them in the second half and Ron sent on Peter Barnes and Peter Withe but Norway held out for the most memorable result in their history. Although Norway had no hope of qualifying for the World Cup, the locals were ecstatic, and rightly so. In the mayhem immediately after the match the radio commentator Bjorge Lillelien, trying to retain a sense of composure while reflecting the full majesty of the achievement, produced one of the best-known passages in the history of football commentary.

'We are the best in the world,' he told his disbelieving audience in a mix of Norwegian and English. 'We are the best in the world. We have beaten England two-one in football. It is completely unbelievable. We have beaten England. England – birthplace of giants! Lord Nelson, Lord Beaverbrook, Winston Churchill, Sir Anthony Eden, Clement Attlee, Henry Cooper, Lady Diana ... we have beaten them all. Maggie Thatcher! Can you hear me? Maggie Thatcher, your boys took a hell of a beating. I have a message for you. We have knocked England out of the football World Cup. Maggie Thatcher, as they say in your language in the boxing bars in New York: "Your boys took a hell of a beating!"'

Can't argue with that, can you? He hadn't got all his facts quite right, though. While there was no disguising England's humiliation, Norway had not dismissed us from the World Cup. There were still more twists to come in this protracted and tortuous path to Spain. We still had to play our final game against Hungary at Wembley and, although we remained top of our group, Romania, Switzerland

and Hungary all had games in hand which could take them above us. Qualification was no longer in our hands.

Ron weathered the inevitable storm and there must have been times when he wished he had stuck by his decision to retire. The media revived their demands for Ron's head and all sorts of accusations were hurled at the players, including a new insult – we were all mercenaries who cared only about how much money we could make. The truth is, of course, that upsets will always happen at every level in football. Norway rose to the occasion. They were playing England and that lifted them. In a sense we paid the price for our reputation. It had happened before (USA 0-1, 1950), has happened since (Norway again, 1-2, 1993) and will almost certainly happen again.

Watching that extraordinary defeat from the comfort of my home I suspected that my hopes of competing in a World Cup tournament were over. All over the country people were working out goal difference calculations on the backs of envelopes but, realistically, we needed a miracle. And we got one! Other results went our way. Our benefactors were the Swiss. They beat Romania in Bucharest, lost in Hungary to spoil their own chances and then drew their return game at home to Romania. This meant that if we drew our final game, at home to Hungary, we would go through on goal difference.

It wasn't until a week before the decisive Hungary game that we knew precisely what we had to do. No one was in any doubt about what was at stake. The Football League cleared the Saturday before the match of all but two First Division fixtures. We had a clear week to prepare. Within two days the game was a 92,000 all-ticket sell-out. The Oslo defeat was forgotten. We were all about to become heroes again! The mood was positive, but there was a similarity between our situation and that of Sir Alf Ramsey's team in 1973. They needed to beat Poland at Wembley in their final match to qualify for the 1974 World Cup. And we know what happened there: they were famously held to a draw, thanks largely to the goal-keeping of Jan Tomaszewski.

Ron got our preparation just right. We were all saddened, though, when our coach Bill Taylor had to leave in the middle of the build-up. He had undergone surgery a year earlier, and was unwell again. Originally appointed by Don Revie, he was hugely popular with the players. He watched the big match on TV but sadly died a fortnight later at the age of 42.

We stayed in familiar surroundings that week, in our usual hotel at West Lodge Park, and on Saturday night Ron took us all to see a show at the Whitehall Theatre. The following day we trained as normal at Arsenal's ground at London Colney and then were given the rest of the day off. Ron said that we could do whatever we wanted as long as we were back in the hotel by 11.30 that evening.

Ray Clemence, who had just moved from Liverpool to Spurs, went with Glenn Hoddle and one or two other players for a drink at a club in Tottenham. Inevitably they were spotted and the news-papers got calls from people saying that England's World Cup players were out drinking. Reporters rang the hotel and talked to the players. Instead of saying they were out with the manager's per-mission, they denied the whole story. Mistake! The papers made a big issue of it a couple of days before the match.

As it turned out, neither Clemence nor Hoddle were due to play against the Hungarians. Ron had made up his mind about the team at the beginning of the week. He'd decided that Peter Shilton, who had played against Poland in 1973, was the goalkeeper in form. I was fit again, having played nine consecutive matches for West Ham. I missed the start of 1981–82 – the season three points for a win was introduced – but was happy to get back into a newly pro-moted West Ham side that stayed in the top five for the first half of the season.

I was pleased to see that Ron had called my West Ham team-mate Alvin Martin into the side for his third cap, preferring him to Russell Osman. Steve Coppell was also recalled, replacing Trevor Francis. Sadly, he would end the match with a bad knee injury, the result of an over-zealous tackle by Jozsef Toth. It was the beginning of the end of his career.

So, Shilton and Martin apart, this was the team that had beaten Hungary 3-1 in Budapest five months earlier. It was to our advantage that Hungary had already qualified so they didn't show much appetite for the game. The result was never in any doubt. The only goal came in the 14th minute when my shot, which I think was going wide, hit Paul Mariner and ricocheted into the net. Later Paul headed wide of an empty net, I had the ball nicked off my toe just as I was going to shoot from inside the area and Tony Morley hit a fabulous shot that the goalkeeper saved. Yes, it was a bit like the Poland game. We were all over the opposition, but this time we got the result we needed.

It had been a long and winding road to Spain but we got there in the end. The crowd was singing. In Fleet Street the newspapers were preparing triumphant headlines. We were heroes again! As I walked off the pitch I thought of that line often used on TV by my old West Ham team-mate Jimmy Greaves: 'It's a funny old game!'

CHAPTER 10

ESPAÑA '82

ROOM 204 IN LOS TAMARISES, a small, elegant hotel over-looking a wide sweep of beach outside Bilbao, was quickly christened the Royal Suite when England's World Cup entourage arrived on a cloudy June afternoon in 1982. It was the room allocated to me and Kevin Keegan. We roomed together most of the time when we travelled with England. Why 'Royal'? Neither of us had any regal pretensions but a few days before we flew out to Spain, the England captain was awarded an OBE. A year earlier I had been appointed an MBE and the mickey-takers in Ron Greenwood's squad were quick to spot a new source of amusement.

Sadly, neither of England's 'Royals' would have much to do with Spain '82. I had a groin injury and Kevin had a back problem. Far from bowing and scraping when in the vicinity of Room 204, most of the players tried to avoid it completely. Just before our second match against Czechoslovakia, Bryan Robson invited himself to our room for a cup of tea. A bad move! He was injured against the Czechs and missed the next game. This gave the rest of the squad even more ammunition. From that moment on the Royal Suite was deemed to be cursed.

It may well have been. The occupants were certainly in need of a bit of good fortune or some divine intervention. Kevin and I spent days in Room 204 bemoaning our fate. Spain '82 was the only chance I had of playing in a World Cup final tournament and, in the end, neither Kevin nor I played more than a few minutes. Considering the difficulties we had in qualifying, Spain '82 became perhaps the most ironic chapter in my playing career.

The year had started so well for me. It seemed that whenever I turned on the TV someone was still repeating the clip of the goal that wedged in the stanchion in Budapest. For eight consecutive Saturdays that winter the Football League programme was seriously disrupted by the Arctic weather conditions. TV companies had no choice but to show old film of old matches. After missing the first few games of 1981–82 because of injury, I was back to my best when I scored twice in the 3-3 thriller with Leeds at Elland Road. West Ham were comfortably in sixth place – not bad for a team newly promoted to the big time – but then the weather hit and sport simply ground to a halt.

In January when the World Cup draw was made in Spain there were serious worries that the large number of postponements would jeopardise England's World Cup preparations later in the season. The draw pitted England against France, Czechoslovakia and Kuwait, and England and France immediately agreed to cancel their friendly match arranged for 24 March in Paris. For the first time there were 24 competing nations split into six groups of four. The winners and runners-up in each group progressed to the second round.

England's first match of World Cup year was against Northern Ireland at Wembley. Ron Greenwood had about three months to decide upon the make-up of his 22-man squad for Spain and was going to use the British Championship matches to consider his options. He looked at Aston Villa winger Tony Morley, Brighton centre-back Steve Foster and West Brom striker Cyrille Regis against the Irish. England won 4-0. A few weeks later we beat Wales 1-0 in Cardiff and this time the manager ran his eye over Manchester City goalkeeper Joe Corrigan, Ipswich centre-half Terry Butcher and Aston Villa striker Peter Withe. The surprise absentee from this match was Kevin Keegan. It wasn't clear why he had been left out, though hints of a mystery back problem began to circulate.

The loss of the French as warm-up opponents was a bit of a blow – FIFA wouldn't allow World Cup rivals to play each other in friendly matches – but Ron still had four more full international matches scheduled, plus two more games that were less exacting but would serve a good purpose. The first of these was a benefit match for the late Bill Taylor, Ron's England XI beating Manchester City 3-1 at the old Maine Road stadium.

The second was really a public relations exercise – but it would prove to be a very useful one. As the seeded nation in Group 4 England had the advantage of playing all three first-round matches at one venue – Bilbao. Ron wanted to ensure we had the locals on our side in each of those games and agreed to take another England XI to play a testimonial match against Athletic Bilbao. It was for local hero Francisco Roca and took place in the San Mames stadium, which would stage our three first-round matches.

The three-day trip was a huge success. Although it obviously wasn't a full international match, Ron took a really strong group of players. He also invited his old friend Ronnie Allen, who was then manager of West Bromwich Albion. This was a masterstroke. Ronnie had spent three years as manager of Bilbao and was still a very popular figure among the Basques.

The locals were very hospitable and did everything they could to make our stay both enjoyable and useful. We visited the hotel and the Athletic training camp that we would be using a few weeks later. The facilities were first class but, as is nearly always the case, there were one or two little issues that we could have done without. A newspaper photograph of a dead dog on the beach, with our hotel in the background, portrayed the area as a bit of a dump. It wasn't a dump at all. Like any beach in winter it looked a bit unloved. By the time we returned in June the beach had been cleaned and looked picture perfect.

The San Mames stadium felt comfortable and familiar. It was English in design, with the terraces coming down to pitch level, and the playing surface was superb. The match attracted a 35,000 crowd and at the end of a competitive 1-1 draw they gave us a standing ovation. I played along with Kevin, Bryan Robson, Kenny Sansom and Steve Coppell. I also remember that Manchester United goalkeeper Gary Bailey and Manchester City centre-back Tommy Caton – who died so tragically of a heart attack in 1993 at the age of 30 – were in the squad that travelled. On the way home Ronnie Allen, who played for England himself in the fifties, told me that the locals were delighted with our visit. 'The England team have done themselves nothing but good in the last couple of days,' he said.

Coppell was probably the best player on the field that day in Bilbao and he, Kevin, Tony Morley and Peter Withe peppered the Athletic goal. I thought the Athletic goalkeeper might have a bit of a future between the sticks. Andoni Zubizarreta was Spain's Under-21 keeper at the time. He went on to have a record-breaking career, spending a decade with Barcelona and winning 126 caps for Spain.

Holland were next on England's World Cup warm-up agenda, but just before facing them Ron named his provisional squad of 40 players for the World Cup. This had to be trimmed to 22 by 4 June. The 40 included one or two unexpected names, such as West

Ham's Alan Devonshire and Paul Goddard, Liverpool's Sammy Lee, Tottenham's Garth Crooks and Steve Perryman and Aston Villa's Gary Shaw and Dennis Mortimer.

Beaten by hosts Argentina in the 1978 final, Holland had failed to reach Spain largely because they'd dropped three points to a very talented Republic of Ireland team in the qualifying programme. The Dutch still had some good players in their line-up, including Rudi Krol, Rene van de Kerkhof and Arnold Muhren. Ron tried Steve Foster again and my West Ham team-mate Devonshire. We won comfortably enough, with Paul Mariner and Tony Woodcock scoring our goals.

A few days later we travelled to Glasgow for the match that would decide the outcome of the British Championship. Scotland needed to win to snatch the title from us and, as usual, their fans gave us an intimidating welcome as we approached Hampden Park in the team bus. Ron had picked probably his strongest team and I was pleased to be included. It was my 45th cap and I knew there would not be too many more. Kevin was the only player with more caps in that team. He had 61.

Significantly, Ron had chosen Peter Shilton to play in goal. It was Peter's 37th cap. His great goalkeeping rival Ray Clemence had 58 caps and probably thought he was the senior of the two. Ron had made it clear to both that he rated them equally. As he had the great luxury of two of the world's best goalkeepers at his disposal he'd told them that he would alternate them. He'd also told them that if England reached the finals he would make a choice between them. Now, with the World Cup only weeks away, it was nearly time to choose. It was something he wasn't relishing.

Shilton played against the Scots – Paul Mariner's goal gave England a 1-0 win and the British title – and waited to hear what the manager had decided. There were two matches still to play. On 2 June Ron sent a B team to play a full international against Iceland in Reykjavik. Joe Corrigan was in goal and the outfield players, in a 1-1 draw, included Goddard and Perryman, each winning his one and only cap.

Twenty-four hours later the senior side played Finland in Helsinki. I was delighted to be included, as was goalkeeper Ray Clemence, winning his 59th England cap. Hilkka, my lovely Finnish wife, turned up to watch the match with her family. She asked if I could supply 17 tickets for the game. 'All together if possible,' she smiled sweetly.

We won 4-1 – Bryan Robson and Paul Mariner each scored two goals. The next day Ron named England's official World Cup squad of 22 with shirt numbers. The number one went to Clemence, number 13 to Corrigan and number 22 to Shilton – the three goalkeepers in alphabetical order. But Shilton, Ron said, would be his first-choice goalkeeper. He was certainly the man in form. Ray had not had the best of times in his first season with Tottenham. Even so, he was not happy to be told he was second choice. The outfield players were also given shirt numbers in alphabetical order which meant Viv Anderson was number two and I was number three.

The number three shirt was a bit of a novelty for me but I wondered whether I'd get the chance to wear it. I felt a tweak in my groin late on against Finland and asked to be taken off. I'd had the same problem in the past. I didn't know how bad it was this time but, to be honest, I feared the worst. I had treatment in the dressing room while the match continued. I was desperate to be fit for the big kick-off. The opening World Cup game against France was just 13 days away. We flew home from Helsinki and were given a two-day break before gathering again for the flight to Bilbao. There was an air of anticipation and excitement at the airport but my mood was one of concern. I already knew that my participation in the World Cup depended on a cortisone injection. I spoke to Ron

Greenwood and the England team doctor Vernon Edwards before we flew out and told them that, from past experience, I knew that this was a deep-seated injury and therefore would require an injection with a *long* needle.

I made my feelings quite clear to Ron and the doctor. I explained to them that the West Ham doctor Brian Roper, a surgeon, had successfully given me the injection in the past. Dr Edwards said: 'It needs a chance to settle down.' I stressed to both of them that I needed the injection with the big needle as soon as possible if I was to have any chance of playing. 'I know what I'm doing,' said Dr Edwards. That day, when we arrived in Spain, the FA doctor gave me the cortisone injection with a small needle. As he prepared to administer the injection I saw the needle and said to him: 'It's not going to work with that needle.'

Dr Roper had always used a long needle because the source of the problem was deep in my groin. Dr Edwards gave me the injection with his little needle and I waited for the reaction. I knew it wouldn't work – I'd had plenty of experience of cortisone. It reduces inflammation but has to be delivered to exactly the right spot. It was a tricky business. Ron knew Brian Roper, of course, but didn't want to diminish Dr Edwards' role or question his opinion. He didn't want to cause any friction.

I had osteitis pubis, which in layman's terms is inflammation of the pubic joint. I had treatment on a daily basis for the next week. Ron wasn't making a big issue of it but there was no hiding the fact that two of his senior players were injured and unlikely to be fit enough to face France in the first game. The relationship Kevin and I had established on the field provided much of England's attacking impetus. A lot was made of a supposed 'telepathic understanding' between us but, in fact, it was far simpler than that. In my midfield role I was always looking to pass the ball forward and create opportunities for the front-running players. No front player did more running than Kevin. As a creative midfield player you are always looking at the options ahead of you. You might have two or three but usually only one is the right option. Kevin was almost always the right option for me. He made most of the runs and most of the best runs. He was always moving into space to make himself available to receive the ball.

He was a great team player and we had been together in the same England team for eight years. You develop a good understanding after all that time. You learn to trust each other. Kevin knew that if he kept working and running I'd find him with a pass. I got to know his strengths and his habits. I could find him with a pass without looking up. I think that's how the 'telepathy' theory took root. The truth is that it's the same with most good players. I had a similar understanding with Bryan 'Pop' Robson at West Ham. Intelligent players invariably make themselves available. Kevin was bright as a button and had the speed of a greyhound. Whenever I looked up he was there, demanding the ball. I knew he was going to be a big, big loss if he failed to recover for the World Cup.

The England squad, Kevin and me included, had flown out of Luton airport in a blaze of flashlights six days before the opening game. I think we were the last of the 24 nations to arrive in Spain. Ron told us that he would prefer to train in the peace and quiet of our Hertfordshire hotel and travel out as late as possible. The players felt much the same.

I remember a strong feeling among us that we wanted to do well for the manager. The bond between the manager and players had grown appreciably during the protracted qualifying programme. It was a good, experienced squad. At 33, I was the oldest of the outfield players. The average age, 28, made us the oldest squad at the tournament. There had been suggestions that the heat would be a big problem for 'Dad's Army' but we were greeted in Bilbao by typically damp British weather. Jesus, the affable proprietor at Los

Tamarises, presented each player with a wine bottled in the year of their birth. Ron, who was a bit put out because there was none from 1921, suggested that corks stay in bottles until we headed home!

During the first week in Bilbao it became clear to Ron that neither Kevin nor I would be fit for any of the three first-round games. This meant that the manager had to appoint a captain until Kevin was ready to return. Mick Mills, the warrior defender from Ipswich, was given the job of leading the team from right-back – England's first World Cup captain since Bobby Moore 12 years earlier. While Kevin and I spent our time in the treatment room, Ron worked with the players who would represent England in the opening game. Kevin and I had speculated about the team line-up, but there were no real surprises: Shilton; Mills, Thompson, Butcher, Sansom; Coppell, Robson, Wilkins, Rix; Francis, Mariner.

On the day Ron named the team the Falklands War ended. Argentina surrendered their brief grip on the British islands in the South Atlantic and a sense of relief coursed through the World Cup family. Argentina, champions in 1978, were in Spain along with, unusually, three British representatives – England, Scotland and Northern Ireland. No one really wanted to consider the implications of a World Cup tie between warring nations.

After a week of mild temperatures, the big day dawned hot – and got hotter. At kick-off the temperature on the San Mames pitch was 100 degrees, though this wasn't an issue when the first goal went in. Terry Butcher headed on a Steve Coppell throw-in – a ploy worked at on the training pitch – and Bryan Robson raced unmarked into the French penalty area and hooked the ball home. He was fresh as a daisy, not even puffing! The official time of the goal was 27 seconds – the fastest in World Cup history. Inspired by the artful Michel Platini, France equalised through Gerard Soler in the 24th minute and for a while they were in control. But Ron made some tactical changes at half time, giving us a sturdier presence in midfield. A second goal from Robson and another from Paul Mariner secured a 3-1 win. The heat had taken a toll, though. Mariner lost nearly a stone and Graham Rix had lost 6lb. Rix was so dehydrated that it took him two hours to produce his urine sample for the mandatory drug tests.

Back at the hotel afterwards the mood was euphoric. Bobby Charlton, who played in the heat of Mexico when England were defending the trophy in 1970, sought out Rix to congratulate him. Had I been fit he may not have played, but he made the most of his opportunity. Bryan Robson was full of praise for Ron's tactical intervention at half time. 'He changed Graham's role on the left and it worked for us,' he said. Ron himself praised Don Howe for his role in working on the set-piece move in training that led to Robson's first goal in 27 seconds. 'All credit to Don for that,' said Ron. It was one of those memorable occasions when you couldn't stop smiling. Everyone was slapping everyone else on the back. We were all happy, but Kevin and I were beginning to feel that time was running out for us.

I should have made a fuss and said that I would go back to London to get the injection done properly. Instead I waited for the reaction to an injection that I knew hadn't worked. Had the injection hit the spot it would have frozen the damaged area. That would have been followed by about 36 hours of soreness, with the blood then dispersing and easing the inflammation. That hadn't happened. I told Ron it hadn't worked. Twelve days after Dr Edwards gave me the injection Ron finally agreed that I should see Brian Roper. The following day Brian very kindly flew in secret to Bilbao. He gave me the injection with a long needle.

I knew it had worked almost immediately but I would not be ready to play for at least another ten days. If England went out in the first round I would go home without kicking a ball. Back then you were totally reliant on the expertise of the doctor in delivering the cortisone to the right spot. These days this kind of serious inflammation is picked up much earlier by an MRI scan and the injection is guided to the right spot by a scanner. Stewart Robson, of Arsenal, and Jonathan Woodgate, of Leeds, both had similar conditions that threatened their careers.

Czechoslovakia were our next opponents and Ron wisely cautioned against overconfidence. The fact that unfancied Algeria had beaten West Germany 2-1 was a timely reminder of the dangers of taking things for granted. Ron was so pleased with the team's performance against France that he named the same eleven. They didn't let him down. A 2-0 win on a cool day – Mariner and Francis scored – ensured a place for us in round two. Kevin and I might still get a chance to play. Kevin had spent 24 hours in hospital being examined by a back specialist in Bilbao. He was depressed and frustrated and returned to Room 204 in a bad mood. He felt he was letting people down and thought it would be better to go home rather than mope about the hotel.

I felt sorry for him. We'd been good mates for a long time, on and off the pitch. We spent many hours playing cards with Emlyn Hughes and 'Shilts'. Kevin was a winner, the most committed, strong-willed and ambitious player I knew. He'd worked really hard to make himself a success. If you wanted the classic example of a footballer who practised until he was perfect, it was Kevin Keegan. He maximised his strengths and worked on his weaknesses, in much the same way, for example, as Chelsea's Frank Lampard in the modern game.

Sitting around feeling sorry for himself wasn't for him. Late one evening he bumped into Ron Greenwood in the hotel. He knew the FA had just flown Brian Roper out to Bilbao to treat me. Kevin told Ron that there was a back specialist who had treated him successfully in Hamburg, where of course he played for three years. Kevin wanted to fly to Germany to see him. Ron was dubious but

Kevin convinced him. He came up to the room and told me he was going to Hamburg. 'Don't tell anyone,' he said. 'The boss wants to keep it quiet.' Kevin borrowed a small car from a hotel receptionist and set off at 1am to drive 250 miles to Madrid. He got the first available plane from Madrid to Hamburg. Few people knew where he was and those who did wouldn't say. You wouldn't be able to keep a story like that from the papers these days.

On his return he was a different person. His smile was back. He wasn't fit enough to play, but he could join training. His presence lifted the whole squad. As France had drawn their final first-round game with Czechoslovakia we knew we would finish as group winners whatever the result in our final game against Kuwait. We were in a buoyant mood when the FA invited the media to Los Tamarises for an 'open day'. The media is kept well away from team hotels by high-level security at all of the big football tournaments. The chance to get an 'inside' look and take photographs is usually much appreciated by the journalists.

This was no different to any other similar occasion organised for the media, except that the guest list included the 'London Ballet' company. An earlier call to an FA official asked if the London Ballet, working in Bilbao, could attend the gathering. It sounded harmless enough to Ron, but as soon as we saw the girls we knew they weren't ballet dancers. They were dancers all right, but they were go-go dancers going by the name of the 'Playmodel London Ballet'. They were appearing at a local nightclub and clearly knew how to enjoy themselves. From their point of view this was a photo opportunity not to be missed, but the players quickly realised that posing with the girls might not be appreciated by everyone back home!

Ron made one or two changes for the game against Kuwait. Glenn Hoddle, who had replaced the injured Robson against the Czechs, came into the starting line-up along with Steve Foster, who

took the place of Butcher. The Ipswich centre-half had been cautioned against the Czechs and Ron didn't want to risk a second
booking, which would have meant suspension. Ron also wanted to
give Ray Clemence a game in goal. But Peter Shilton, now established as the first-choice goalkeeper, claimed that he had not had
much to do in the first two games and felt that he should face
Kuwait just to keep himself sharp. Poor Ray missed the chance of
his one and only World Cup appearance. As it turned out, Shilts had
practically nothing to do in a very poor game against Kuwait. Trevor
Francis scored the only goal of the game but Ron made us aware
afterwards that he wasn't happy with our performance.

The morning after the Kuwait victory we said farewell to our
friends in Bilbao and moved camp to a quiet hotel in the hills about
an hour's drive from Madrid. The training ground was close by, discreet and well-equipped. The FA had done their homework well.
We were one of only two nations – Brazil were the other – to have
won all three first-round matches and there was a growing feeling
that England might have some influence on the outcome of the
tournament.

Our next opponents were the other 'old enemy', West Germany,
in the Bernabeu in Madrid. This was the business end of the tournament. There were many memories to be revived, particularly by
Geoff Hurst. He was now one of Ron's coaching assistants and had
been a significant figure in the World Cup battles with the
Germans in 1966 and 1970. The West Germans were the reigning
European champions and hadn't lost to another European country
for nearly five years. They had, though, just been beaten by Algeria
before allegedly coming to some kind of agreement with Austria in
their final group game. An early headed goal by Horst Hrubesch,
Kevin's former strike partner at Hamburg, gave them a 1-0 lead
and a lack of effort from both teams for the remainder of the match
meant that the Germans and Austrians progressed while Algeria,

with the same number of points, went home muttering darkly about a stitch-up.

Spain, the hosts, were the other nation in Group B, having qualified despite drawing 1-1 with rank outsiders Honduras and losing 1-0 to Billy Bingham's Northern Ireland team, who had played most of the second half with ten men after Mal Donaghy was sent off. The winners of Group B would face the winners of Group D – France, Austria or the Irish – in the semi-finals. Kevin and I were both progressing well in training but Ron decided to take no risks. The side he chose to face the Germans was the one that had beaten France and Czechoslovakia in the earlier round.

To be honest, it wasn't much of a match and the 75,000 who had turned up expecting another titanic England–West Germany clash must have been bitterly disappointed. We couldn't break down Germany's man-to-man marking and, although we had more chances to score, they had the best one when Karl-Heinz Rummenigge hit the bar. Ron sent on Tony Woodcock, who had played for FC Cologne for three seasons and was used to tight German marking, in the hope that he might find a chink in their armour. There was a lot of booing and jeering at the end of an unimaginative game which now meant that progress to the semi-final depended on the remaining two matches in the group.

Germany were to play Spain next in Madrid. The fact that we had a full week to rest before our game against Spain was a bonus and meant that we would know what we had to do to reach the last four. Kevin and I had a week to build up our training programme. Neither of us was 100 per cent, but we were getting close. Kevin was playing tennis most days after training and his old exuberance had returned. He clearly felt that he was ready.

The players watched the Spain–Germany match on the TV in our hotel. Ron went to the game with his coaches, Don Howe and Geoff Hurst. The Germans knew they had to win to put pressure on us. They made changes and called in Pierre Littbarski and Klaus Fischer to give them a more attacking edge. It was a good move. They won 2-1 before a 95,000 crowd with goals from, yes, Littbarski and Fischer. But Spain looked very average.

That night there was excitement and apprehension in the England camp. We now knew that a semi-final place was well within our reach. We had to beat Spain by two goals to reach the semi-final. For a while we thought that a 2-1 victory would be good enough but FIFA ruled that if we won 2-1, as Germany had done, we'd have to draw lots with the Germans. The simple fact, of course, was that the ball was in our court. Spain were out of the tournament and had nothing to play for but pride. How would they react? Would their fans get behind them? We had seen enough of Spain to know that we could beat them by two goals. We were the form team. We were unbeaten for 11 consecutive matches. In that time we had scored 20 goals and Mariner, Francis and Robson were finding the net regularly. The prize for us was a semi-final against France, the team we had already beaten 3-1 in our opening match. For England, it was a fantastic position to be in.

Kevin and I trained well during our week of preparation and we both felt fit enough to play. We'd worked hard but if Ron and Don Howe were both taking a training session we tended to drift towards Ron. Eventually the group would be split in two and those selected to work with Don seemed to do twice as much running as those working with Ron! We'd done our share of running over the years. The question now was: would we be selected to start against Spain? The day before the match we had a full-scale practice game – 'probables' against 'possibles'. Steve Coppell had injured a knee against the Germans so Kevin and I knew that there was at least one vacancy in the team for an attacking player. Ron put Kevin in the 'probables' eleven, playing up front with Paul Mariner. Trevor Francis moved out to the right to fill the role vacated by Coppell. This looked like the starting line-up against Spain.

The 'possibles' won the match 1-0 – T. Brooking scoring the goal – but that evening we all thought the team of 'probables', with Kevin at the front alongside Paul Mariner, would line up to face Spain the next day. I was pleased to have scored but even more pleased that I had come through the match unscathed. I knew I was fit enough to start the match if selected, but I went to bed that night quite relaxed about it all.

Something was nagging away at me, though. I had wondered about some aspects of the build-up. This was a match where we needed to go for the jugular. But some of the training had suggested a more cautious approach. Don Howe was a very good coach and a strong disciplinarian. He was 'hands on' and liked a rigid team struc-ture. You had to play the way he wanted. Ron was much happier to delegate some responsibility to the senior players. He used to say: 'If it's not working, just change it. Don't wait for me to tell you.' This wasn't the way Don worked. I don't think he was happy on the one or two occasions when Kevin or I changed things on the pitch.

His approach to the game was very different to Ron's. He'd been a top-class defender himself of course and played for England in the 1958 World Cup in Sweden. He joined Ron and the England squad late in that season and immediately admitted that he was a far more abrasive figure. 'I'm a shouter and Ron's fatherly,' he said. 'We should blend well.'

Ron and John Lyall were the only coaches I had at club level and they both wanted their players to express themselves. The empha-sis was always on playing to your strengths. That's what I was used to. Don's priority, on the other hand, was to stop the opposition from playing. In some ways their different styles made them a good partnership but for the Spain game we needed Ron's approach. It was a situation made for a positive team with an attacking strategy.

I think Kevin and I should have been in the starting line-up. Kevin thought so too. But when Ron announced the team we were both on the substitutes' bench. Woodcock for Coppell was the only change to the side that had drawn with the Germans. I was gob-smacked. I couldn't believe that Ron had overlooked Kevin, and when I got the chance I told him so. Kevin was fuming. Tony was a good striker but Kevin was a talismanic figure. He was the England captain.

All kinds of conspiracy theories emerged. Kevin was convinced that Don had played a big part in Tony's selection. Don was assistant to manager Terry Neill at Arsenal and who had Arsenal just signed? Tony Woodcock. They paid £500,000 to FC Cologne to sign him on 8 June – just one month before the match against Spain. Kevin felt that Don had pressurised Ron into picking Tony. Don could be a prickly, stubborn figure. Ron hated confrontation of any sort. If challenged, he would often tend to change the subject to avoid a row. When I was a young player he would keep a senior player in the team rather than leave him out and risk a set-to.

Naturally Ron had his own point of view. Basically he argued later that he selected neither Keegan nor Brooking to start the match because he didn't believe we were fit enough. He felt neither of us would have lasted the full 90 minutes and, if someone else had been injured too, he would have been in trouble. I know I could have started. Would I have lasted 90 minutes? I don't know. I do know that I aggravated the injury during my 27 minutes as a substitute but I didn't feel that until afterwards. I think Kevin could have played for the entire 90.

When we had our team talk in the dressing room before the match Ron and Don both had contributions to make. Ron had his say. Then it was Don's turn. He said: 'It's not a race. You've got ninety minutes. Be patient.' To sum up, his message was: take your time. It was contrary to what Kevin and I and most of the players felt. We had talked about it the previous evening. Our feeling was that we had to go for it straight from the kick-off. That day it was the 'Don' team talk that stuck in the mind when we really needed a 'Ron' team talk.

Kevin and I sat on the substitutes' bench throughout the first half, boiling with frustration. We were both finally called to action in the 63rd minute. We replaced Graham Rix and Woodcock. Although Spain had nothing to play for, they frustrated us with their defiant defending. We created and wasted our chances. We had 20 shots on goal; Spain had two.

With the clock ticking, Kevin and I, for the first time in our long careers, stepped on to the World Cup stage. The England fans greeted us warmly and we were soon into the rhythm of the match. Kevin had a fabulous chance to score when Bryan Robson, with a cross from the left, put the ball on to his forehead. Somehow Kevin missed an empty net. I had a chance, too, but my shot, at the end of a long run, was well saved by Luis Arconada.

It finished 0-0. England's World Cup was over. Heads were on chests in the dressing room. Kevin was furious and kept muttering about a missed opportunity. But it was no time for recriminations. Ron was going round to each player, thanking them for their efforts. It was a sad moment. For Ron, it was the end of a career. He moved into quiet retirement in Brighton. Kevin and I didn't realise it then but neither of us would play for England again.

We'd done our best in Spain, but sometimes that's not good enough. You need something else. How on earth, for instance, had the Germans got to the final? They lost to Algeria in their opening game, fought tooth and nail to hold us to a goalless draw and were 3-1 down to the French in their semi-final before going through on penalties after extra time. We finished the tournament unbeaten in five matches. We'd conceded just one goal. We'd battered the French with some fine attacking football. Yet England were on their way home and West Germany were in the final, where they would lose 3-1 to Italy. My experiences in that World Cup were among the most frustrating of my career. We should have beaten Spain. We were good enough to have reached the final.

We might not have won it because Italy were a good team. After a shaky start they went on to beat Brazil and Argentina and they deserved their success. Others saw the injustice of England's situation. No team had beaten us but we were out. FIFA thought it was unfair. Rules were changed and a knockout process was introduced after the first round at future final tournaments. It was the right thing to do, but too late for us. I met Ron Greenwood many times in the years before he died in 2006 and we often ended up talking about that summer in 1982.

He always stuck to his guns. He insisted that, at the time, he didn't think Kevin or I were fit enough to start the match. It was unlike him to be so cautious. He changed a lifelong set of beliefs about the way the game should be played for one match. I'd have preferred to lose 3-1 knowing that we had at least had a real go at them. And, deep down, I think Ron would have preferred that too.

FAREWELL TO UPTON PARK

WHAT NOW? That was the question I asked myself in the late summer of 1982. The events in Spain remained an enduring source of regret, a disappointment enhanced by the knowledge that my chances of having a second stab at the World Cup were precisely nil. The opportunity of a lifetime had been and gone. I was approaching 34 and had just been told that my groin injury – the reason I was unable to play a more significant role in Spain – would require major surgery.

Dr Brian Roper, the West Ham surgeon, was quite graphic and detailed when he described the options available to someone with my condition. 'We can sort it out but if you don't have the operation you'll have problems for the rest of your life,' he said. 'Even getting in and out of a car will become painful.' If I had the surgery he reckoned that I'd be out of action at the very least for six months, probably longer. I still felt that I had a bit of life left in me.

I wanted to play for a season or two longer at West Ham, although I had already accepted that my brief appearance against Spain in the World Cup in June had been my last cap for England. Forty-seven wasn't bad but I had been hoping to finish with 50 caps.

Bobby Robson, anointed as Ron Greenwood's successor before the World Cup, took the reins officially at the start of 1982–83. He worked under Ron as manager of the B team, and was scouting in Spain, and his promotion to the top job was precisely the graduation process that Ron had envisaged when he originally appointed his team of coaches. Bobby's first match in charge was against Denmark in Copenhagen in a European Championship qualifying tie. He was often accused during his eight years as manager of being indecisive – but there was nothing indecisive about his first squad.

To everyone's surprise he left out the England captain Kevin Keegan, who learned from the press that his reign was over after 63 caps. Considering Bobby's experience as a manager, I was a bit taken aback that he had not personally informed a player of Kevin's stature that he was being left out. I believe he could have used a player of Kevin's knowledge and standing in the game. Kevin was 31. He was furious when he learned that he'd been axed. Having been let down by the outgoing England manager he now found himself let down by his successor as well.

Several of Ron's squad were 30 or over and Bobby clearly felt that he had to plan for the longer term. Ray Wilkins, at 26, was made captain though that appointment was not to last. I knew I wouldn't get back into the squad, but I felt sorry for Kevin. I wonder now how Bobby felt a year later when it became obvious that he would fail in his first challenge as England manager – qualifying for the 1984 European Championship. Kevin's fabulous form at Newcastle at the time suggested that he might have made the difference had he still been in the England team.

As for me, I had worked through the pre-season training with West Ham but it was clear that my groin injury was still a problem. I discussed my future in some detail with the West Ham manager, John Lyall, and he agreed that it would be best for me to have the operation. The inflammation in my pubic joint was getting worse and as a result I was in considerable pain if I turned sharply.

I had the operation, which involved a bone graft from my hip, in September 1982 and for the first four weeks after surgery I had to lie on my back in bed. I was not allowed to move. Finally, the great day came and I was helped very carefully out of the bed. I had to use crutches initially but gradually, as my strength returned, I was able to have hydrotherapy in a local pool. It was a long, slow process. It was worth it, the doctors assured me. Brian Roper said I'd miss the best part of the season but I'd have no further problem for the rest of my life. So far he's been proved correct.

It was a frustrating time. I wanted to be playing because I knew time was running out for me. While I was confined to bed West Ham hit a rich vein of form, beating teams like Liverpool, Arsenal and Manchester City. Alan Devonshire was playing some of the best football of his career and Paul Goddard, Francois Van der Elst and our penalty specialist Ray Stewart were all scoring prolifically. Meanwhile, Billy Bonds made his 545th league appearance for West Ham, breaking Bobby Moore's all-time record, and Frank Lampard made his 500th league appearance. They had been my team-mates for years and I felt that I should have been a part of all that.

It took all of six months before I was able to return to serious training but, towards the end of the season, I felt I was recapturing the kind of fitness you need to play at this level. My groin was perfect and no longer gave me pain. John Lyall asked me if I felt ready to play. He put me in the team for the last home match of the season. We lost 3-1 to Arsenal, but I was delighted to be back. I was like a youngster making his debut. It was a wonderful feeling. We finished in eighth place, which gave me reason to believe that we might do well the following season.

I played the full 90 minutes against Arsenal. Yes, I was a bit rusty but I felt good. I had no problems during the match or afterwards. What I needed was more football. The club helped me arrange a summer job in Hong Kong. I spent a couple of months playing in hot and humid conditions. My former West Ham team-mate Graham Paddon was out there. So was Don Shanks, the former Luton, QPR, Brighton and Wimbledon full-back. Don was a close friend of Stan Bowles. They used to go racing together. A very funny guy, he was one of the 'personalities' on the London football scene in the seventies and eighties. Somehow, he'd wangled a side-line as a racing columnist in a newspaper for expats in Hong Kong. He'd give tips and write about the runners and riders.

On the last day of the Hong Kong Festival Don was one of the jackpot winners. He picked up something like £40,000, which is a lot of money (and was even more in those days!). He was jubilant. It was the biggest win of his life. He wanted to convert the cash to sterling and take it home with him. So Graham and I accompanied him to a series of money-changers. He had the cash stuffed in a rucksack. How we got through that day without being mugged, I'll never know. On our last night together he took us out for a slap-up meal. He was a really genuine and generous bloke. Aware that he was an enthusiastic gambler, Graham and I suggested to him that he should invest some of his winnings in an apartment. We thought we had convinced him. He said he would move into property but, as I remember it, I heard that he'd lost the lot by September!

I returned from Hong Kong ready for the challenge of a new season. I knew that it would, in all probability, be my last. I had about ten months left on my contract at West Ham. As I recall I was earning about £1,200 a week at the time. I was one of the highest-paid players at the club. A new contract, if they offered me one, would start in June 1984 when I would be just a few months short of my 36th birthday. I thought it unlikely that they would make much of an effort to keep me.

I trained well and was injury-free in pre-season but as the big kick-off approached I wondered whether I'd be selected and, if so, how I would do. I shouldn't have worried. John Lyall put me in the team for the opening match against Birmingham City at Upton Park. We won 4-0, with 18-year-old Tony Cottee, called up to deputise for the injured Paul Goddard, scoring twice in five minutes.

I missed the next game, a 1-0 win against Everton at Goodison Park, with a thigh strain, but was back to face Tottenham at White Hart Lane. My old England team-mates Ray Clemence and Glenn Hoddle were in the Spurs side that day. We won 2-0, which meant three wins out of three without a goal conceded. We were at the top of the old First Division table. We then beat Leicester City, including a young Gary Lineker, 3-1 and recovered from 2-0 down to beat Coventry 5-2 at Upton Park. With a maximum 15 points from our first five games we were emerging as the shock troops of the season.

I was surprised at how well I was playing. I was helped, of course, by the fact that we were playing well as a team. We had become hard to beat. John Lyall shared many of Ron Greenwood's qualities and beliefs, but he was a steelier character. He'd worked hard on the training pitch and in the transfer market to improve West Ham's defence. Attacking football was still our priority but now we were a much sounder defensive unit. Phil Parkes, the world's most expensive goalkeeper, was enjoying outstanding form. He was protected by the best back four in West Ham history: Ray Stewart, Alvin Martin, Billy Bonds and Frank Lampard.

It was Bill's 37th birthday on the day we suffered our first defeat – 1-0 against West Brom at the Hawthorns. It was a minor blip. I scored my first goal of the season as we beat Notts County

3-0 and hit two when we thrashed Bury 10-0 in the Milk Cup. We were comfortably in third place in the table when we beat Spurs 4-1 on New Year's Eve.

Then it all started to go wrong. First, Alan Devonshire was seriously injured. He and I enjoyed a great rapport but we played our last game together in the third round of the FA Cup in January 1984. He tore his cruciate ligament in a 1-0 win over Wigan and didn't play again for 15 months. Then, another key player, Alvin Martin, broke six ribs in a car crash. He missed most of the rest of the season. We were still fourth when European champions Liverpool thumped us 6-0 at Anfield in April but failure to win any of our last six games meant that we slumped to ninth.

We finished with two home games and lost them both – a sad farewell to Upton Park for me. Nottingham Forest knew they would have to beat us to finish third behind Liverpool and Southampton. There was a surprise for me before the match when the Forest manager Brian Clough made a presentation to me on the pitch – a cut-glass bowl to mark the end of my career. It was a nice gesture. An even bigger surprise followed when my six-year-old son Warren walked out as our match-day mascot. I had no idea he'd been selected for the job.

We took the lead on 19 minutes when Ray Stewart scored from the penalty spot after Chris Fairclough had brought me down. But Garry Birtles and Peter Davenport scored to give Forest a 2-1 win. Two days later, on a Monday evening, we faced Everton in our final match. Five days after that Everton were due to meet Graham Taylor's Watford in the FA Cup final. Nonetheless, they fielded nine of the side that played at Wembley. They beat us 1-0 to climb above us in the league table and finish seventh.

John Lyall was furious in the dressing room afterwards. He launched into us and accused us of complacency and missing a great opportunity. He said we should have finished in the top four instead of which we let it slip in the last weeks of the season. He was probably right though I remained more than satisfied with my own contribution that season – I was surprised that it had gone so well. John had obviously told the coaching staff not to let anyone in the dressing room while he was addressing the players. His coach Mick McGiven and the youth-team coach Tony Carr were guarding the doors. I was taking my socks and boots off and could hear someone thumping on the dressing-room door. Eventually, the 'doormen' relented and the club chairman, Len Cearns, peered through the steam.

He looked at John and then he looked at me. 'Sorry, John,' he said. 'But the crowd won't go home until Trevor goes out and says goodbye.' So I put my gear back on and went on to the pitch amid great cheering. I ran round the pitch, waving to the crowd and picking up the scarves they threw at me. It was an amazing and emotional experience, but what surprised me more than anything was that it seemed virtually everyone in the stadium had stayed behind to bid their farewells. Quite unforgettable. I was lapping it up while the rest of my team-mates were getting a rollicking from the manager!

I stuck by my decision to retire, though it wouldn't have taken much for me to change my mind. Alan Devonshire's long-term injury was a factor. I knew he wouldn't play much the following season and that would place a lot of the creative burden on me. Did I want that kind of pressure at the age of 36? I wasn't sure that I did. That apart, a very talented youngster, Alan Dickens, was beginning to make an impression. He was a creative midfield player already dubbed Brooking Mark Two. Tony Cottee, with 19 goals in my last season, was clearly a star in the making and, of course, John would shortly sign Frank McAvennie from St Mirren. Together they formed a formidable striking partnership and were key factors in the club's best-ever finish – third – in 1985–86. This was something of a transitional period for John's squad and I believe that if they thought I had a role to play they would have offered me a new contract. I think they were quite happy to get me off the payroll.

I had no interest in continuing my playing career in the lower divisions. Many players took that route in those days but I had a couple of business interests and there was no pressing financial need for me to continue playing. It had always been my intention to retire at the top and Hilkka agreed with that. We had talked long and hard about my future and she was quite happy for me to retire from football. She didn't want me to continue playing or begin a new career as a coach.

My wife and children all had a say in my future. They knew I'd been playing well and that some were suggesting I should play on. But, in the back of my mind, I'd always thought that this would probably be my last contract. I'd been gearing up for it for two or three years and there was a general feeling in the family that it would be nice to go out at the top. The fact that I'd had one or two informal approaches from the BBC, suggesting that I might like to do a bit of work for them, helped me make up my mind. If they wanted me, and I was good enough for them, it would keep me involved in the game from a safe seat in the stands.

I also had a great affinity with West Ham and Upton Park and all the fans who had watched me play over the years. I felt that in some way it would be a betrayal to play for another club. So, when John Neal, the Chelsea manager, asked me if I would go and play for him at Stamford Bridge I explained to him that I would find it very difficult, particularly as they were one of West Ham's London rivals. Chelsea had just won promotion, thanks largely to the goals of Kerry Dixon, David Speedie and Pat Nevin, and John Neal thought I would be a good influence in midfield in their first season back in the big time.

It was a flattering offer and the fact that they had approached me at all confirmed my own view that I had played really well in my last season. Further compliments came from the England manager Bobby Robson. I was asked to play in a testimonial match against an England XI and Bobby said to me afterwards: 'Why are you retiring when you're playing so well?' The fact that others thought I could still do it made me think. I was voted Hammer of the Year for 1983–84 and whenever I met any West Ham fans they urged me to reconsider. I had always told myself that I would quit while I was still playing well and my form in my last season enabled me to fulfil that wish. So, I said farewell to Upton Park and flew off to New Zealand, where I played as a guest for an Auckland team for six weeks. I'd always wanted to go to New Zealand and one of the benefits of retirement, of course, is that you can do what you want!

Around the same time I was approached by the BBC and asked if I was interested in joining Peter Jones, Bryon Butler and their distinguished team of radio commentators and pundits. I had done some TV and radio work but this was a serious commitment. 'Yes,' I said, 'I'd like to have a stab at that.' I had another request from an unexpected source. Out of the blue, I was contacted by the Sports Council asking me if I would consider becoming chairman of their Eastern Region at the end of the year.

The Sports Council, formed in 1972, was responsible for the development of sport in the UK. Their motto was 'Sport for All' and they were involved in promoting around 110 different sports. In 1997 the council became UK Sport. Established by royal charter, UK Sport currently has a staff of around 90 and a budget of more than £100 million. It is now the nation's high-performance sports agency and is accountable to the Government through the Department of Culture, Media and Sport.

I had no real idea of what was involved when they first approached me but it was something worthwhile and a challenge that appealed to me. I wasn't to know in the autumn of 1984 that I would devote the next 15 years to sports administration. I gained a huge amount of knowledge and experience of sports politics in that time. I was eventually elected to the national council, became vice chairman and then chairman, and my work in those years probably influenced the FA's thinking when they started looking around for someone to help with the development of football from grass roots to the elite level.

I knew the start of the new season would be a bit of a wrench for me. I was expecting to miss the buzz and excitement of it. After all, I'd shared the sense of optimism that fills every pre-season dressing room for years. As it turned out, West Ham started 1984–85 badly, with a goalless draw against Ipswich Town at Upton Park. Two days later they lost 3-0 to Liverpool at Anfield. As I suspected, the absence of Alan Devonshire proved critical. At the end of the season they were just two points clear of the relegation zone.

Although I had bid farewell to the big time I couldn't bring myself to hang up my boots. I still wanted to play, which was why I agreed to try a new experience – Sunday morning football. I started my debut season in Sunday morning football with a goal and a 3-0 win over the Red Lion pub. I finished the season with a trophy in the league cup competition. I'd been persuaded by friends to join a Sunday morning team that played about one mile from West Ham's training ground at Chadwell Heath in east London. I spent about eight years playing for them and enjoyed every minute, although I never fully mastered the knack of putting up the nets! It was a bit of an eye-opener at first, but it wasn't until I played Sunday morning football that I really appreciated just how fast I was ...

CHAPTER 12

HOUNDS AND CLOWNS
OF THE SEVENTIES

I'M OFTEN ASKED WHETHER I believe the footballers of my era could cope with the pressures of the modern Premiership. I have no doubt that football at the highest level today is faster than when I was playing and has benefited from huge advances in things like diet, medicine and the quality of playing surfaces. There are other differences, too, that have fortunately favoured the creative player over the defensive player.

Some argue that the Trevor Brooking of the seventies simply wouldn't be quick enough to be effective in today's game. I believe quite the opposite. I think my type of player would be even more effective today than in the seventies. The reason for that is easily explained. In the seventies players of my type did not receive the protection from referees that is standard in the modern game. The type of tackling I had to live with has been outlawed and the game as a whole has benefited from that.

The seventies was a wonderful period in which to play professional football. The old First Division was top-heavy with skilful players and great personalities – but they weren't all angels. Some were spiteful, aggressive and violent. The game had tolerated that type of player for a long time. But in the early seventies there was recognition from the sport's authorities that the game had to change.

Football was in decline. The boom that followed England's World Cup victory in 1966 was slowing significantly. More than 30 million fans watched football across the four divisions in 1967–68. By 1973–74 that number had dropped to 25 million. Growing hooliganism was one problem but the game was also suffering as a spectacle. The tough guys ruled and the quality of the entertainment suffered as a consequence. Some of the football was at best functional and at worst seriously boring.

Action was needed to change the direction of the game and one of the first to accept this was Alan Hardaker, the long-serving secretary of the Football League. A Yorkshireman and serving Royal Naval officer on the Atlantic convoys in the Second World War, Hardaker was a man used to getting his own way. With the backing of his management committee, he instructed the League's referees to clamp down on foul play. There would be, he insisted, a less liberal interpretation of the Laws of the Game in future. He ordered that the laws, and lists of misdemeanours subject to cautions, be displayed in every dressing room in the League. The tackle from behind, for instance, was banned altogether.

The effect on the game was dramatic. The first Saturday of hard-line refereeing in season 1971–72 produced four dismissals and 120 bookings. By Christmas there had been more than 1,100 bookings. The Football Association, still responsible for administering discipline, was snowed under with appeals – 140 by January when a normal season would perhaps attract ten in total. The FA granted many of the appeals and, in matters of discipline, were clearly not singing from the same song sheet as the Football League. A compromise had to be reached. The League relented, agreeing that referees could apply greater discretion when interpreting the rules. In return, the League won the introduction of a totting-up system with penalty points for offences and an automatic two-match ban for a player amassing 12 points.

Previously, suspensions covered a time period, which meant that some players missed more matches than others. Banning players for a number of matches rather than a number of weeks seemed fairer to me. Agreement was also reached to end appeals against cautions, many of which were lodged by clubs for tactical reasons in the hope that their players would be free to play in important matches. Similarly, I felt that automatic suspension was a fairer method.

The message had hit home. Football was now placing greater emphasis on skill and was at last prepared to protect those who had it. This was good news for me and players like me. When I started playing seriously in the mid-sixties football still clung to some of the sporting values that had been so admired by the rest of the world in the first half of the last century. Looking back, it's astonishing to think that the Tottenham double-winning team of 1960–61 attracted just one caution for the season. Let's be clear, that was one booking between 17 players in 49 matches – impossible in the context of today's game.

And those days were long gone by the time Johnny Giles, Peter Storey, Nobby Stiles and Ronnie Harris were queuing up to kick lumps out of players like me in the seventies. Some teams, like Leeds United, had a long cast list of players skilled in the dark arts. I remember little Bobby Collins, just 5ft 3in but a real terrier with a nasty bite, providing Don Revie's early Leeds team with real menace in midfield. He was the first of several of his type at Leeds. Giles, a great passer, could also bring your contribution to an abrupt halt with a fierce tackle. Norman Hunter and Jack Charlton were formidable centre-backs and little Billy Bremner was another tough Scot in the Collins mould.

Whenever I played against Leeds in those days I was always happy to receive the ball early because there was so little time to settle. The pitches were usually heavy which meant that the ball stuck but more pertinent still was the inevitable tackle. You knew it was coming. Defenders were upon you within a second or two. You had to be able to take the knocks and ride the tackles. The only option was to try to move the ball on the instant you received it. If anything, defenders in today's game are swarming over the man with the ball even more quickly than they were in my day. The difference is that they have to be a little more conservative and cautious with their tackling. Happily, many of the challenges that were commonplace a generation ago have all but disappeared.

Every creative player in my day needed an unofficial minder. Mine was my long-time pal Billy Bonds. I was big enough and strong enough to ride most tackles but occasionally a really bad one would flatten me. 'Bill! Bill! Did you see what he did to me?' was my usual cry as I climbed back to my feet. Bill wasn't in the 'vicious' category but he was as tough as old boots and very few tried to test themselves against him.

Some observers, probably with justification, regard the early seventies as a barren period for English football. We'd lost our grip on the World Cup in Mexico in 1970, attendances were in decline, TV revenue was minuscule in comparison with today and the refereeing clampdown tended to suggest that carnage on the pitch was a regular occurrence. This wasn't true of course. But what was true was that players, benefiting from the 1963 High Court ruling that the 'retain and transfer' system was illegal, were becoming more aware of their own power. It was unheard of, for instance, for a player to decline the honour of playing for England, but Paul

Madeley, Alan Hudson and Colin Todd did just that at various times in the early seventies.

It was becoming harder to justify the regular claim that the Football League was the strongest, most competitive in the world. It was certainly the toughest but at the elite level of the European game our clubs were second rate. After Manchester United's success in 1968, we had to wait seven years for another English club to reach the European Cup final – Leeds United, who were beaten 2-0 in Paris by Bayern Munich.

Notorious for their cynicism, Leeds were nonetheless a team of many talents and were the dominant force in English football for a decade from the mid-sixties. In that time they won the old First Division title twice, were runners-up five times, the FA Cup once, runners-up three times, the League Cup once and the old European Fairs Cup twice. Don Revie, their manager, took criticism as a personal affront and, to be fair to him, he was always trying to present his team as top-of-the-bill entertainers rather than as a force of destructive warriors.

I remember him deciding to introduce a showbiz style warm-up routine before Leeds United matches in the hope of winning over any doubters in the crowd. Every team warmed up before a game, but Revie decided he wanted something the crowd could watch and enjoy. He turned the Leeds United warm-up into an event in itself. Before the FA Cup quarter-final with Tottenham at Elland Road the Leeds players went on to the pitch in tracksuit tops with their names emblazoned across the back, and name tags holding up their stockings. They all performed an exercise routine that had clearly been rehearsed – and then beat Spurs 2-1. This became their regular pre-match ritual as they progressed to the FA Cup final where they beat Arsenal 1-0 at Wembley – the first leg of their bid for the double.

Within an hour of the final whistle at Wembley, Revie and his

Leeds team were on their coach heading back to Yorkshire. Much to Revie's annoyance, Leeds had been ordered by the Football League to play their final league game against Wolves at Molineux on the Monday evening, 48 hours after the Cup final. Providing Leeds didn't lose they would add the league title to the FA Cup. Wolves had lost their previous four home games so the smart money was on Leeds to finally achieve the coveted double. But it wasn't to be. They had two penalty claims, both for blatant hand-ball, rejected and lost 2-1. That result, plus Liverpool's goalless draw at Arsenal on the same night, handed the title for the first time to Brian Clough and Derby County who, having finished their league programme, listened to the unfolding drama on the radio at their holiday hotel in Majorca.

Some took pleasure in Leeds United's failure but it was hard not to feel sorry for some of their players. They had one or two truly outstanding talents and when they were playing at their best as a team they were exceptional. The BBC film of their 7-0 demolition of Southampton at Elland Road in 1972 has become an iconic piece of football memorabilia. 'Poor Southampton don't know what day it is,' BBC commentator Barry Davies told the nation as the goals went in. 'It's almost cruel.'

Giles and Bremner were perhaps the best all-round footballers in that Leeds team, but my personal favourite was the Scotland winger Eddie Gray. He was one of the most gifted players of my era. He made his debut for Leeds as a 17-year-old on New Year's Day 1966 and held down a first-team place for nearly 20 years. I liked him because he was a winger in the classic mould. He used skill, pace and craft, qualities that were never more apparent than in the 1970 FA Cup final against Chelsea, when he roasted his marker David Webb on a sand-covered pitch at Wembley. The match ended 2-2 and, for the replay, Chelsea used the uncompro-mising Ronnie Harris to mark Gray. One ferocious tackle from

Harris slowed Gray significantly and reduced Leeds United's attacking potential for the rest of the match. Chelsea won the replay 2-1 with, ironically, Webb heading the winner.

Sadly, Eddie had long battles with injury, which explains why he made only 12 appearances for Scotland and missed the 1974 World Cup. In later years he had two spells as Leeds' manager but it is as a player that he is most warmly remembered at Elland Road. In 2000 the fans voted him the third greatest ever Leeds player behind Bremner and John Charles, and club connoisseurs widely regard his goal against Burnley in 1970 as the best Leeds United goal of all time.

What is extraordinary is that Eddie played in a team of hard men in an era of hard men but was never booked himself. There were times when he had plenty of reason to retaliate. But he didn't. He just got on with his job with the stealth of an assassin. Revie once said of him: 'When he plays on snow he doesn't leave any footprints.' Eddie was the kind of crowd-pleaser who attracted the attention of the tough guys among rival teams. The truth is, of course, that in those days lots of teams had lots of crowd-pleasers in their ranks – Rodney Marsh, Charlie George, Stan Bowles and Alan Hudson come to mind. The players who attracted most attention, on and off the pitch, were usually strikers or goal-scoring midfielders.

Today, when we are discussing England strikers for a major tournament, we might have five or six realistic contenders. At any time in the seventies you might have had a dozen or more to select from – Hurst, Keegan, Channon, Worthington, Bowles, Clarke, Macdonald, Johnson, Boyer, Pearson, George, Francis, Mariner, Latchford and Woodcock are among those I can think of. Some played only a match or two for England, but others such as Kevin Keegan, Trevor Francis, Tony Woodcock and Paul Mariner had substantial international careers. Geoff Hurst, as we all remember, was England's

World Cup hat-trick hero from 1966. I'd grown up with him on the training ground at Chadwell Heath and watched him develop from a left-half of limited potential to a world-class striker.

Ron Greenwood, the West Ham manager at the time, decided to move Geoff to the front because he was so poor defensively. Geoff accepted the challenge. He worked and worked and worked and learned how to time his runs, take the ball on his chest and draw others into attacking positions. Sturdily built, he took everything the tough guys threw at him with a resigned shrug. Often, in the dressing room after matches, you would see him with his back and legs covered in bruises. He never complained. It was all part of being a top-class centre-forward in those days. As a self-made sporting hero, Geoff was a fine example to others.

One of the others was Kevin Keegan, who had the same work ethic as Geoff. For me, Kevin was the best of them. In fact, I think he was the best I played with at any level. He was an exceptional player at Liverpool and, after six years at Anfield, became an even better one when he moved to SV Hamburg in 1977. His three years in Germany, where he twice won the European Footballer of the Year award, broadened his game further, teaching him in particular how to deal with man-to-man marking. His willingness to learn and determination to continually improve were elements I came to admire as we became firm friends and room-mates on England's trips abroad. Nothing illustrated this commitment more than his battle to overcome a back injury during the 1982 World Cup in Spain. It was a long, painful process for him but he wouldn't let it beat him. One morning, I remember, he got into a hot bath to soak. I went down to breakfast. When I came back an hour later he was still in the bath, unable to get out because of his bad back.

For me, he remains the classic example of the self-made superstar. His ambition, focus and work ethic took him from humble beginnings at Scunthorpe to Liverpool, Hamburg, Southampton,

Newcastle and global stardom. He wanted to be the best. He was a comedian and motivator in the dressing room and an outstanding captain who conducted himself as befits a top sporting personality. Short and stocky, he reached high balls he had no right to get and, in full flow with the ball at his feet, he reminded me of Maradona.

The standards he set for himself he expected from others. He was totally committed and expected the same from those around him. I think he was disappointed when he went into coaching and management to discover that not all players felt the same way as he did. When he was playing he said he'd never be a coach. He retired as a player in 1984, then, after six or seven years in retirement in Spain, Newcastle invited him back to become their manager. He won promotion and, in 1995–96, Newcastle finished as Premier League runners-up to Manchester United. Remember that season? Newcastle's 12-point lead was whittled away and they lost one of the classic Premier League encounters – a 4-3 defeat to Liverpool in a match that perfectly illustrated Keegan's dedication to attacking football. Then there was the famous TV rant. As he came under increasing pressure, he directed his outburst at Manchester United manager Alex Ferguson: 'I will love it if we beat them. Love it!'

He had a chequered management career and the way he walked out on England, quitting in the Wembley dressing room after a 1-0 World Cup qualifying defeat to Germany in 2000, was further evidence of a complex and demanding character. He found the mix of personalities in the dressing room a challenge and a source of frequent frustration.

If he was totally committed to the job why couldn't all the players feel the same way? He couldn't understand a lazy or indifferent attitude. He could quickly fall out with players who were not as dedicated as he was. As a player he drove himself on and always gave 100 per cent. On the day he could no longer give 100 per cent he quit. That day came in January 1984. He was playing for

Newcastle against his old club Liverpool in the FA Cup at Anfield. Newcastle lost 4-0 and there were moments in the game when Kevin simply couldn't match the pace of the man who was marking him, Mark Lawrenson. He knew what he wanted to do but no longer had the physical prowess to do it. He was a perfectionist. Second best wasn't good enough. He knew it was time to go.

Although he was no publicity seeker he was fortunate in some ways to capitalise on the public's growing appetite for fame and celebrity. This had been sharpened considerably by George Best's seven or eight successful years with Manchester United. He was one of the greatest individual talents since the war and it was a privilege to play against him. Rebellious, good looking, easily led astray by a short skirt or magnum of champagne, George's adventures took football off the back pages and on to the front.

Sir Matt Busby was as fatherly as any manager could be in the circumstances. But no one was really surprised when George announced he was quitting the game at the age of 27. It was a great shame. Those five years between 27 and 32 are often the most productive of a footballer's career. George left behind some wonderful memories – his fabulous dribbling ability, the balance and ease with which he rode tackles, and a catalogue of great goals. He was at his peak in 1968 when he picked up the European Footballer of the Year award after winning the European Cup. I played against him early in my career – he scored a hat-trick against us. I scored a goal myself but my enduring memory of that day is the way George played. I remember him taking a short corner, receiving a return pass, dribbling past three defenders before selling Bobby Moore a peach of a dummy and tapping the ball into the net.

It was a memorable game at Old Trafford. United won 4-2 with George's hat-trick and another goal from Bobby Charlton. They very nearly got a fifth but Bobby Moore dived to head Denis Law's shot off the line. With Best, Charlton, Law, Willie Morgan and

Brian Kidd, United were probably the most glamorous team in the old First Division at that time. It was back in the 1971–72 season and the triple alliance of Best, Charlton and Law was coming to an end. They were the Gods of the game and for a young player like me it was an awesome experience playing against them at Old Trafford. What a great example Bobby Charlton was to young players, on or off the field. You couldn't help but admire him. He started as a winger but, in the end, could play almost anywhere. It didn't matter whether the ball was on his right or left foot. It made no difference. He was genuinely two-footed and I couldn't tell you, even now, which was his best. He was a great passer with a wonderful shot and surge of power and was deservedly voted European Footballer of the Year in 1966.

My dad had used Bobby Charlton as an example to stress the advantages of being able to play with both feet. 'No one knows how best to challenge him,' he explained. He was right. A defender facing Bobby Charlton in full flow wouldn't know whether to channel him to the right or the left. He didn't have a weak side. He could go past a defender on either side. He was a wonderful player but for me George Best, equally adept with either foot, was on another level.

Playing alongside Charlton and Best at this time was 'the king' of Old Trafford – Denis Law. Skilful, daring and volatile, he bemused and bewitched a generation with his theatrical interpretation of the game. He was an original and there have been plenty of imitators in the years since. I loved the way he tucked the sleeves of his shirt into his fists and how he would raise one arm to salute a goal. His mop of blond hair became a trademark much admired and copied, most notably by the pop singer Rod Stewart. As a schoolboy in Aberdeen he wore glasses to correct a squint, but when he turned up at Huddersfield for a trial they knew they had unearthed something special. He then went on to Manchester City,

Torino, Manchester United and City again in a 17-year career that produced more than 300 goals. He took pleasure in them all – except one. In 1974 United let him return to City on a free transfer and at the end of the season he back-heeled the goal that sent United down to the Second Division for the first time in 36 years.

Law played for Scotland on 55 occasions between 1958 and 1974 and was chosen to play alongside Di Stefano, Puskas, Eusebio, Yashin and Gento for the Rest of the World against England in the FA's centenary match at Wembley in 1963. Law relished such exalted company and it gave him particular delight to score against England that day. The following season he became the first and only Scotsman to be voted European Footballer of the Year.

It says much for Manchester United's status as the flag-bearers of the English club game that in the space of five years Law, Charlton and Best were all voted European Footballer of the Year. Each was a worthy winner, but there were others, equally deserving, who were overlooked. Jimmy Greaves, for instance! Has there been a more consistent goalscorer? Jim scored England's 90th-minute winner against the Rest of the World at Wembley and is still considered by many to be the greatest goalscorer in the history of the English game. He finished third in the 1963 European vote behind the legendary Moscow Dynamo goalkeeper Lev Yashin and Italy's Gianni Rivera.

Jimmy was a natural goalscorer and the statistics show just how instinctive he found the business of putting the ball in the net. He scored 357 goals in 516 league games for Chelsea, Tottenham and West Ham and a further nine in 12 games during his brief stay with AC Milan. He scored 44 goals in 57 matches for England, a rate unmatched by Bobby Charlton, Gary Lineker or any of England's top marksmen in the modern game such as Michael Owen or Wayne Rooney.

If you include his goals in cup competitions and for the England

Under-23 side the grand total is 518. He headed the old First Division scoring list on five occasions and scored on every debut he made. Sadly, I missed his debut for West Ham because of injury. Nonetheless, he maintained his record, supplying two ice-cool finishes in the 5-1 win over Manchester City at Maine Road in March 1970. People who say that he wouldn't have survived in today's game are wrong. Players with his ability will always score goals and will adapt to the circumstances and demands made on them.

Unfortunately, when I played with him at West Ham, he was coming to the end of his career and I suspect that the problems that would engulf his private life were already gnawing at him. Jim always says that if you ask the Chelsea fans which were his best years they will say those at Chelsea, and if you ask Spurs fans they will say those at Spurs. But if you ask West Ham supporters they will say those at Chelsea or Spurs!

To be honest, Jimmy didn't do much apart from score but when you could score as regularly as he did you didn't have to do much else. He was stealthy, alert and absolutely deadly in the penalty area. There was no flamboyance about his game. He glided past defenders, wriggled around goalkeepers and almost invariably 'passed' the ball into the net. He made it look easy and that was the beauty of his game. I often wondered how he came to terms with the fact that Sir Alf Ramsey chose Geoff Hurst ahead of him for the World Cup final in 1966. He had originally lost his place because of injury but had fully recovered and, as England's leading goalscorer, was entitled to believe that he would be reinstated for the final. He wasn't. On the morning of the final he left the room he was sharing with Bobby Moore with his bags packed. As soon as the match finished he left Wembley with his wife and went on holiday. I think that his disenchantment with football began that day. He was desperately unlucky to miss the final. Had he played he might have won wider recognition in Europe. The fact that the English football writers never voted him Footballer of the Year remains a mystery to me.

At least my West Ham team-mate Bobby Moore won that national accolade. But the closest he got to the European title was second in 1970 when he was just edged out by Gerd Muller, the opportunist West Germany and Bayern Munich striker whose goal in extra time in Mexico ended England's tenure of the World Cup that year. That defeat was probably the biggest disappointment of Bobby's long and illustrious career. Lionised by his fellow professionals, he was the embodiment of all that was great about English football. His international career spanned nearly 14 years and 108 games. Bobby was captain for a record 90 matches, and England lost only 13 times when he led the team out.

Bobby enjoyed his celebrity status but never lost sight of his East End roots. He'd often sit quietly in a corner of one of his favourite London pubs, chatting to the locals. One Christmas he was sitting in just such a pub with a freshly plucked turkey on the bar in front of him. It was the turkey West Ham traditionally gave to their players on Christmas Eve. Tina, Bobby's wife, was at home, waiting to stuff the turkey. She was ringing round trying to find him and, in desperation, called Bob's mum, Dot. 'I bet I know where he is,' she said. She went straight to the pub. 'Get home with that turkey now,' she told the England captain in front of a sniggering audience. 'Leave off, Mum,' said Bobby. 'I'm nearly thirty now!'

Bobby liked a drink but, from my earliest days at West Ham, I'd been deeply impressed by his work ethic on the training ground. He was a good role model for youngsters. One Sunday morning early in my first-team career, I was having treatment from our physiotherapist, Rob Jenkins, at Upton Park. Rob, whose father Bill had been the club physio before him, was always in the treatment room on Sunday mornings, working on injured players. On this particular morning Bobby Moore turned up in a sweat suit and started lapping the Upton Park pitch. 'What's he doing?' I asked Rob. 'He always does that on Sunday morning if he's had a big Saturday night out,' Rob explained.

No argument about the greatest defender of the time is ever likely to end in agreement, but all such debate must start with Bobby Moore. Others, such as Italy's Facchetti, Germany's Beckenbauer or Argentina's Passarella, might have been stronger, more elegant or quicker but none had Bobby's combination of talents. Those who saw him play will know what I mean. Those who didn't are unlikely to understand. Bobby wasn't the quickest, the tallest, or the toughest, but he had a matchless mix of skills that gave him composure and a presence that were a fine example to those around him. Critics who said he couldn't run, couldn't head the ball or couldn't tackle were really missing the point. His thought process was the quickest thing on the pitch. He was always ahead of everyone else. Trying to sneak the ball past him was like trying to sneak the sunrise past a rooster.

Bobby was already an established international star when I went to Upton Park as a boy. His career seemed to run forever. He played in the days of Johnny Haynes and Billy Wright and was still playing when Kenny Dalglish, a big name from a much more recent era, suddenly burst upon the scene. They played against each other for the first time when Bobby marked Kenny in the Scottish FA centenary match in February 1973.

In those days Scotland drew most of their players from the English clubs. Leeds, Liverpool, Manchester United, Manchester City, Arsenal, Tottenham, Derby and Newcastle regularly supplied the hard core of the Scotland team. Kenny was still learning the basics of the game at Celtic when he lined up with George Graham, Martin Buchan, Lou Macari, Billy Bremner and Peter Lorimer for his first taste of the 'auld enemy'. It was a bitter experience for the

Talking to interim England manager Joe Mercer before training for a game in Belgrade against Yugoslavia in June 1974, just at the beginning of my international career. *(Getty Images)*

Dave Watson (left), one of England's finest defenders, made his England debut with me in Sir Alf Ramsey's last match as manager in Portugal in April 1974. Gerry Francis made his debut six months later in Don Revie's first match as manager and, although he was made captain, injury restricted his international career to just 12 appearances in two years.

Chasing Brazil's Zico in Los Angeles on the Bicentennial tour of 1976. Brazil beat England 1-0 but my outstanding memory is of Rivelino's 60-yard pass – the best pass I saw in my career.

Ray Wilkins made an outstanding debut as England overturned a two-goal deficit to beat Italy 3-2 in New York on the Bicentennial tour in 1976. Tempers flared at times and the Italian defender in this picture – one Fabio Capello – shows England's other debutant, Gordon Hill, little sympathy with this tackle.

I was delighted to be back in the England team for this World Cup qualifier against Italy in November 1977, but sadly we were unable to qualify for the finals in Argentina. *(Getty Images)*

Mrs Thatcher outside No. 10 with Ron Greenwood and the England squad prior to departing for the European Championship in Italy in 1980.

Battling in midfield against Spain during that tournament. I scored, and we won the game 2-1, but unfortunately we did not progress to the next stage of the competition. *(Getty Images)*

Shielding the ball during England's World Cup qualifier against Switzerland in November 1980; it was my 40th cap. *(Getty Images)*

Celebrating my favourite goal, against Hungary in 1981, when the ball lodged in the stanchion. *(Getty Images)*

Backed up by Bryan Robson, who was already emerging as a key figure in the side in 1981, I move forward in attack. *(Getty Images)*

Kevin Keegan and I look dejected after injury ruled us out of England's 1982 World Cup opener against France. *(Getty Images)*

Wearing the unfamiliar number three shirt, I shoot for goal during my one and only brief appearance in the World Cup finals. *(Getty Images)*

I was honoured at a Football Writers' Association tribute night in 1985. The guest list reflected my time with West Ham and England – Don Howe (left), Geoff Hurst, Bobby Robson, John Lyall, me and Ron Greenwood.

Back in the claret and blue strip of West Ham, I played Sunday morning football for the same Havering team for about eight years. Our home ground was around a mile from West Ham's training ground at Chadwell Heath.

What a line-up! This was a 70th birthday lunch for Ron Greenwood. The front row (left to right) is: Billy Bonds, Geoff Hurst, Ron, Dave Sexton, John Lyall and me. The back row (left to right) is: Dennis Signy of the Football Writers' Association, journalist Brian James, ITV commentator Brian Moore, journalist Michael Hart, Don Howe, journalist Reg Drury, England physiotherapist Fred Street and FA administrator Alan Odell.

Commentating on England v Tunisia in the 1998 World Cup in France. I hugely enjoyed my time working with the BBC. *(Getty Images)*

I had a couple of brief spells as manager of West Ham. Working with Paolo Di Canio was one of the more interesting challenges in the job. *(Getty Images)*

In my role as Director of Football Development at the FA, it was important I worked closely with England managers such as Fabio Capello. *(Getty Images)*

I've always enjoyed working for charities and good causes, whether it's a big fundraiser in London with Princess Diana, a Lady Taverners' ball with the former US president Bill Clinton as chief guest, or meeting and greeting at the local church garden fete.

With Hilkka at Buckingham Palace in the autumn of 2004, when I was honoured to receive my knighthood from the Queen.

Hilkka and I were thrilled to be invited to the wedding of Prince William and Kate Middleton at Westminster Abbey in April 2011. Prince William, of course, is the President of the FA – and an Aston Villa fan.

raw Dalglish. On a snowy Hampden Park Willie Ormond's Scotland were beaten 5-0 by England.

Dalglish matured into a wonderful player who, if selected, would have graced the long and distinguished list of European Footballer of the Year winners. His best finish was second to Michel Platini, of France and Juventus, in 1983 when he was at the height of an illustrious playing career. He'd joined Liverpool from Celtic for £440,000 at the start of 1977–78, the replacement for Kevin Keegan, and within weeks the fans on the Kop had unfurled new banners that read: 'Kenny's From Heaven!'

Keegan, who had picked up the mantle of greatness once it slipped from George Best's shoulders, handed it on to Kenny, who accepted the responsibility with enthusiasm. A model professional, Dalglish took just 100 games to score his first 50 goals for Liverpool. His strike rate never faltered. A superb all-round creator and finisher, his only weakness was probably a lack of genuine pace. It was something we had in common! He won a record 102 caps for Scotland, three European Cup-winner's medals and seven League Championship titles.

He scored spectacular goals and I remember in particular the one against West Ham in the Milk Cup final replay at Villa Park in 1981. We were leading 1-0 when Terry McDermott chipped a ball through to the right of our goal. Kenny was already in the penalty area and as the ball floated over his shoulder he slid and hooked it in one movement across the face of the goal into the far corner of the net. It was a remarkable goal and laid the foundation for Liverpool's 2-1 victory.

In the summer of 1985, when Joe Fagan stepped down as manager following the Heysel Stadium disaster in the European Cup final in Brussels, Kenny was elevated to player-manager. His success continued unabated with the league and FA Cup double in his first season as manager. I rate him among the truly great players of that era and what few people know is that Kenny and I could have been team-mates. Before he joined Celtic he had trials with a number of clubs in England, including West Ham. He spent a week at our training ground at Chadwell Heath. Ron Greenwood, the manager, said later that his talent was obvious as soon as he saw him play. West Ham were keen to sign him as an apprentice but, sadly, young Dalglish was homesick and went back to Glasgow where he signed for Celtic.

When he was at the pinnacle of his game what particularly impressed me was his speed of thought. A bit like Bobby Moore, he always seemed a second or two ahead of everyone else. That compensated for any lack of pace. He was two-footed, shielded the ball well and was always aware of the runners around him. He had the knack of picking the right pass at the right time.

Although he came along a little later than Kenny Dalglish, I'd have to put Gary Lineker right up there as one of the great goalscorers of his day. I first played against him in 1979 when Leicester were on their way to the old Second Division title, but I particularly remember a game against him two or three years later when Leicester City savaged West Ham at Filbert Street. They won 4-1 and young Lineker was the player who caught my eye. I thought then that he was a future England striker, though I seem to recall someone telling me that he was Scottish! He was, of course, born in Leicester and was destined to become one of the great strikers of the eighties.

The thing that impressed me about him was his lightning speed and astute reading of the game. The timing of his runs was excellent. That is what set him apart from other strikers who were merely quick. He made his England debut in 1984 and two years later established himself as a global star when he finished the 1986 World Cup in Mexico as the leading marksman with six goals. It was his hat-trick against Poland in Monterrey that pulled England back from the brink of a shameful World Cup exit.

After seven seasons at Leicester he had moved to Everton but his success in Mexico put him on the international market. Just weeks after returning from the World Cup, and after only one season at Goodison Park, Everton reluctantly accepted a £2.75 million offer from Barcelona. Gary, who finished his England career with 48 goals, just one behind the all-time record scorer Bobby Charlton, formed a productive attacking partnership with Peter Beardsley. They became key figures in Bobby Robson's eight-year reign as manager.

Remarkably, Gary was never cautioned in a professional career spanning nearly two decades. His exemplary behaviour on and off the field was recognised by FIFA with their Fair Play award. He was, and continues to be, an excellent ambassador for the English game and is now instantly recognised as a TV personality and football pundit. The place where he really came alive, though, was the penalty area. His knack of suddenly changing the direction of his run regularly generated chaos in opposing defences. He knew which causes to chase and which to leave alone. As a midfield player, I would have enjoyed delivering the ball into his path. I'd retired from international football when he made his debut against Scotland in May 1984 but, happily, I was privileged to play alongside many players Gary would list among his England team-mates.

Notable among these was the Manchester United captain Bryan Robson, who was once described by England manager Bobby Robson as 'the bravest, most committed and strongest player I ever had'. It was no exaggeration. Bryan possessed a depth of commitment that bordered on the reckless, a fact borne out by the number of injuries he sustained. I have seen estimates that his injuries cost him about 30 England caps. As it was, he played for his country 90 times and scored 26 goals – a remarkable return for a midfield player. But he was no ordinary midfield player. Bobby Robson christened him 'Captain Marvel'. He was three players in one –

defender, midfielder and goalscorer. He tackled, passed and scored goals. You couldn't ask for much more.

I played a few games with him towards the end of my career and, unfortunately, was a spectator when he produced perhaps his finest performance, in England's 3-1 win over France in Bilbao in the opening match of the 1982 World Cup. It was England's return to the World Cup stage after a 12-year absence and we made an instant impact with the quickest ever goal in the tournament – Bryan Robson's strike after just 27 seconds. He provided a second goal and gave a stirring performance in midfield that earned praise from around the world.

That team included some of the best England players of my time – among them Peter Shilton, Terry Butcher, Kenny Sansom, Ray Wilkins and Steve Coppell. Shilton's place in goalkeeping folk-lore is safe, with his record 125 caps in a 20-year international career. Many consider him the finest England goalkeeper of all but I think Gordon Banks has an irresistible claim to that title. England's World Cup-winning goalkeeper would have earned more than his 73 caps had it not been for the car accident that robbed him of the sight in one eye, dramatically cutting short a wonderful career. His value to England was never more apparent than at the 1970 World Cup, when Alf Ramsey considered Gordon's enforced absence to be the main reason why England lost to West Germany. Similarly, I recall with some frustration just how valuable he was to Stoke in the four-match League Cup semi-final epic against West Ham in 1971–72. Gordon's outstanding contribution included a remarkable save from Geoff Hurst's penalty.

Like Bryan Robson, Terry Butcher broke into the England team in 1980 and stayed for a long time. He won a total of 77 caps and but for injury – he missed the 1988 European Championship, for instance – would have won a lot more. He was still a fledgling inter-national in 1982 when he played in all the games that mattered at the World Cup in Spain. Terry stood 6ft 3in, passed well with his left foot and was as brave as a lion. The English public will always remember the image of him trudging, bandaged and blood-stained, from the pitch at the end of a match against Sweden. At his best he was one of the most consistent and reliable centre-backs in the world but, in my opinion, the defender he succeeded was equally as good.

Dave Watson, of Sunderland, Manchester City, Werder Bremen and Southampton, was from the old school of England centre-halves. He had started his career as a striker with Notts County but by the time he got into the England squad he was a powerful and uncompromising centre half. Not the tallest of centre-backs by today's standards, he was nonetheless outstanding at attacking the ball in the air, as he demonstrated with the immense header that led to the first of England's four goals against Hungary at Wembley in 1978.

Dave made his England debut at the same time as me in Sir Alf Ramsey's final match in Portugal in 1974. Sadly, his career coincided with the 12 years of England's exile from the World Cup so he never got the opportunity to play on football's biggest stage. Whenever we travelled with England you always knew which room Dave was occupying because of the noise! He invariably took a big music box with him. He loved heavy rock and particularly Status Quo. He'd often go to recording studios to listen to bands making records and, at that time, I would not have been surprised had he turned up with a guitar one night on *Top of the Pops*!

His mate in the England squad was Steve Coppell, who was a bit of an academic but shared a passion for heavy rock. His career was unorthodox in that, rather than sign for a club as an apprentice, he went to Liverpool University to study economics. Tranmere Rovers thought enough of his football skill to play him as an amateur in their Third Division team.

He was a winger at a time when wingers were unfashionable but the Manchester United manager Tommy Docherty spotted his potential and bought him for a bargain £50,000 in February 1975. Docherty played him for ten of the last 11 games of the season – eight wins and three draws – so Steve played a significant part in helping United win the old Second Division title.

Sadly, his playing career was cut short by injury. A tackle by the Hungarian Jozsef Toth at Wembley in November 1981 damaged his knee and, although he played on for a year or so more, the knee condition worsened. He was able to play in the first four games of the 1982 World Cup but the problem flared up after the goalless draw with West Germany and he had to miss the decisive match against Spain. He had become an essential element in the team and it would be a long time before England found another wide player as smart and energetic as Steve.

It was Sir Alf Ramsey, of course, who had stunted the development of wingers in the sixties but by the time Steve joined United, coaches were again looking for wide players who could both attack and defend. Steve fell into that category. He had the pace to reach a 30-yard pass, the skill to wriggle past a defender and send over the perfect cross. But he also had the energy to run back and provide cover for his defensive team-mates on the right flank. It was this willingness to work up and down the right flank that set him apart from so many other wingers at that time. When his team lost possession Steve didn't hang about on the flank waiting for someone to win it back. He wanted to win it back himself. He was involved all the time – a quality that is a prerequisite for today's wide players.

Steve made his England debut against Italy in 1977 along with Manchester City's Peter Barnes, who played wide on the left, and Everton's Bob Latchford, who played up front alongside Kevin Keegan. I remember it particularly well because I scored in our 2-0 win. For a while the front four of Coppell, Latchford, Keegan and Barnes looked a very promising formation. Whenever they were available Ron almost always picked them and two years later, when all four played against Scotland at Wembley, Coppell, Keegan and Barnes all scored in a 3-1 win.

I clearly recall manager Ron Greenwood stressing to Coppell and Barnes before each match that they would have to do their share of donkey work in midfield. Why? Because at that time Ray Wilkins and I were playing in the centre of midfield and neither of us had a reputation for tackling. Therefore if we lost the ball in midfield we could be terribly exposed. This is exactly what happened a few weeks after that win over Scotland.

Our 'famous' front four lined up with Ray and myself in midfield to face Austria on a sultry night in Vienna. I have to say that Steve did his fair share that day, scoring one of our goals, but Ray and I struggled to protect our back four. It was exciting, but we lost 4-3. Ray was one of the great England players of my time and when we meet these days we still have a chuckle about the times we roomed together. I used to share with him before being 'upgraded' to share with Kevin Keegan. As a player Ray was neat, tidy and precise – the same qualities he demonstrated off the field. I don't share his obsession with tidiness, something he's happy to tell everyone he meets. He claims I was the most untidy player it was his misfortune to room with. He was always complaining because I'd left my socks on the floor or I hadn't shut the wardrobe door. I survived his constant moaning by burying my head in a book. Even today Ray will tell you: 'I always knew when I was boring Trevor because he'd suddenly pick up a book and start reading.' It's true. I always had a book on the go, usually a thriller of some sort, when I travelled with England. Ray and I were great pals and, somehow, still are.

He was a wonderful player with a fantastic passing range. I never understood those who criticised him for passing backwards or square. He simply didn't want to give the ball away. And he didn't. He was a natural leader, the captain of Chelsea at 18. He had a broad vision of the game and was probably more appreciated by coaches than the man on the terraces. Nonetheless, he was hugely valued by Chelsea, Manchester United and AC Milan and was capable of moments of inspiration – his goal against Belgium in the 1980 European Championship being a classic example of that.

That tournament in Italy provided an opportunity for a swathe of top-quality England players to experience tournament football for the first time. Failure to qualify for the 1974 and 1978 World Cups meant that England were absent from tournaments from the 1970 World Cup in Mexico until the Euros in 1980. So for players like me, Kevin Keegan, Ray Wilkins, Dave Watson, Steve Coppell, Kenny Sansom and Glenn Hoddle the trip to Italy in the summer of 1980 was a new experience.

Some rose to the challenge in spectacular fashion, others were more cautious. Then there were those, like Glenn Hoddle, who just wanted the chance to show what they could do on the inter-national stage. Probably the most talked-about player of the time, Glenn went on a pre-tournament trip to Australia with England. Ron Greenwood had still to finalise the make-up of his squad and had to make a choice between Hoddle and Bryan Robson in mid-field. Hoddle scored in a 2-1 win in Sydney and got the vote. His fans were jubilant. There were those who couldn't find enough superlatives to describe him. But he did have his detractors; those who felt he didn't work hard enough or contribute sufficiently to defensive duties. It seemed to me at the time that whenever he played for England he was on trial and had something to prove. That was an unfair burden to place on a player who, for me, was as gifted a footballer as I'd seen since George Best drifted out of the game.

He'd been a regular in the Tottenham side for three years when

Ron Greenwood gave him his England debut on a foggy night against Bulgaria at Wembley in 1979. Glenn scored with a long-range shot, but it probably took him three or four more years before he considered himself a regular in the England side. There was much about his game that reminded me of the great South American players – his ability to pull the ball down from shoulder height with either foot, the weight and range of his passing and the precision with which he trapped the ball. He started only one match in the Euros in Italy and only one in the 1982 World Cup in Spain but by the time the 1986 World Cup came round Bobby Robson was convinced of his value. He played in all five games and Gary Lineker described him as, 'A striker's dream. I would make runs never seen by most people but always seen by him.' Glenn won 53 caps in the years between 1979 and 1988 and would prob-ably have played many more times for England if it weren't for his tendency to drift out of games. But you can't have everything! I thought he was brilliant.

One of his closest pals in the England squad was Arsenal's Kenny Sansom, who made his England debut in a goalless draw with Wales in 1979 and established himself as a left-back of truly outstanding potential in the 1980 Euros. For me he was as good as Ray Wilson, England's world-class left-back of 1966. As an attack-ing left-back Kenny had few rivals and was almost unchallenged until the emergence of Stuart Pearce in 1987.

Initially Kenny benefited from the shrewd tutelage of Terry Venables in the young Crystal Palace side that was tagged the 'Team of the Eighties'. I remember playing with him for an England XI in a testimonial match at Aston Villa and I've never for-gotten the surging runs he made on the left. He was like an orthodox left-winger playing at left-back. He and John Barnes pro-vided England with a formidable partnership on the left. Barnes, a little like Hoddle, was a complex and unpredictable talent. He had his fans – and his detractors. But there was no doubting his talent. He demonstrated this spectacularly in Brazil in 1984. I was fortunate enough to be in Rio in my new role with the BBC when England, touring South America, faced Brazil in the old Maracana stadium. England won 2-0 and John scored with a goal that was Brazilian in concept and execution. A searing run at the heart of the Brazil defence carried him past lunging tackles and into the area, where he casually slid the ball past the goalkeeper.

It was a wonderful goal, his first for England, but in some ways it became something of a curse. People came to expect the same magic in every match he played. Such moments are not easily replicated. He was a powerful runner with a thudding shot and I suspect he was frustrated when not given more opportunities in a central role. He could play as a central striker but Bobby Robson preferred to use him on the wing. Predominantly left-footed, there's no doubt that his ability to whip in crosses from the left considerably enhanced Liverpool's appeal and their goal-scoring record.

John won a total of 79 caps in a 12-year international career and for much of that time played with the other great England winger of the time – Chris Waddle. Another purist who had much in common with John, there were times when they appeared to be taking turns in the England shirt. Eventually, Robson realised the threat they posed when they played together – as they did in the first five matches of the 1990 World Cup in Italy.

Chris made a total of 62 appearances for England but was discounted early in Graham Taylor's reign. I guess he presented Taylor with the usual dilemma a manager faces when dealing with an unconventional talent – how best to exploit it. Some players present no such problems. My great friend Billy Bonds, for example. You didn't have to exploit him. You just sent him out on to the field knowing that for 90 minutes he would give you everything he had. He did that for West Ham for 21 seasons – a record 804 first-team games and 61 goals. Ron Greenwood signed him as a right-back from Charlton Athletic for £47,500 in May 1967. Ron agreed to pay a further £2,500 if Bill was awarded an England cap.

Charlton very nearly got the extra £2,500 14 years later. Greenwood, then England manager, selected Bill for his first cap against Brazil at Wembley in May 1981. He'd also called up West Ham's young centre-half Alvin Martin for his debut and felt that Bill's familiar presence alongside him would be helpful. Sadly for Bill, four days before the international he cracked two ribs in the final league game of the season against Sheffield Wednesday. Had he got into the England team on that occasion he would have been hard to shift. Instead, he finished a remarkable career without playing for his country and, for me, he remains the best uncapped player of my time in the game.

He was certainly the best signing West Ham ever made. Apart from his 21 seasons as a player he was also youth-team coach and manager for four years. As a player his fitness was legendary. He was still playing at 42. He put the rest of us to shame. A family man who enjoys country walks, bird watching and Thomas Hardy novels, once he got on to the pitch he was transformed into a warrior who could hold his own with the rogues and tough guys of the time. Players like Tommy Smith, Mike Doyle, Johnny Giles, Graham Roberts, Graeme Souness, Jimmy Case, Peter Storey and Ronnie Harris would never take liberties with Billy Bonds.

He was the best captain I played under. Bobby Moore led by example, but Bill encouraged us in a way that brought the best out of us. Whether at right-back, centre-back or in midfield, he was a dominant, inspiring figure on the field, but very shy off it. He was more than happy to keep a low profile. An incident just before the 1980 FA Cup final illustrated his attitude to TV and the media in general. We were staying at a hotel in Hendon the day before the match and the TV cameras were due to film us that afternoon. I was sharing a room with Bill and just before the TV crew arrived he said he was going to 'pop to the betting shop for five minutes'. Three hours later he returned, assuming the interviews were over. He was horrified to discover that because of technical hitches the recording had been put back to that evening. He agreed to co-operate providing he could sit in the background and didn't have to answer questions!

Billy Bonds had no equal. Thirty years after my retirement from professional football I can still say that there is no player I would rather have in my team than Bill. It was a great shame that he never won the cap he so richly deserved. With that foremost in mind I have selected what I believe to be the best England team drawn from those I played with or against in the years 1966–84:

Banks (Stoke);

Bonds (West Ham), Watson (Manchester City), Moore (West Ham), Sansom (Arsenal);

Coppell (Manchester United), Charlton (Manchester United), Robson (Manchester United), Barnes (Liverpool);

Keegan (Liverpool), Hurst (West Ham).

CHAPTER 13

WHO'D BE A FOOTBALL MANAGER?

WHO'D BE A FOOTBALL MANAGER? It's one of those jobs you know will almost certainly end in tears unless you have a record like Sir Alex Ferguson at Manchester United. Just ask David Moyes. I had two brief spells managing West Ham and it was enough to convince me that I was right to decide when I finished playing that I would not be extending my football career into management on a permanent basis.

Let me be clear. I enjoyed the two periods I had in charge at Upton Park. Yes, I was sad that the first one ended in relegation. So, in a sense that ended in tears! But I'd obviously made a good impression because when a second opportunity came along I was the first choice to take over again on a short-term basis. I had often wondered what it would be like to manage a big club like West Ham. Most fans think they can do it. But it's not as straightforward as it seems, especially not in the modern game. I had been involved in professional football for nearly 40 years when I was given my first chance and I have to admit that it was an eye-opening experience.

Ron Greenwood and John Lyall, who between them managed West Ham for almost 30 years, were the men who shaped my thinking about football management. Both top-quality coaches, they were honest, uncomplicated and committed to their jobs at Upton Park. I learned a lot from both of them. They were fortunate to work at a time when trust and loyalty were still considered virtues. At the time of John Lyall's sacking in 1989 the club had employed just five managers in 87 years. In the 25 years since John's departure the club appointed a total of nine managers. How times change!

I have followed the fortunes of the nine with interest because of my affinity with the club. The inevitable newspaper speculation following John's sacking suggested that the frontrunners for his job were Peter Shreeves, Ray Harford, Don Howe, Harry Redknapp and Steve Coppell. They were even tipping me as an outsider. But John's successor was eventually unveiled as the Swindon manager and former Scotland striker Lou Macari, who made a goal-scoring debut for Manchester United against West Ham at Old Trafford in 1973. I missed that game through injury but remember it because United were bottom of the table at the time and their team that day included eight Scots. Another Scot, Tommy Docherty, was manager. Lou was a far better player than he was manager and after just eight turbulent months in charge at Upton Park he resigned, explaining that he wanted to fight to clear his name of FA allegations about unauthorised betting while manager of Swindon. His 229 days represented the shortest tenure by a West Ham manager. He had 40 matches in charge and won just 15 of them.

For Lou it all came to a head in February 1990. The rumblings of dressing-room disharmony were cruelly exposed on the plastic pitch at Boundary Park where Oldham beat West Ham 6-0 in the first leg of the Littlewoods Cup semi-final. Four days later West Ham faced Lou's old club Swindon in a critical Second Division promotion clash. That Sunday, the team bus was late leaving the usual meeting place for the players, the Swallow hotel at Waltham Abbey on the M25. Lou had not turned up at the allotted time so his coaching assistants Billy Bonds and Ronnie Boyce ordered the bus to leave with the players, hoping that Macari would join them at Swindon. He didn't. He had decided to resign. The mounting problems at the club combined with the tabloid coverage of the betting scandal persuaded him that it was time to go despite reassurances of support from the West Ham board.

On the team bus that day was Ludo Miklosko, the 6ft 4in goal-keeper Lou had signed from Banik Ostrava for £300,000. Identified as the long-term replacement for Phil Parkes, Ludo had waited two months to receive his work permit and must have wondered what kind of club he'd joined as he sat on the bus travelling to Swindon. He was expecting to make his long-awaited debut. But where was the manager who had signed him?

Having hastily been placed in charge of the team, Billy Bonds and Ronnie Boyce agreed that Ludo should make his debut as planned. He played well and produced two particularly critical saves that ensured West Ham drew 2-2. Twenty-four hours later Lou's resignation was announced officially, kicking off another round of managerial speculation. Peter Shreeves, Harry Redknapp and Ray Harford were again the names thrown into the mix. There was even a suggestion that John Lyall, sacked just eight months earlier, should be asked to return. That was a non-starter but I detected a feeling that the club wanted to return to the tradition of appointing from 'inside'. Macari and Ron Greenwood were the only managers to arrive at Upton Park with no previous association with the club.

After 23 years as player and coach Billy Bonds had an intimate knowledge of what made the club tick. His managerial experience was scant, but did that matter? He was a man of loyalty and integrity and the fans loved him. The decision was left to the club's new chairman, Martin Cearns. He had just succeeded his father Len, who had been a director for 42 years. Martin, wisely, decided that Bill was the man for the job. Bill immediately appointed another West Ham stalwart, Ronnie Boyce, as his number two. They were 'family' and received a rapturous welcome from 20,000 fans at their first game in charge – a 1-1 home draw with Blackburn Rovers.

In the next game a Martin Allen goal at Middlesbrough gave Bill his first win and a few days later Oldham came down to Upton Park to defend their six-goal lead from the first leg of the Littlewoods Cup semi-final. There was no realistic chance that West Ham would recover the deficit but when Julian Dicks hit the bar, with West Ham already leading 3-0, you began to wonder. In the end the aggregate score was 6-3, but Bill was already restoring pride and confidence.

Bill's promotion to the top job galvanised West Ham and brought stability and hope. When they played Harry Redknapp's Bournemouth in April they were back in eighth position and a play-off place was just a possibility. Harry's boy, Jamie, making his first start, got an early taste of life at this level. Bournemouth were swamped as West Ham cruised to a 4-1 win. At the end of the season Harry and Bournemouth were relegated while Bill got West Ham to within one place and two points of the play-offs.

Bill had four seasons in charge and his first full season, 1990–91, was his most successful. There was a sense that this was a new beginning. Two old stalwarts, Phil Parkes and Alan Devonshire, had gone, along with Liam Brady. Record goalscorer Frank McAvennie, who broke a leg in Macari's first match at the start of the previous season, was back in action. He'd made a couple of appearances as a substitute at the end of the previous season, but we saw what we'd been missing when he scored in the first home match of the season – a 1-1 draw with Portsmouth.

West Ham were unbeaten for the first 21 league matches – a run of results that included a 3-1 win over John Lyall's Ipswich – and were top of the table when they finally stumbled, losing 1-0 at Barnsley over Christmas. The second half of the season was just as productive, although the FA Cup provided a prolonged distraction. Wins against Aldershot, Luton, Crewe and Everton secured a semi-final date with Nottingham Forest at Villa Park – an infamous episode for all West Ham fans. The result hinged on a 26th-minute decision by referee Keith Hackett and his interpretation of the newly introduced 'professional foul' law. When Tony Gale collided with Gary Crosby about 25 yards from goal, Hackett decided it was a 'professional foul' and gave Gale his marching orders. It was his first dismissal in a long and distinguished career. At that moment the match was evenly balanced at 0-0. But in the second half the ten men gradually tired and Brian Clough's Forest put four goals past Ludo Miklosko.

The consolation for Bill came a month later on the last day of the league programme. West Ham led the table by two points from Oldham and by some strange fixture quirk the leading four clubs were playing each other: West Ham (1) v Notts County (4), Oldham (2) v Sheffield Wednesday (3). As long as West Ham could match Oldham's result they would finish as champions.

Before the kick-off Ludo was presented with the Hammer of the Year award for keeping 21 clean sheets – just one short of Parkes' all-time club record. Sadly, it was quickly apparent that Ludo would not be matching Phil's record that afternoon. Within 27 minutes Mark Draper had given County a two-goal lead. George Parris pulled a goal back for West Ham and 2-1 was how it finished. Up at Boundary Park, where the match was now in injury time, it was

2-2 and a single point would not be enough to lift Oldham above West Ham.

West Ham were champions! Or were they? Champagne corks were already popping as Football League and Barclays Bank officials carried the championship trophy and players' medals to a table, decked out in claret and blue, on the pitch. Suddenly they stopped. There was a moment of obvious confusion and embarrassment. Then they started retreating. Up at Oldham, in the last seconds, Neil Redfearn had scored a penalty. Oldham had won 3-2 and they were about to be crowned as champions. West Ham had fallen at the final hurdle, but they were promoted as runners-up. It said much for the progress Bill had made in 15 months in charge that he and his players were bitterly disappointed to have finished second.

Sadly, the club failed to build on that progress. Bill knew the first season back in the old First Division would be challenging. West Ham were installed among the early favourites for relegation in 1991–92 and by mid-September were languishing in 18th place after just one win from the opening eight games. Bill was unfortunate in the sense that the implementation of the Taylor Report, which decreed that every stadium would have to be all-seater within two years, meant that already meagre financial resources had to be spent on ground safety measures rather than on strengthening the playing staff. Bill had less than £1 million to spend in the transfer market and, in order to trim the wage bill, he released players such as Ray Stewart and Stewart Robson on free transfers and sold Iain Dowie to Southampton for £500,000 after he'd played just 12 games for the club.

At this time the club was considering either redeveloping Upton Park or relocating. Redevelopment was the preferred option even though it was going to cost £15.5 million and would take three years to transform Upton Park into a 25,000 all-seater stadium. To help finance this, the club launched the 'Hammers Bond' scheme. The idea was that supporters would pay up to £975 for the right to buy a season ticket. No Bond meant no season ticket and therefore a scramble for the 6,000 remaining 'un-Bonded' tickets, which were available essentially for visiting fans. This caused huge ill feeling among the fans. Although the scheme had influential backers – Billy Bonds was not among them – there were all kinds of sit-ins and protests and regular chants of 'Sack the Board!'

It was not a good atmosphere in which to conduct a relegation fight and, not surprisingly, highlights on the pitch were few and far between. A wonderful goal from Mike Small produced a 1-0 win at Arsenal in November but West Ham won only two of the next 20 matches and, by the time they faced Manchester United at Upton Park in mid-April, they were locked at the bottom of the table. Second-placed United had to win to have any chance of presenting Alex Ferguson with his first title. It was the last season of a championship that had begun in 1888–89.

Ferguson's United would win the first FA Premier League title the following season, but he was not to know that when he complained bitterly about the 'obscene' effort West Ham had put into denying his team the last old First Division title. West Ham had failed to score in nine of their previous 12 games and United, one point behind Leeds with a game in hand, saw this midweek fixture as the ideal opportunity to leapfrog them to the top. But they had not taken full-back Kenny Brown into the equation. In the 66th minute a right-wing cross from Stuart Slater was inadvertently driven against Kenny by United centre-half Gary Pallister. The ball bounced off Kenny into the net and although some thought it a bit of a fluke Kenny claimed he got a significant touch. Whatever, we were all delighted, especially the goalscorer whose dad, also Ken, was in the stands. Ken Brown senior had played for West Ham from 1952 to 1967.

The 1-0 win was not enough to save West Ham from relegation.

Three days later they went to Coventry, themselves in the relegation fight, and lost 1-0. That confirmed West Ham's demise. But a woeful season had one ironic twist left. The last game was against Nottingham Forest at Upton Park and Bill decided to make Frank McAvennie substitute. As he had just been handed a free transfer, this was the last chance the 31-year-old Scot had to bid farewell. He had developed a real rapport with the Upton Park faithful during his two spells with the club. Bill decided to put him on at half time and Frank responded by demolishing Des Walker, who had just completed a big-money transfer to Sampdoria. A prolific marksman in his heyday, Frank scored a hat-trick in 25 minutes. It was a rare moment to savour in an otherwise unedifying season.

Bill decided a bit of a staff reshuffle was in order at the start of 1992–93. His friend of many years and one-time team-mate Harry Redknapp had quit as Bournemouth manager, declaring that he 'needed a break from the game'. It was a short break. Bill offered him a job as first-team coach and ushered long-serving one-club loyalist Ronnie Boyce into a scouting role. Tony Carr, one of the great youth coaches of recent times, took over the development of the youth section while Paul Hilton succeeded him as reserve-team coach.

There was a sense that Harry was coming home to the East End. He and Bill had formed something of a partnership on West Ham's right flank in the sixties. I always got on well with Harry when he was a player. My parents got on well with his dad because they would sometimes travel together to matches when we were kids. As he established himself at the club he got a bit of a reputation as a ducker and diver because he would sometimes turn up at the training ground with a car boot full of stuff he wanted to sell. He introduced the car-boot sale years before it became popular!

Harry was an old-fashioned winger and a big favourite with the fans. The die-hards on the old Chicken Run terrace loved him, and his fiery red hair made him a very distinctive figure. Like me, he wasn't a natural tackler but he could still summon a bit of temper and belligerence. I remember, for instance, how unwise he was to kick Billy Bremner in the shins at Leeds in October 1968. Small, Scotch and ginger (like the drink!), Bremner was the captain of Leeds and a formidable opponent who never took kindly to being kicked. On top of that, West Ham's relations with Don Revie and Leeds United had been strained ever since we humiliated them with a 7-0 win in a League Cup tie at Upton Park in November 1966.

Memories of that result were still a source of irritation for them when we went to Elland Road two years later. Leeds were top of the table at the time and stayed there all season. They had obviously identified Harry as a menace and Bremner went after him from the kick-off. After one particularly spiteful tackle, Harry kicked out in retaliation. Referee Tom Pallister immediately sent Harry off – only the second player dismissed under Ron Greenwood. We were already one goal down but the ten men played gallantly and held out until the 62nd minute. The artful Bremner rubbed it in, swallow diving theatrically in the penalty area. It was a dubious claim, but the referee gave Leeds the penalty and Johnny Giles scored past Bobby Ferguson. So Harry and Bill had plenty of history in common when they came together again with the intention of restoring West Ham to a place among the elite of the game. This was the inaugural season of the Premier League, a competition that would develop into the multi-million-pound business we see today. West Ham were not part of it. Instead, the club were in the renamed First Division – from which they had just been relegated!

An Alan Pardew goal gave Charlton a 1-0 win in West Ham's opening home game and then Kevin Keegan's Newcastle confirmed just how difficult promotion was going to be when they won 2-0 at St James' Park in the early days of the new season. Julian

Dicks was sent off in that match and, in fact, received his marching orders three times in the first four months of the season. The Newcastle defeat was followed by an eight-match unbeaten run that lifted West Ham to second in the table. The fans, though, remained largely unimpressed. Just 11,921 turned up for the Watford match and even fewer – 10,326 – for the visit of Sunderland. They had still not forgiven the board for the ill-conceived 'Hammers Bond' scheme.

But the mood had changed dramatically by the time West Ham faced Sunderland at Roker Park on 27 February. The match ended goalless, but the result hardly mattered. Three days earlier Bobby Moore, the greatest Hammer of all, had died at the age of 51 after a long fight against bowel and liver cancer. Bobby's death unleashed a wave of emotion nationwide but it was probably among West Ham fans that the loss was felt most deeply. Supporters from both clubs laid wreaths and a minute's silence was impeccably observed. A week later the biggest crowd of the season – 24,679 – was at Upton Park to watch West Ham face Wolves. Geoff Hurst and Martin Peters, who had shared many of Bobby's great triumphs, and former West Ham manager Ron Greenwood carried a floral tribute in the shape of Moore's number six shirt on to the pitch. No player wore the number six shirt that day. Ian Bishop wore number 12 instead.

The match was incidental, but the result important to Bill and Harry, who had both played for many years with Bobby. West Ham came from behind to win 3-1. They were well on course for promotion and, in a sense, the death of Bobby Moore had a unifying effect on the fans. Perplexed and disheartened by the 'Hammers Bond' scheme, they now began to return to Upton Park in greater numbers and late in the season, as Bill and his men clinched the runners-up spot and promotion with four consecutive wins, the scheme was finally shelved.

It was a difficult start to life in the Premiership. Upton Park looked like a building site when Wimbledon arrived for the opening match of the 1993–94 season. Their owner Sam Hammam inexplicably scrawled graffiti over the visitors' dressing room before watching his team secure a 2-0 win. When West Ham faced Glenn Hoddle's Chelsea at Upton Park in October they had won only two of nine games. Before the Chelsea kick-off Bobby's widow – his second wife Stephanie – was joined by Geoff Hurst, Martin Peters and club chairman Terry Brown in sealing a time capsule into the foundations of the proposed new Bobby Moore stand. Bobby would have been quietly pleased that they had seen fit to name a stand after him. He would also have been delighted with the result. A Trevor Morley goal secured a 1-0 win, lifting West Ham to 17th.

Things were looking up by December. A 2-0 win over Southampton – the eighth clean sheet in 11 games – lifted West Ham to 10th in the table. The board were obviously happy with the progress under Bill because in January they offered him and Harry new three-year contracts. Bill said that Harry had done a great job in the 18 months they had been together. Harry said that he'd enjoyed every minute of it.

Six months later, after West Ham had finished a respectable 13th in their first Premiership season, it had all turned sour. The true circumstances of Bill's departure remain something of a mystery. It is a matter that Bill and Harry still refuse to agree over. They were friends for many years – Harry was best man at Bill's wedding – but that is no longer the case.

Harry made his debut for West Ham in August 1965, two years before me, replacing Peter Brabrook in a 1-1 home draw with Sunderland. But it wasn't until my first season – 1967–68 – that he began to wear the number seven shirt regularly. Sadly, he didn't win anything with West Ham. The nearest he came was the League Cup in 1972, when we were beaten in a semi-final marathon with Stoke. It was, in fact, a foul on Harry by Gordon Banks that gave

Geoff Hurst the penalty that the England goalkeeper saved. But for his save we would have progressed to the final.

Later that year Harry was transferred to Bournemouth where he went on to make a name for himself as a coach. He led them to the Third Division title in 1986–87 with a record number of points and spent nine years there, establishing a reputation for himself as a wheeler-dealer in the transfer market. He always enjoyed coaching and got all the qualifications he needed. Years later, long after Bill had left West Ham and the pair of them had gone their separate ways, Harry claimed that he had told Bill that Bournemouth had made him an offer to return to Dean Court that he simply couldn't refuse. Harry claims that Bill's reaction was: 'I don't know what I'll do without you, Harry. If you go, I'll go.'

Bill has kept a dignified silence over the exact circumstances surrounding his resignation. I think he's the most genuine person I've known in football and, considering his reputation at West Ham, I don't think Harry or the club came out of it as they should have done. I don't think Bill was very well treated at the time. I also think it's fair to say that my relationship with Harry suffered because he knew that Bill had confided in me. Publicly, what is known is that during a pre-season tour in Scotland in August 1994 Bill was summoned to a hurriedly arranged board meeting in the team's hotel. It was suggested to him that he become director of football, with a job for life, while Harry took charge of first-team affairs. A few days later Bill resigned, ending his 27-year association with the club.

Harry had seven seasons in charge at Upton Park and his start wasn't encouraging. West Ham failed to score in their opening three games and by the time they registered their first win – 1-0 against Aston Villa – they were 17th in the table. Harry was still agonising over the circumstances of Bill's exit, even though the club's managing director, Peter Storrie, insisted that Bill had resigned before they offered him the job of director of football and that at no point was he told that the board preferred Harry as first-team manager.

It was a long time before Bill went back to the club – then as a match summariser for a London radio station – but within weeks of his departure he was back in the claret and blue strip. My Sunday morning team-mates, who wore West Ham's cast-offs, were delighted when Bill agreed to make a few guest appearances on park pitches in places like Romford and Brentwood.

Another West Ham legend, Frank Lampard senior, Harry's brother-in-law, was installed as assistant manager. It would not be too long before young Frank Lampard was challenging for a first-team place. Young Frank was one of several outstanding graduates in the club's youth scheme. The progress made at youth level would prove critical in the coming seasons and earn the club millions of pounds in the transfer market.

Harry bought Tony Cottee back from Everton and he quickly re-established his scoring credentials. He finished as the season's top marksman with 15 goals, even though he was absent with injury at the end when points were critical. A 3-0 win over Liverpool and a 1-1 draw with Manchester United in the last game – again denying United the title – was enough to secure 14th place and keep West Ham in the Premiership. That had been the main aim for Harry and Frank at the start of the season.

Harry's reign at West Ham coincided with big changes in the game. Suddenly the new Premiership, financed by Sky TV, was the place to be. The big clubs were spending big money on foreign players, who all wanted a taste of life in the Premier League. Suddenly, interpreters became familiar figures in dressing rooms up and down the country. Spurs, among the biggest spenders, now had a Romanian, Ilie Dumitrescu, and a German, Jurgen Klinsmann, in their team taking instructions from an Argentine – Ossie Ardiles. I remember the Spurs manager saying at the time that transfer prices were 'stampeding'. His point was that fees didn't necessarily reflect the quality of the players coming into England. 'Abroad the price is a truer reflection of players' ability,' he insisted.

Flocks of overseas players came to the UK – Eric Cantona to Leeds United, Basile Boli to Rangers, Stefan Schwarz to Arsenal, Bryan Roy to Nottingham Forest, Jaime Moreno to Middlesbrough. It was a lucrative market and Harry made sure that West Ham weren't left at the starting gate. The changing rooms at Chadwell Heath and Upton Park were once citadels of cockney wit and rhyming slang, occasionally interrupted by a high-pitched Scot or a deep Suffolk burr. Now the dressing rooms were multi-lingual, as a stream of foreign players arrived from all over the world – Marc Rieper, Paulo Futre, Florin Raducioiu, Marc Keller, Hugo Porfirio, Eyal Berkovic, Samassi Abou to name just a few. Some represented value for money and among these I would place Paolo Di Canio, a £1.7 million buy from Sheffield Wednesday, and Slaven Bilic, a £1.6 million buy from Karlsruher.

Others, like the Dutch striker Marco Boogers, who cost £800,000 from Sparta Rotterdam, were not such good value. Poor Marco! He played only four games and during the second was sent off for a high tackle on Manchester United's Gary Neville. He returned to Holland claiming that he was suffering from stress. Harry needed a reliable goalscorer to take over from Tony Cottee but didn't really find one until he signed John Hartson from Arsenal for a club record £3.2 million. The previous season Cottee had finished as the club's top scorer with just 12 goals and it looked as though full-back Julian Dicks would finish as top marksman in 1996–97 until Harry signed Hartson, and Paul Kitson from Newcastle for £2.3 million, in February 1997. The timely arrival of Hartson and Kitson proved crucial and their goals helped West Ham avoid the drop by just two points.

Those two astute signings, combined with the emergence of

youngsters like Rio Ferdinand and Frank Lampard, transformed the atmosphere around Upton Park. The optimism was fully justified. The following season West Ham finished eighth in the Premiership and reached the quarter-finals of the FA Cup and Coca-Cola Cup. In both competitions they were knocked out by an Arsenal side reforming impressively under new French manager Arsene Wenger.

Hartson repaid a big slice of his fee by finishing the season as top scorer with 24 first-team goals and Ferdinand demonstrated the value of a buoyant youth policy by capturing the Hammer of the Year vote. Sadly, Hartson, struggling with his weight, lost his way the following season and played just 17 Premiership games, scoring four goals. Ian Wright carried the scoring burden and although he finished as top marksman he scored only nine goals. It was, though, to be Harry's best season in the Premiership. West Ham finished fifth, the second highest position in the club's history, despite conceding more goals than they scored. And, encouragingly, Joe Cole was the latest to emerge from a youth team that had just won the FA Youth Cup. Those young players would provide the club with a fabulous financial return on their original investment.

In his first five years in charge Harry had turned over around £80 million in transfer fees, giving the club a profit of some £10 million. Even so, with a ground capacity limit of 26,000 imposed on the club, he knew he didn't have the spending power to attract the very best players and challenge consistently for a place in Europe. This year, at least, West Ham had the chance to experience European football after a gap of 18 years.

With the Premiership season kicking off early because of Euro 2000 the following summer, 1999 saw the shortest closed-season break in memory. On 17 July Harry's boys faced Jokerit of Finland in the Intertoto Cup, with the 17-year-old Joe Cole replacing Berkovic, who had been sold to Celtic for £7.75 million. West Ham won 1-0 and played three more Intertoto Cup ties before the Premiership season had even started. In mid-August, with Cole, Lampard and Ferdinand all involved, West Ham gave a magnificent performance in France, beating Metz 3-1 to secure a place in the UEFA Cup.

A 6-1 aggregate win over NK Osijek of Croatia in the first round of the UEFA Cup produced the kind of European tie West Ham last experienced when I was playing. Steaua Bucharest, European Cup winners in 1986 when they beat Terry Venables' Barcelona on penalties, were the opposition in round two. A fractious first leg, on a rain-swept autumn evening in Bucharest, was West Ham's 19th match of the season. The Danish referee, Claus Bo Larsen, suggested to Harry that he take off Paolo Di Canio before he sent him off. The Romanians won 2-0 and held West Ham to a goalless draw at Upton Park. The European dream was over.

Sadly, the domestic cups were no more fruitful. Aston Villa knocked West Ham out of the Worthington Cup in a replayed quarter-final – replayed because West Ham had given cup-tied Manny Omoyinmi a six-minute appearance as a substitute not realising that he was ineligible to play. There were no such technical problems in the FA Cup, just West Ham's traditional vulnerability when playing against teams from a lower division.

This time the team was John Aldridge's Tranmere Rovers from Division One. They won 1-0 and with West Ham's FA Cup exit came the first murmurings of dissent from Di Canio, who was substituted midway through the second half. Temperamental and unpredictable, Paolo was revered by the fans. He was a showman and they loved him for it. He finished the season as top marksman and, not surprisingly, was voted Hammer of the Year. He hit a 'wonder' goal against Wimbledon – the BBC's Goal of the Season – and was probably relieved to miss the next match, a 7-1 thumping by Manchester United at Old Trafford. It was a long, hard season and once again there was no silverware to show for it. But there were some consolations for Harry, particularly the emergence of Michael Carrick, the latest from the youth team conveyor belt to break into the senior side.

Publicly, Harry was saying that players like Carrick, Cole, Lampard and Ferdinand were the future of the club but, behind the scenes, the reality was different. The Bobby Moore and Centenary Stands had already cost £11.5 million and now the club were starting work on the new 15,000-capacity West Stand. How would that be financed?

Harry probably had a fair idea. His last season in charge started disastrously and probably set the tone for what was to follow. The first ten matches produced one win, four defeats and five draws, their worst start since relegation in 1992. When they lost 2-1 to Arsenal at Upton Park in mid-October they were 18th in the table, and there was increasing speculation in the newspapers about what the future held for some of the outstanding young players West Ham had produced.

Leeds United, for instance, had made no secret of the fact that they admired Rio Ferdinand and Frank Lampard. West Ham had resisted big-money offers from Leeds for Ferdinand but when they went to Elland Road in November few knew that it would be Rio's last game for the club. West Ham won the match but lost the player. Nigel Winterburn headed his first West Ham goal to secure a 1-0 win and Leeds splashed out a world record fee for a defender of £18 million to buy Rio.

The realities of football finance and an ever-increasing wage bill finally won the day. A fee of £18 million was too good to turn down. Harry was given some of the money to strengthen his squad and he bought Rigobert Song (£2.5 million), Titi Camara (£1.7 million), Christian Dailly (£1.75 million), Ragnvald Soma (£750,000) and Svetoslav Todorov (£500,000), and he took Sebastien Schemmel on loan from FC Metz. Some, of course, were only squad players. In all Harry used 35 players in the first team that season.

Was it necessary to have so many players? Some were beginning to wonder. There was a feeling that Harry and the club chairman, Terry Brown, were on a collision course. At least a 3-0 win over Southampton in the last home game of the season meant that West Ham could go into their final match, at Middlesbrough, with their Premiership status intact.

Before that game there was a break for the FA Cup final and, during that week, Harry drove from his home at Sandbanks in Dorset for a meeting with the chairman, believing that they would finalise a new four-year contract worth £1.6 million annually plus bonuses. A couple of hours later he learned that his seven-year reign as West Ham manager had come to an end. Only Harry and the chairman knew what was said in the heated debate that led to his departure.

John Barnwell, the chief executive of the League Managers' Association, said after speaking to Harry: 'You can assume that a Premiership manager with two years remaining on his contract is unlikely to have resigned.' I don't know what happened in that meeting, but if it is true that he didn't resign then either he was sacked or he left by mutual agreement. Steve Blowers' excellent book *Nearly Reached the Sky*, a modern-day history of West Ham, claims that the chairman was upset by what Harry had said in an interview with a fanzine.

It also claims that nearly all observers agreed that the row between Redknapp and Brown was triggered by different perceptions of the 2001–02 transfer budgets. The book states that Harry bought 67 players for around £56 million and sold 66 for around £68 million. He was the game's most accomplished wheeler-dealer and when he left West Ham they had made a decent profit in the transfer market.

Harry was the longest-serving manager in the Premiership after Sir Alex Ferguson and felt that he deserved to earn what his players earned. He thought it wrong that a squad player, who only made an occasional first-team appearance, should earn more than the manager who signed him. Terry Brown acknowledged the debt the club owed Harry, who had spent 17 years at West Ham as player, coach and manager. 'He loved the club and signed some great players but merely spending money in the transfer market does not automatically guarantee success on the pitch,' he said.

I thought Harry did okay as manager of West Ham. The statistics are inconclusive. He had 325 first-team matches in charge. He won 121 and lost 122 with 401 goals scored and 413 conceded. It's not impressive but it was enough to keep West Ham in the Premiership, and that is what is so important in today's game. Frank Lampard senior departed with Harry, and Glenn Roeder, who had been appointed as reserve-team coach by Harry, took charge for the last match of 2000–01 – a 2-1 defeat at Middlesbrough.

It wasn't a good start for Glenn. Who'd be a football manager?

CHAPTER 14

THE BOSS: PART ONE

I WAS INVITED TO JOIN the board of directors at West Ham a couple of weeks after Glenn Roeder succeeded Harry Redknapp as manager. Harry left in May 2001 and after a month of intense speculation Glenn was given the top job. For many, his appointment was a surprise. Glenn was an accomplished coach and a popular figure at Chadwell Heath, but he had no experience of managing in the Premiership.

There were plenty who had, and they made it known that they were available in the days immediately after Harry's departure. Alan Curbishley, who had done a good job on a tight budget at Charlton Athletic, was probably considered favourite. He was well known to the locals because he had spent four or five years in and out of the West Ham first team in the seventies.

Other significant names emerged, such as Ruud Gullit, George Graham and Steve McClaren, who had been an impressive number two under Alex Ferguson at Manchester United. But Middlesbrough offered him the job vacated by Bryan Robson and he decided to take that. Even Stuart Pearce tossed his name into the ring. The enormously popular former England defender had just been voted Hammer of the Year but, approaching 40, he was talking about hanging up his boots. Like Roeder, though, he had no Premiership management experience and eventually decided to play for another season under Kevin Keegan at Manchester City.

Charlton were reluctant to release Curbishley who, in the end, withdrew from the race. With McClaren installed at Middlesbrough, West Ham decided to promote Glenn. He took over in June 2001. 'I feel a bit like Foinavon in the 1967 Grand National,' he said with a smile. 'I'm the only one left standing!' But a self-effacing personality hid an iron will and a prodigious work ethic.

He had been a footballing centre-back with Leyton Orient, QPR, Newcastle and Watford and spent three years managing at Vicarage Road. He'd also helped Glenn Hoddle coach the England team, so he knew his way around a training programme and was used to working with big-name players.

Glenn's first task was to appoint an assistant and he chose the former QPR, West Ham and Newcastle striker, Paul Goddard, as first-team coach. Ludo Miklosko became goalkeeping coach and long-serving former player Roger Cross was given responsibility for the reserves. All three coaches knew the West Ham way of doing things. Before I accepted the invitation from the board I asked if Glenn had been informed of the idea. They confirmed that they had asked him and that he'd said he would be very happy to talk to me regularly. On that basis I accepted the position. Once the appointment was made official I organised a meeting with Glenn. I wanted to satisfy myself that he was comfortable with my position on the board of directors. I didn't want him to think that I would be constantly hovering over him. I told him that I'd visit the training ground once a week and if there was anything he needed, or I could help with, he had only to ask. I would always give my opinion if asked, but I told him that I tended to wait to be asked.

Peter Storrie, the club's managing director who'd established a close working relationship with Harry, had also left the club and the chairman Terry Brown believed the board would benefit from a non-executive director who had a sound knowledge of football-related matters. Terry and most of the board felt that there had been difficulties discussing football matters with Harry. When questioned, I'm told, Harry's response was almost always the same: 'That's what I'm paid for and I expect you to accept what I say.'

One or two of Harry's transfer deals had been questioned by club directors and they felt they needed someone on board with football expertise. They wanted someone who could represent the board-room view and discuss football issues with the manager on a firmer footing. They felt they had never been able to challenge Harry properly because they simply didn't have the knowledge. There had been issues related to transfers where they had been unable to communicate meaningfully with the manager. That would be my job in future.

Harry had helped re-establish the club's credentials in his seven years in charge and had nursed through a number of talented young players. But it had gone badly wrong in his last season, when many of the players signed with the Rio Ferdinand money were simply not of the quality required. Players like Titi Camara and Rigobert Song were not good enough for the Premiership, nor were Ragnvald Soma or Svetoslav Todorov. The best investment by far was the Scotland defender Christian Dailly, who cost £1.75 million from Blackburn Rovers in January 2001. He was Harry's last cash buy for West Ham. The crowd at Upton Park were slow to take to him, but the fact that he won 67 caps for Scotland and played 191 first-team games for West Ham in seven seasons says something about his quality.

Let's compare him and his record to that of Aboubacar 'Titi' Sidiki Camara, signed from Liverpool for £1.7 million in December 2000. A Guinea international striker, he announced on his arrival: 'I'm here to score goals!' He didn't. In three years he played a total of 14 games and scored no goals. Rigobert Song's contribution was better. A Cameroon international defender, he played 27 games in his two years with the club. He was Harry's first defensive signing following the loss of Rio and he cost £2.5 million from Liverpool in November 2000.

What you have to realise is that these players were among the top earners at the club. Camara's salary was more than £1 million a year. People used to ask: 'What happened to the rest of the Ferdinand money?' Well, much of it went on salaries. We had one of the highest wage bills in the Premiership at the time. The following season we paid out £30 million in players' salaries. That was a huge sum. There were others, such as Gary Charles and Scott Minto, who were earning fortunes but hardly playing.

Gary was a classy full-back who had played for East London Schools before Brian Clough's Nottingham Forest spotted him. He was the target when Tottenham's Paul Gascoigne famously tore his cruciate ligament with a reckless tackle in the 1991 FA Cup final. Gary spent three injury-troubled years with West Ham, playing a total of six first-team games, before accepting medical advice to retire. Harry had signed him from Benfica in 1999 and he had cost the club £4.4 million in transfer and salary payments.

When I had my first meeting with Glenn we looked through the first-team squad and agreed that we probably had ten players earning Premiership wages who were not in fact good enough to play in the Premiership. In a sense, Glenn was locked into that situation for at least two or three years until the contracts of those players ended. Even had he wanted to give them away he couldn't because no other club would be foolish enough to match the wages they received at West Ham. Most of the ten we identified were quite happy to sit tight and go through the motions in the reserves until their contracts ran out. That's just what they did until the end of 2002–03 when quite a few contracts expired. The strategy was to get some of the big earners off the wage bill. Then we felt we'd be in quite a strong position to strengthen the squad. That was the plan. It was wrecked by relegation and the fact that life in Division One was going to cost us £20 million a year in lost revenue.

Glenn's first games in charge confirmed his belief that playing reinforcements would be necessary. After five matches we were at the bottom of the table and out of the Worthington Cup, beaten on penalties by Reading. Frank Lampard's £11 million sale to Chelsea had created a void in midfield and there were constant stories about further imminent departures. Paolo Di Canio, for instance, was the subject of constant transfer speculation. Glenn was aware, too, that England debuts by Joe Cole and Michael Carrick in a 4-0 win over Mexico at Derby were already exciting interest among the club's big Premiership rivals.

Glenn signed Sebastien Schemmel, originally on loan, from Metz for £465,000. He then bought his former Watford team-mate David James from Aston Villa for £3.25 million. The England goal-keeper was immediately injured and had to wait until November for his West Ham debut. A further £10 million was spent on two more experienced players – Czech central defender Tomas Repka from Fiorentina and Don Hutchison, who returned to the club from Sunderland six years after becoming Harry Redknapp's first signing. Sadly, Don suffered a cruciate knee ligament injury in February that would keep him out of action for the best part of a year.

Repka and Schemmel, along with James, would become key elements in a West Ham defence that struggled, throughout the season, to find some confidence. On three occasions they conceded five goals – against Everton, Chelsea and Manchester United – and in October suffered their record Premiership defeat: 7-1 against Blackburn. There were rumblings of discontent from the fans even though they were turning up in ever greater numbers. In November the lower tier in the new West Stand was opened and for the first time since the Taylor Report attendance figures topped 32,000. Her Majesty the Queen, in her Golden Jubilee year, visited the East End in May and officially opened the West Stand. The stadium was now one of the best equipped in the country, but that didn't stop the first whispers of an eventual move to the proposed Olympic Stadium in Stratford.

By the time Di Canio and Fredi Kanoute scored to secure a 2-0 home win over Charlton Athletic in early April, West Ham had climbed to seventh and some were even speculating about a place in Europe. Defeats against Arsenal and Newcastle ended that dream but a 2-1 win over Bolton on the last day of the season ensured a seventh-place finish.

It had been a difficult baptism for Glenn. Many of his best players had been injured at some stage during the season. Christian Dailly was the only player not to miss a match. There were good signs, though. I'd seen enough of Glenn's coaching to know that his sessions were comprehensive and producing results. I remembered him as a cultured centre-back famous for his step-over. He always liked to play football from the back and knew the value of keeping possession. He was also a workaholic. His enthusiasm knew no bounds. He lived and breathed the game. I thought we had established a rapport quite easily. He invited me to come to the training ground whenever I wanted. In my own mind, I sometimes wondered how I would feel if I was in his position. I was very conscious of keeping a low profile. I didn't want to be intrusive or become a busybody.

I wasn't the sort of director of football most clubs have these days. I didn't work full time. The modern director of football is much more involved in the day-to-day running of the team. I received an honorarium. In real terms 'non-executive director' meant that I went to matches, to the training ground once a week to talk to the manager and to board meetings once a month. I was involved in most of the policy consultations and debates but not the everyday decisions taken by the executive.

I hadn't seen all of West Ham's matches because I was still contracted to do 40 games a season in the commentary box for BBC Radio Five Live. When West Ham asked me to join the board I had to check with the BBC to ensure there was no conflict of interest. As I was an official of West Ham FC, it was possible that another club might complain to the FA that I had made derogatory remarks about them or their players. That never happened. I tried to keep my comments fair and constructive. I knew my BBC commitments would mean that I missed some of West Ham's games but the club were quite happy about that.

In Glenn's first season the team's form at Upton Park had been excellent – just three defeats, a home record bettered only by Liverpool, who finished runners-up to Arsenal. Inexplicably, the home form in the new season, 2002–03, was dreadful, undermining the sense of optimism generated by the seventh-place finish the previous season. Such was the feel-good factor that the club had sold a record 20,000 season tickets but, after just a few weeks, the fans were beginning to show signs of serious impatience.

The season started woefully – a 4-0 defeat at Bobby Robson's Newcastle with Lomana LuaLua from Congo, who apparently supported West Ham as a kid, scoring the first two. Glenn spent six years at St James' Park and I suspect that this was a defeat that irritated him. The next game, at Upton Park, was against double-winners Arsenal, unbeaten in 23 matches – a run that stretched back to the previous December. Cole and Kanoute secured a two-goal lead before Thierry Henry pulled one back. But then Kanoute missed a 75th-minute penalty and Sylvain Wiltord snatched an equaliser two minutes from time. Later in a long, difficult season some fans would claim that Kanoute's missed penalty was the start of West Ham's decline. It was a 2-2 draw that day but we were brilliant at times and completely outplayed them. The fans were impressed with the quality of our play and, had you told them as they left the ground that we wouldn't win a home game for another five months, they'd have laughed at you. But that was how it was.

After six matches – four defeats and two draws – West Ham were bottom of the table. The first win came in the seventh match, when Paolo Di Canio scored an 84th-minute winner against Chelsea at Stamford Bridge. But at home? Nothing! We were losing home games to teams like Charlton, West Brom, Birmingham and Southampton. We were marooned at the bottom unable to win a match on our home turf. We were making elementary errors and passing the ball badly. People were blaming a lack of atmosphere in the newly refurbished stadium, but I think that was irrelevant. The fans were really restless when, late in January, Jermain Defoe came off the substitutes' bench to score an 89th-minute winner against Blackburn at Upton Park.

It lifted them off the bottom but the omens were not good. No team at the bottom on Christmas Day had escaped relegation and West Ham were bottom on 25 December. The injury situation was a critical factor in our relegation. Looking back you could trace our demise to the absence of the injured strikers Kanoute and Di Canio. One of the things I noticed was our inability to hold the ball at the front. This meant that our defence was always under pressure. We were so short of strikers at one point that Glenn asked defender Ian Pearce to play up front. A £1.6 million capture from Blackburn Rovers in 1997, Ian was a tough, versatile defender who had made a good recovery from a broken leg. He did a good job for us as a makeshift striker in difficult circumstances.

With hindsight it was a mistake not to have another experienced striker available. Once the season had started we couldn't bring one in after 31 August because FIFA introduced the new transfer restrictions in 2002–03. We had to wait until the January 'transfer window' and then Glenn tried to sign the experienced Tottenham striker Les Ferdinand. Nowadays, of course, clubs realise the value of having four or five quality strikers to cover for all eventualities during the course of the season. I'm sure the current West Ham manager, Sam Allardyce, following his experiences with the injured Andy Carroll in 2013–14, would agree with me.

Les Ferdinand was a good signing. The 36-year-old former QPR, Newcastle and England striker was in his sixth season at Tottenham and manager Glenn Hoddle was using him sparingly. Injury limited his first-team appearances but I knew he would make a good impression in the dressing room. He'd been linked with a move to West Ham on numerous occasions so it was no real surprise when he finally signed for £200,000 at the end of the January transfer window. We had hoped to complete the deal earlier in the month but Tottenham were reluctant to release him until they had signed a replacement.

The Upton Park crowd soon discovered why he had been dubbed 'Sir Les'. He was a class act on and off the pitch. He played in 14 of the last 15 Premiership matches of the season and made a huge difference. He held the ball up, supported the other strikers, Kanoute and Defoe, and took it upon himself to go back and help out when we were defending set pieces. He was a really good example to his team-mates in the dressing room at a time when we needed strong characters. He made his debut for us in a 4-2 defeat at Charlton, but a week later was in the side that beat Blackburn Rovers 2-1 on 29 January – the first home win of the season.

It was a result that lifted West Ham off the bottom of the table and briefly eased the pressure on Glenn. The crowd was getting on his back, but he never hid or complained. He invariably stood in front of the dugout throughout matches and always faced the media afterwards. He wasn't a natural delegator. He wanted to take responsibility for everything. He wouldn't hide from his critics. It's an admirable trait, but it meant that he was taking the weight of it all on his shoulders. I thought he was very dignified and stoical during a difficult time in his career.

In similar circumstances Harry would have been far more animated. He'd have a funny comment for most occasions. He could often turn a negative into a positive with an appropriate quip. I also think he found it much easier to build a rapport with the West Ham fans because he had played for the club. Glenn found it much tougher. Most fans realised that he wasn't the first choice for the job. Initially I don't think there was a big sense of expectancy on the terraces. I think the supporters were a bit surprised by the success Glenn had in finishing seventh in his first year. In a way, that set the standard for Glenn during a period of financial constraints at the club. With relegation becoming more of a reality week by week, the chairman Terry Brown told the fans that Glenn was 'manager at a time when we need to show financial caution and does not have the funds that have been made available to previous managers'.

Paolo Di Canio had returned from injury against Blackburn – and found the team much changed following his two-month absence. Apart from the introduction of 'Sir Les', Rufus Brevett, a free transfer from Fulham, was in the number three shirt. The number two shirt went to an 18-year-old who had been on loan at Millwall. Glen Johnson featured in 14 of the final 15 games of the season at right-back and, such was his precocious talent, he was an immediate hit with the fans. You can imagine how they felt a few months later when he was sold to Chelsea for £6 million after England manager Sven-Goran Eriksson had told the new Stamford Bridge owner Roman Abramovich that the two best young players in the country were at West Ham – Johnson and Joe Cole.

The newcomers certainly made West Ham harder to beat at a critical stage of the season. A 2-1 win over West Brom at the Hawthorns lifted us to 18th and was the start of a really impressive run of form. Of the ten matches that remained, we won five, drew four and lost just once, at Bolton. Sadly, Di Canio wasn't in the starting line-up for any of the final ten games. What no one knew at the time was that the West Brom match would be his last start for the club. After a couple of minutes of the second half at the Hawthorns, Glenn had decided to make a change. The number ten flashed up on the sub's board and Paolo was not happy to be taken off. In fact, he was very unhappy, jabbing Glenn in the chest as he left the field. The truth was that he had pulled up violently just before the break and, despite insisting that he was fit to continue, it was obvious that he wasn't. When Paolo flew home to Italy for specialist treatment, most people thought that we were unlikely to see him again that season.

Had he been fit he would have been invaluable at Bolton, in the thick of the relegation fight with us. Our form until then offered a bit of a lifeline and we felt that the last five matches would produce enough points for us to stay up – Bolton (A), Middlesbrough (H), Manchester City (A), Chelsea (H), Birmingham (A). We played at the Reebok Stadium on Easter Sunday in what was essentially a 'six-pointer'. Bolton won 1-0 with a 38th-minute goal from Jay-Jay Okocha, who ran from the halfway line and chipped the ball over David James. Ian Pearce was later sent off and there was a bit of a rumpus at the end involving Joe Cole and Rufus Brevett, who were later charged by the FA. With just four matches remaining West Ham were 18th, six points behind Bolton. If, instead of losing that match, West Ham had drawn, the final points total would have been 43. In that scenario Bolton, then managed by Sam Allardyce, would have had a total of 42 points and they would have been relegated.

The deeper truth, of course, is that West Ham's relegation could be traced back to the abysmal home form before Christmas and the club's inability to sign replacements for injured strikers because of the introduction of the transfer window. My opinion is that had we been able to sign Les Ferdinand earlier in January, rather than at the end of the month, we would have had a great chance of avoiding the drop. In the first half of January we drew at home to Newcastle and lost at Arsenal. With Les in the side I think we would have picked up more than one point from those two games.

Two days after the Bolton match we were at home to Middlesbrough, Trevor Sinclair providing the goal in a 1-0 victory. Sadly, West Ham remained pinned in 18th place. Beneath us, Sunderland and West Brom had been doomed for some time and, above, the other candidates for the third relegation spot, Aston Villa, Bolton, Leeds and Fulham, kept picking up enough points to remain ahead of West Ham.

The fans were still trooping out of Upton Park, mulling over the various permutations following the Middlesbrough win, when the issue of relegation suddenly became very academic for Glenn Roeder. He was sitting on the sofa in his office when he suddenly collapsed. Club doctor Ges Steinbergs treated him until an ambulance arrived to rush him to the Royal London Hospital in Whitechapel. He was sedated for five days until brain specialists were able to confirm that he had a tumour that had caused the blockage of a blood vessel. I'd talked to Glenn immediately after the match and there was no suggestion that anything was wrong.

I left the ground about an hour after the end of the match and was driving home when I took a call on my mobile from the club's managing director, Paul Aldridge. He told me that Glenn had just collapsed and was on his way to hospital. No one knew the severity of his condition. It was Easter Monday and I'd just been talking to friends about the importance of the visit to Manchester City. Suddenly that didn't seem very important at all.

Paul called me again at home the next morning. Glenn, apparently, was sedated in hospital and his condition was critical. It seemed likely that he would need brain surgery. Paul said that there was no way he would be fit enough to work before the end of the season. He asked if we could meet the following day to discuss the options available to us. When we met, the initial suggestion was that we try to appoint an experienced coach just for the last three games. We eventually dismissed this because of the practical problems involved in finding someone at such short notice. The second option was to appoint Paul Goddard and Roger Cross, Glenn's two coaches, to take over. Both were accomplished coaches, but we spoke with one or two senior players who felt that neither would be strong enough for what would be a daunting climax to the season. I told Paul that I would be prepared to help the two coaches. Perhaps the players would be happier if there were three of us involved in the job.

We then wondered whether a couple of the senior players might be capable of doing the job. Those mentioned were David James, Steve Lomas and Les Ferdinand. Again, discreet enquiries among the players suggested that there would be too many arguments in the dressing room if we took this route. We met again the following day. We went through the options again. We were running out of fresh ideas. When Paul Aldridge suggested that I do the job for three games, there were not many alternatives left to explore. I said I'd do it as long as the players were happy with the decision. The next morning – 48 hours before we played City – I met the players. I spoke to a few of the senior lads – Steve Lomas, Les Ferdinand, Joe Cole, David James and Trevor Sinclair.

I explained that the board had suggested I take over in the short term. For it to be successful, I told them that I needed their support, and that anything they weren't happy with they should talk to me about. I also told them that there was one important decision I had to take and I needed their advice. Paolo Di Canio hadn't played since Glenn substituted him against West Brom. My feeling was that, if he was fit, we'd be better off with him than without him. In the back of my mind I knew it would be handy to have him on the bench in case we needed a goal, although I wasn't happy with some of the things he'd said and done. We would probably need to win three games to have any chance of staying up and he had the skill to score the goal that might just make the difference.

Paolo and Glenn hadn't got along all season. Paolo was hotheaded and temperamental. He had exchanged blows with previous managers such as Fabio Capello and Ron Atkinson. The ill feeling between him and Glenn had been festering for months and came to a head in the game with West Brom. Everyone thought he'd tweaked his hamstring. I didn't expect to see him come out for the second half. Glenn told me later that he was going to take him off at half time but Paolo insisted he was fit enough to play on. When he took him off Paolo started his usual histrionics, waving and shouting. When I walked into the dressing room after the match he was the first player I bumped into. I said to him quite innocently: 'How's the hamstring?'

'The hamstring! There's nothing wrong with it,' he barked. 'I had no problem. I shouldn't have been taken off.' We all thought he was injured – all, that is, except Paolo. The day after the match, when the players reported for a warm-down, Paolo rang to say he had a gastric bug and wouldn't be in. The players had the following day off, but Paolo came in. He worked in the gym. The day after that, all the lads reported, including Paolo. But he didn't feel right and he worked on his own in the gym again. The next day, a full training session in preparation for the match against Tottenham, he called in and said he wasn't feeling well. He said that he was going back to Italy to see a doctor he knew at a clinic in Bologna. He often went there when he was ill or injured.

He wanted his doctor to assess the progress of his knee and give him strengthening exercises that would occupy him while he was unwell and unable to train fully. The Monday after the Tottenham game, he called to say that he would be staying in Bologna for another week to do rehabilitation work. In the end he stayed there for three weeks. The club paid the bills. We still didn't know the extent of the hamstring injury or if indeed he had one at all. When he finally declared himself fit again, he still wasn't able to train on a regular basis because of a recurring gastric problem. He had the same problem when I took over from Glenn nearly two months later.

So, I didn't want to invite him back into the fold if his presence was going to upset the other lads in the dressing room. He had been injured for much of the season and hadn't played since his touchline tantrum in February. It was pretty clear that he would be leaving the club at the end of the season. What I had to decide was whether to bring him back for a salvage operation for the last three games, against Manchester City, Chelsea and Birmingham. The senior players I spoke to were not happy with some of the things he'd said and done but all felt that we were better off having him as an option on the subs' bench than not having him at all.

I called him at his house in Loughton, in Essex. We had a long chat. He went over some of the background, outlining the various reasons for his discontent. I didn't want to go over all that and I told him so. It was in the past. We had to think about the immediate future. I asked him about his fitness. I told him that I needed him for the last three games. He said his legs were still a little weak but he was willing to have a go for me. I was delighted and put the phone down feeling quite pleased with myself. Football management? Nothing to it!

I knew that as a player Paolo Di Canio was a class act. But he could be difficult to handle. For some managers he was a dream to work with but for others he was a nightmare. Certainly, many thought that Harry Redknapp had taken a massive gamble when he signed Paolo for £1.7 million from Sheffield Wednesday in January 1999 after he'd served an 11-match ban for his infamous push on referee Paul Alcock. But he responded brilliantly to Harry's management, finishing top scorer with 17 goals, one of which was the stunning volley against Wimbledon that won the BBC Goal of the Season competition.

The fans loved Paolo's style and his eccentricities but I'm not sure that Harry always shared their enthusiasm. Paolo's decision to catch Trevor Sinclair's cross rather than shoot, while Everton goalkeeper Paul Gerrard lay on the pitch injured, won him praise from FIFA president Sepp Blatter. But there was an argument that his sportsmanship had cost West Ham two points. 'It was unusual, wasn't it?' observed Harry, having had to settle for a 1-1 draw. Paolo made friends and influenced people at Lazio, Juventus, AC Milan and Celtic, and even now, in the autumn of his long career, he retained great technical ability and superb vision. In tight areas he could still demonstrate high-quality ball control and I thought that if we could get Fredi Kanoute, Les Ferdinand and Paolo Di Canio on the pitch at the same time we would have the kind of firepower needed to keep us in the Premiership. There had been only a couple of occasions, back in January, when Glenn had all three fit simultaneously.

I wanted Paolo to be fit and available. I knew he could provide that little something extra that is often the difference between winning and losing. He was one of the great strikers of his time and I'd put him up there with the all-time great West Ham goalscorers like Geoff Hurst, 'Pop' Robson and Tony Cottee. With Paolo you had an added bonus – he was a great entertainer and crowd-pleaser. But, sadly, he wasn't always fit. That was probably one of the reasons why Glenn Roeder didn't get the best out of him. Now that we really needed him he still wasn't 100 per cent fit. He trained but wasn't sure whether he'd be ready for the game against Manchester City on Sunday. In the end he didn't make it. He called and sounded genuinely disappointed. He said that he'd report for training the day after the City game and was fairly confident that he'd be able to give me 100 per cent for the final two matches.

I can't pretend that my first three days in the job were easy or straightforward. There was much I had to get a grip on and I had to do it quickly. Paolo's fitness was only one concern. I have to admit that I was quite anxious on the Friday as I prepared to talk to the players as a group. I'd been a player myself so I knew what they'd be thinking and saying to one another. They were quite happy to stand in front of you and give their opinion but that didn't mean they were saying the same thing behind your back. I had no reason to believe they were taking the mickey when I wasn't looking but, even so, I knew the result of the first match would be crucial in establishing a platform and giving me the credentials with which to work in the days ahead.

One of the first things I did when I was appointed was watch three videos of Manchester City. One film concentrated solely on their attacking players and showed how they had scored most of their recent goals. My old England pal Kevin Keegan was their manager. His team and tactics looked settled. When I got the players together I told them to be particularly aware of Shaun Wright-Phillips. He ran well with the ball. I identified him and Nicolas Anelka as the biggest dangers to us.

I decided to spend time on our set pieces. Our delivery from corners and free kicks had been shocking against Middlesbrough. I put on a session specifically to address this problem. I asked Rufus Brevett to try crossing the corner kicks with his left foot from the right side. All the lads laughed: 'Rufus! Oh, no!' He hit four and three were really good deliveries. He got the job. On the other side of the pitch we had Jermain Defoe. I'd seen Thierry Henry whipping them in to the near post for Arsenal and Jimmy Floyd Hasselbaink doing the same for Chelsea. Jermain did just as well. Joe Cole had taken a lot of set pieces in the past and I didn't want to leave him out of the equation. So I asked him to take the near post and, at every other corner, run out to meet the kicker and play a one-two. I'd seen Shaun Wright-Phillips do the same thing for City.

Safe in mid-table, Manchester City had held us to a goalless draw at Upton Park in September. We flew up to Manchester 24 hours before the match. It was 20 years since I'd travelled as a player and most of the travelling in my time was done by train. I used to eat steak on match days but that's frowned upon now. I remember towards the end of my career being told that red meat was not good for me. I had to check what they wanted for their pre-match meal. It was all carbohydrates, white meat, fish and vegetables.

Sitting in the hotel in Manchester I watched the Saturday football shows on TV. My appointment was one of the main subjects for discussion. Rodney Marsh, the former QPR and England striker, said: 'I can't believe they've brought him in. Can you imagine how long his team talk will be? They should've looked for someone else. Anyone but Brooking!' Some were more supportive. The former West Ham striker Tony Cottee said: 'What more could they do with just three matches to play?'

It was really amusing listening to the opinions. I didn't take it too seriously. I had other things to worry about. Similarly, I stayed away from the telephone. I didn't really want to talk to people. I got a lot of text messages, from Billy Bonds and other friends. That meant a great deal to me. On the way to Maine Road I sat at the front of the bus – a new experience for me – convincing myself that I had picked the right team. The options were few. Fredi Kanoute was fit again but I decided to retain Les Ferdinand, who had played well in the Middlesbrough win, in an unchanged side. Fredi was on the bench. It was important that I got it right because this was the match that would set the tone for the other two games. A lot of people were doubtful about my appointment. I'd never done this sort of job before and I'd been out of the professional game for a long time. If we got beaten by three or four goals I knew it would be virtually impossible to rescue the situation in the final two games. It would create an air of depression around the club because people would realise that relegation was the only conclusion. A win would mean that we were still in with a shout and it would keep the dressing-room spirit bubbling. I think I was more nervous before this game than before the others. To be honest, I felt more anxious than I had ever felt as a player.

We didn't play well in the first half. City kept possession better than we did. Our midfield was passing poorly. We had chances but it was goalless at half time. A single point from a draw was no good. We had to win. At the interval I decided to start the second half with Fredi Kanoute and play with three strikers. I decided to take Edouard Cisse off. He was playing as a holding central midfield player. He hadn't done too badly in the first half, but if we were trying to win there was no point in taking off an attacking player. When I told him he was being substituted he took it really badly. He took his boots off and threw them across the dressing room. He then sauntered across to the showers and said to me: 'I hope you enjoy your brief time as manager.'

I laughed. I wasn't too bothered about who I upset. I had nothing to lose. We needed to win and I had to do what I thought was right in the circumstances. We started the second half impressively and then, as luck would have it, Les Ferdinand got carried off after 53 minutes. I was playing with three up and I'd suddenly lost one of my main three. I decided to push Joe Cole forward to support Kanoute and Defoe, and bring Don Hutchison off the bench and play him in midfield. He passed the ball really well for us and Joe looked good just behind the front two.

One goal decided it – and for us one goal was enough. With nine minutes remaining Defoe took a short corner to Cole who clipped it in to the near post. Hutchison got his toe to it. Peter Schmeichel, the City goalkeeper, parried the shot but couldn't hold it. He pushed the ball on to a post and Kanoute was there to knock it into the net. It wasn't a classic but it was satisfying to take three points. I was particularly pleased because the goal had originated from the short corner we had been working on in training. As the players left the field I made a point of shaking hands with all of them.

The last minutes were anxious for the new manager, who kept straying animatedly out of his technical area. There were six minutes of extra time and Kevin Keegan, the City manager, complained to the fourth official that I was encroaching in his technical area. 'This new fellow has no idea where he's supposed to be!' he grinned. We had a few moments together afterwards. He was generous in defeat.

It was a great start to my management reign. I spoke to the media and then had to find out what was happening to Les Ferdinand. He had been taken to hospital for X-rays. Happily, I was told that he would be taken from the hospital to join us at the airport for the flight back to London. The mood on the plane home was jubilant, even though we were aware that Bolton had recovered from 2-0 down to draw with Arsenal. I enjoyed the moment of triumph with a Coke, but remember thinking at the time about Glenn Roeder, who was in hospital fighting for his life. It was really his win because this was his

252 | TREVOR BROOKING

team and he had mapped out the following weeks' training programme before falling ill. The players were unanimous afterwards in
saying that they had wanted to win the match for Glenn.

The following morning the newspapers were full of our surprise
win at Maine Road. One tabloid had a selection of photographs of
me shouting, wincing, gesticulating, putting my head in my hands
and jumping up with my fists in the air when Kanoute scored our
goal. It was very gratifying but as all managers say: 'The only match
that matters is the next one.' I was ready to focus on that game –
the big London derby with Chelsea at Upton Park. We'd come
from behind to beat them 3-2 at Stamford Bridge in September. It
was our first win of the season and Claudio Ranieri's first defeat.
Paolo Di Canio scored twice that day and I knew it would be a big
plus for us if he was ready to face them again. Sadly, the news from
the treatment room suggested that Les Ferdinand might not be
available for selection, so I thought it would be really handy to have
Paolo in the squad.

I'd been in enough relegation fights myself as a West Ham
player to know what they were all thinking in the dressing room. It
is a difficult time for players, and confidence – or lack of it – can be
decisive. I sensed a change of mood among them after the City win.
As the week progressed the players became more and more vocal,
more opinionated and more optimistic about the challenges ahead.

That's what winning does for you. On the Monday, for instance,
five of the senior men who had played against City were in the
treatment room with injuries. At that point in the week three of
them were doubtful – Steve Lomas, Joe Cole and Les Ferdinand.
I suspected that by Thursday, maybe even by Wednesday, most of
them would be available. Even Cisse, who had reacted petulantly
when I'd taken him off, had the good grace to apologise to me.

They all wanted to be involved. Well, not quite all. Because of
the injuries and uncertainties surrounding player availability I

named a big squad for the Chelsea match. The list included the full-back Sebastien Schemmel, a French Under-21 international first spotted by Glenn Roeder when he was on a scouting trip for Harry Redknapp, who signed him on a loan deal from Metz in January 2001. When Harry left the club, Glenn signed him permanently. He'd done a good job as an overlapping full-back but had problems in his personal life, fell out with Glenn and on one occasion had to be escorted out of Upton Park by security staff.

When I took over Seb hadn't played for nearly five months and was obviously surprised to be in my squad. He came to see me. 'We have a problem,' he explained. 'As I haven't been playing I've decided to take my family to France on the ferry on Saturday. The season is over. I didn't expect to play again. We're all booked on the ferry.'

I said: 'What do you mean "booked on the ferry"? You are employed by us. This is still part of the football season, the most important part. We need you here with us. I've got a lot of injuries. I may have to move Glen Johnson to centre-half and play you at right-back.'

Not at all put off by my reply, he said: 'So, if everyone is okay can I go then?'

'No, everyone who doesn't play will train after the match. I expect to see you with the rest of the players. With the greatest respect, in nine days you can take a ferry anywhere in the world and stay there for seven weeks. But for now you stay here. We are fighting for our lives, trying to stay in the top division. You will be with the squad on match day and you will report for training on Monday. I hope that is clear.'

He delayed his trip home but he wasn't happy and didn't play for us again. I'd never come across such an attitude from a professional footballer before. In those few weeks at the end of that season I discovered just how much the attitude of players had changed since my playing days. When they're not in the team some don't even want to be on the subs' bench. Some of the overseas players felt, like Schemmel, that they should be allowed to go home for the weekend if they were not selected to play. They didn't want to play in the reserves, something that was unthinkable when I was playing. How can you win back your place in the first team if you don't perform well in the reserves? It was a different world to the one I'd inhabited as a player. The modern professional was rich, many of them millionaires. The car park at the training ground was full of big luxury saloons and four by fours. The day of the Cortina with a roof rack was long gone.

I found the atmosphere in the dressing room challenging – there were so many languages and different cultures for a start. In my day they were nearly all local lads, many had grown up together. There was a natural unity and a shared sense of identity and purpose. They wanted to play and win for the club and the fans. Twenty years later I discovered that some of the players in the dressing room at West Ham were simply professionals contracted for a period of time. That was how they viewed it. Others, I think, had a genuine affection for the club and wanted West Ham to succeed.

Fortunately, Schemmel was an exception. Most of the others were committed to the cause, even though the newspapers claimed it was a lost one. On the Tuesday of that week, Les said that he thought he would be fit enough to start. Paolo declared that he thought he could manage an hour against Chelsea. The mood in the dressing room was building nicely. Chelsea had been playing well and were fighting with Newcastle for third place.

But I sensed that the lads really believed they were going to beat Ranieri's team of multi-national stars including Zola, Gallas, Petit, Hasselbaink, Desailly and, of course, young Frank Lampard. The confidence level would not have been anything like as high had we lost at Maine Road.

Much as I suspected would be the case, they were all available for selection. When we had our team talk I told them that I had experienced relegation and knew how they were thinking. I told them that if they finished the match each believing they'd done all they could, there wasn't much more that could be asked of them. If enough of them felt the same way at the final whistle then I believed we'd get out of trouble and retain our place in the Premiership. I was always honest with them. I always made sure they knew whether they were playing or not. They might not agree with the decision but I thought it was important to be straight with them. No one doubted the talent within the team. The secret was getting them – all of them – to play to their full potential.

I felt that we were going to beat Chelsea. I had felt that all week. Perhaps the players sensed my optimism. We started with Ferdinand, Kanoute and Defoe at the front. I was so pleased that Les was fit. He was a massive influence on and off the pitch. I'd heard good reports about him but you can never be sure about a player until you see them and work with them yourself. Apart from his attacking qualities, he was also one of our best defenders and was a really good influence on youngsters like Jermain.

We had a full house of 35,042 for my first Upton Park match as manager. The crowd had always been good to me and it was no different now. I wanted us to play with a bit of style but it was so much more important just to get the three points. Ten minutes into the second half the game was deadlocked at 0-0. I decided to send on Paolo Di Canio. It would be his final appearance at Upton Park after five seasons with the club. The crowd roared their approval as he started warming up. Chelsea were defending furiously and at times couldn't get out of their own half. This was because our attack had them pinned back. It occurred to me that, had we not had so much bad luck with injuries to attacking players, we may have been able to play this way earlier in the season.

We had all the possession but we needed a goal – and quickly. That's why I sent on Paolo. Les's fitness was starting to fade – a legacy of the previous week's injury – and, sure enough, in a moment of pure theatre, Paolo pulled down the curtain on his West Ham career with the 70th-minute winner. It was a wonderful moment and remains one of my greatest memories. Upton Park was absolutely rocking and for me the tension and drama made the occasion unforgettable. I particularly remember the reaction of the Chelsea manager in the minutes after the match. Claudio Ranieri said 'Well done' when we shook hands at the final whistle, and a few minutes later I saw him again as we prepared for our TV interviews. We shook hands once more and he complimented my team, commenting on how well we had played. I think his disappointment at losing was eased a little because he'd heard that Manchester City had won at Liverpool, which meant that Chelsea's final game, against Liverpool at Stamford Bridge, would determine who finished fourth. Such was his good grace in defeat that I was really pleased for him a week later when Chelsea beat Liverpool to clinch fourth spot. We, of course, had our own worries about the final day. But for the moment our dressing-room mood was one of triumph and jubilation. It soon became apparent, though, that a win against Birmingham City in our last game might not be enough.

The euphoria wore off in stages. First we heard that Aston Villa and Fulham had both won. Then we watched the 5.30 kick-off on TV that evening between Southampton and Bolton. That finished goalless which meant Bolton controlled their own destiny in the relegation battle. Twenty-four hours later, on the Sunday afternoon, Leeds were the most unlikely victors at Highbury, beating second-placed Arsenal 3-2. Those three points lifted Leeds to safety.

So, after two wonderful results against Manchester City and Chelsea, we were still in deep trouble. Now, though, only Bolton and West Ham were contenders for the third relegation spot. West

Brom and Sunderland were already relegated and everyone else, apart from West Ham and Bolton, was safe. If Bolton beat Middlesbrough at home in their final match they would stay up and we would be relegated regardless of our result against Birmingham.

I tried to be positive and confident during that last week of training but our fate was no longer in our hands. Middlesbrough had a poor away record and it was obvious to everyone that Bolton were clear favourites to stay up. I tried to cut away all my other commitments and focus on the job in hand. I avoided talking to the newspapers but I became aware that people were getting a slightly different view of me from the TV. Instead of sitting calmly in a studio, as I had done for years, the football viewing public now saw an animated Brooking making his feelings known in the dugout. I wasn't conscious of it until people started to point it out.

The public were fantastic to me. Everyone was wishing us well in our fight against relegation. Even fans from other clubs would come up to me and say that they hoped West Ham avoided the drop. I wondered whether I should speak to Glenn but decided against it. I sent him my best wishes. Thankfully, he was making progress. The only person at the club with access to him was the managing director Paul Aldridge. On the Friday, the day before we travelled to Birmingham for the final game, the media was crawling all over our Chadwell Heath training ground. We smuggled Glenn's wife Faith into the ground to talk to Joe Cole, the team captain. She said that Glenn was insistent that she wished the lads all the best against Birmingham. It was good of her in the circumstances to find the time to visit us. The players appreciated it.

The win against Chelsea had taken us to 41 points. This was, in fact, one point better than Glenn Roeder's pre-season safety target. That gives some idea how close the fight for survival was that year, and I impressed upon the players that while there remained a chance of survival we should make the most of it. For the final game of the season I selected the team that had beaten Chelsea 1-0. All the planning, though, quickly looked irrelevant because within 20 minutes of the kick-off Bolton were leading Middlesbrough 2-0. We played well at Birmingham and should have won but were trailing until Di Canio came off the bench to score in the 89th minute – his 50th and last goal for the club. His goal gave us a 2-2 draw and 42 points, a record number for a relegated team. Even had we won and finished with 44 points, the same as Bolton, we would still have been relegated on goal difference.

It was a sad time but I was proud of the players. They had fought until the last whistle of the last match and got as close as was realistically possible. I thought their fighting spirit in difficult circumstances was wonderful and, relegation or not, I was sure that Glenn Roeder would have been proud of them, too. As far as management was concerned, that was it for me. I'd done my best and although we had failed to beat the drop we were unbeaten in my three games in charge. I received a text message from my BBC colleague Gary Lineker. It read: 'Quit while you're still a genius!'

The West Ham chairman thanked me for my contribution and explained what relegation would mean to the club. Financially we would lose at least £20 million and that meant reducing the wage bill while still retaining a staff big enough to cope with 46 Nationwide fixtures as opposed to the 38 in the Premiership. I was happy to be standing down and happier still that Glenn was making good progress. Those in the know thought he would be back in action for the start of the new season.

CHAPTER 15

THE BOSS: PART TWO

I HAD MY CHANCE TO GO into football management when West Ham sacked John Lyall. I turned it down and I've never regretted the decision. My brief appointment at the end of 2002–03 was just that – brief. I never intended it to be anything else. I was happy to help out while Glenn Roeder was ill and I enjoyed my three games in charge, but at the end of the season I wanted nothing other than to resume a 'normal' life.

Had I wanted to join the management ranks on a permanent basis I would have explored what West Ham proposed during the long hot summer of 1989. John had just been sacked following relegation. I had been out of the professional game for five years. Martin Cearns, a club director and son of the chairman Len, asked to see me. He would soon succeed his father as chairman, further strengthening the Cearns family's association with West Ham. J.W.Y. Cearns was a founder of the club and a director who served, apart from a three-year break, from 1900 until his death in 1934.

Martin Cearns told me that the directors were thinking of looking outside the club for a manager. But during the conversation he asked me: 'Have you ever considered doing this kind of thing yourself?' I replied: 'No, not really.' For me and my family it would have been a big upheaval; the children were settled at school and I was making a good living from outside the game. 'Just supposing I was interested,' I said, 'what kind of salary were you likely to offer?' As I recall, Martin said it would be around £100,000 a year. The fact was, I was earning more at the time from my other interests, so I said that I couldn't really consider it.

In the years after I retired from playing a number of people encouraged me to have a go at management. This confidence on their part was touching and usually based on the fact that they had heard me on the radio and assumed I knew a bit about it! There was, however, another school of thought that I came across from time to time. This basically assumed that I wasn't tough enough to be a football manager and make hard decisions. I understood why people thought this but I knew it wouldn't be an issue should I ever take the plunge into management. I can be forthright and decisive when I need to be and years later, as chairman of Sport England, I think I surprised some important people by demonstrating this side of my nature on several occasions. I've never been the shouting or abusive type, although there were times during my Sunday morning football career when I verbally assaulted lazy team-mates in the dressing room!

Perhaps Martin Cearns, who was then a Barclays Bank manager, genuinely believed that I had the qualities needed to be a successful manager of West Ham. As it turned out, he was chairman for only two years but remained on the board until 2006 when he resigned, selling his shares in the club to the Icelandic billionaire Bjorgolfur Gudmundsson for more than £7 million.

Once Martin had established that I had no real interest in the job, he asked if there was another candidate I could recommend.

The man I proposed was Gerry Francis, who I knew from the days when we were both in the England squad. He had been a talented, diligent midfield player, a former England captain under Don Revie. I thought he was at least as good as all the other names that had been mentioned. He was the manager of Bristol Rovers at the time and, of course, went on to be manager of Queens Park Rangers and Tottenham.

In the end the board appointed from outside, as Martin had suggested they would. John Lyall's successor, Swindon manager Lou Macari, had no previous association with West Ham. His reign was short-lived and was followed by a return to the traditional method of appointing managers who had a connection with the club. Billy Bonds and Harry Redknapp had both been West Ham players and, although he hadn't played for the club, Glenn Roeder was already on the coaching staff when he was promoted to replace Harry.

Happily, Glenn made a full recovery from brain surgery and was back in the hot seat preparing the players for the new season. I had resumed my previous role as non-executive director and was determined to give Glenn all the support he needed. For him, the priority was to win back West Ham's Premiership status at the first attempt. I knew that would not be an easy task. I had tasted relegation as a West Ham player back in 1977–78. It took us three years to regain our place among the elite of the game. I was at the height of my England career when we were relegated. The newspapers were full of speculation about me leaving because Second Division football would jeopardise my England place. I remember going to see John Lyall in his office at Upton Park.

I told him that I wanted to stay at West Ham and help the team win back their First Division status. I told him that I didn't want to leave but if they had to sell me for financial reasons I'd understand. John didn't have to sell anyone as a result of relegation. He started the first season in Division Two with basically the same side that had been relegated a few months earlier. What's more, the club provided funds to strengthen the squad and, during the period we were in Division Two, he paid a world record fee for a goalkeeper for Phil Parkes from QPR and made three other big-money signings – Ray Stewart, Paul Goddard and Stuart Pearson. I think such a response to relegation would be simply impossible in the modern game. In West Ham's case, for instance, in the summer of 2003 the first task was to cut the wage bill. Relegation was going to cost the club millions in revenue.

I think a total of 19 players left, including most of the big earners such as Joe Cole, Glen Johnson, Lee Bowyer, Edouard Cisse, Sebastien Schemmel, Paolo Di Canio, Les Ferdinand, Frederic Kanoute and Trevor Sinclair. One who didn't leave – at least not immediately – was Jermain Defoe. Within days of relegation he had handed in a transfer request, but it was not a good decision and I told him so. I said the crowd would be on his back and they were as soon as the new season started. His request for a move was initially rejected but everyone realised that he would be back in the Premiership sooner rather than later. He was only 21 and we knew he was a real talent when we signed him from Charlton Athletic in controversial circumstances.

He was one of the few big names left when Glenn named his team for the opening First Division game against Preston at Deepdale. Although Jermain scored in our 2-1 win I suspected his heart wasn't really in it. Sent off against Gillingham in September, West Brom in November and Walsall in December, we realised he would face a long suspension if he was dismissed for a fourth time. As it was, I think he missed seven games that season because of suspensions. We eventually decided to agree to his transfer request and accepted a Tottenham offer for him of £6.7 million plus Bobby Zamora in the January transfer window.

In many ways that period was a deeply depressing and hugely

frustrating time for West Ham. It was as difficult a time as I could remember. Clubs like West Ham were locked into player contracts that reflected how wages had increased since Sky TV began bankrolling the Premiership. When I was a player, most professionals had a one-year contract with a one-year option, or a two-and-two, but in the modern game they are looking at far longer contracts. That backfires if after three months you discover the player is not as good as you first thought. In the early days of the Premiership, if you had a player who wasn't quite doing it, you could move him on to a Nationwide club. It's not so easy now because there's a vast salary difference.

All the Premiership clubs have a list of players they consider not good enough. But it's hard to move them on because of the wage structure, which is why some Premiership clubs pay half of a player's salary while they play for another club in a lower division. We were asked to pay half of Sebastien Schemmel's wages. We wanted him off the wage bill and he told us that Metz wanted to re-sign him. Good news, we thought, until he told us that they wouldn't pay what he wanted as a salary. They would pay only half of what he was getting with us. He asked us if we would pay the other half. We said, 'Non!'

In 2003–04 we tried to persuade some of the bigger clubs to loan players. For many young players at the big clubs making the transition from reserve to first team is almost impossible. Young players need regular first-team football to develop properly and clubs of Champions League status can't allow their young players to develop in the first team. That's where the loan system can help. We, for instance, took a young striker, Neil Mellor, from Liverpool. He wasn't getting a regular game at Liverpool and he came to us because we gave him a chance to impress and make a name for himself. He benefits, we benefit and, in the long term, Liverpool should also benefit.

Neil was just 21 when he joined us on loan. A sturdily built Yorkshireman, he was a centre-forward in the Geoff Hurst mould. We considered it something of a coup. Delighted to be back in the thick of things, Glenn was so pleased with the signing that he ignored David Connolly and put the untried Mellor in the team for the opening game against Preston.

Connolly, a prickly Republic of Ireland international striker signed for a bargain £285,000 from Wimbledon, was seriously upset that Glenn had favoured Mellor, who met his new team-mates for the first time the night before the game. As it turned out, Connolly came off the substitutes' bench to replace Mellor and score the winning goal against Preston. He went on to score 14 goals in 48 appearances for West Ham. Neil Mellor scored just twice in 21 games before he was injured and returned to Liverpool.

Connolly scored two goals four days later in a Carling Cup win over Rushden and Diamonds and was picked ahead of Mellor for the first home game of the season – a lifeless 0-0 draw with Sheffield United. A 28,972 crowd turned up for the match and once again chants of 'Sack the Board!' resounded around the stadium. The chairman took two pages of the match programme to explain the background to the summer exodus of players. Administration had been a real prospect until the club began to implement cost-cutting measures. With income reduced by around £20 million, the club also needed to repay £8 million in loans, which meant a total of £28 million had to be recouped in savings and transfers. The wage bill had been cut by £10 million and £18 million had been received from the sale of players. It was an honest explanation of the club's financial situation and demonstrated just how damaging relegation had become for Premiership clubs in the modern era. In the past, relegation was nowhere near as financially damaging as it is now. When West Ham were relegated in 1977–78 there was no exodus of players. I could have left, along with Billy Bonds, Frank

Lampard and Alan Devonshire. I stayed and bounced back with the team, as did the others. We made up our own minds. The club didn't need to sell its best players and we, the players, didn't have agents urging us to move on.

I realised just how influential agents had become during my spell as manager. Most of them tell their clients that progress on the international front is dependent on playing in the Champions League. Agents were quick to point out to their players that the England manager, Sven-Goran Eriksson, selected the bulk of his team from the clubs playing in the Champions League. Joe Cole, for instance, had never wavered on the issue. He was convinced that he hadn't been picked for England because he wasn't playing in the Champions League. He felt that he had to learn to play in Europe. Agents tell clubs today that they have mapped out the careers of their clients to include Champions League football.

I was reminded of what we'd lost on the playing front when I watched England play Croatia at Ipswich early that season, 2003–04. Our goalkeeper David James kept a clean sheet during his 45 minutes of action and four former Hammers all played some part in a 3-1 win – Rio Ferdinand, Joe Cole, Trevor Sinclair and Frank Lampard junior. A couple of months later Glen Johnson and Jermain Defoe won their first England caps, too. Throw Michael Carrick into the mix – he, of course, joined Defoe and Kanoute at Spurs in 2004 – and you get some idea of the calibre of player West Ham produced at that time.

At least, for the time being, we still had James, Carrick and Defoe. All three featured when we went to Rotherham in August for a match that had a lot more significance than a row over the Millmoor dressing rooms. I missed the game because I was still contracted to Radio Five and was due to work at Chelsea that afternoon. In the week before the match Glenn had mentioned to me that when we'd played at Preston their manager Craig Brown had told him that the changing facilities at Rotherham were cramped. He suggested that we allow our players to change into their kit at the hotel and avoid a crush in the dressing room. It sounded sensible to me.

On the day of the game, I was at Stamford Bridge, BBC headphones on, waiting for Chelsea–Leicester City to kick off. I was listening to all the pre-match chatter from around the grounds. Suddenly I heard a Yorkshire voice suggesting there was a bit of ill feeling towards West Ham that afternoon because their players had arrived at Millmoor, turned their noses up at the dressing-room facilities and returned to the hotel to get changed. What in fact had happened is that they'd arrived in their tracksuits with their playing kit underneath. But there was clearly a feeling among the locals that West Ham were acting like big-time Charlies, demeaning the facilities on offer. That simply wasn't the case. As it turned out Rotherham won the match 1-0 and West Ham played badly, encouraging the local media to speculate that our snubbing of their facilities had wound up the players in the Rotherham dressing room and fuelled resentment among the crowd.

I know Glenn wasn't at all happy with our performance that day. What he didn't know was that the Rotherham defeat would be his last match as West Ham manager. That night the managing director Paul Aldridge called me at home and said that the chairman Terry Brown and some of the directors were appalled at the level of West Ham's performance at Rotherham and were seriously concerned that we were going to make a poor start to the season. They considered it essential that we made a sound start to our bid to return to the Premiership at the first attempt. He said that the fans were already complaining and the general feeling among board members was that it would be disastrous to lose ground in the promotion race early in the season.

All this, of course, was absolutely true, but we had played only three league games – a win, a draw and a defeat. It was really early in the race to make judgements, but it was clear to me that the mood among the directors was swinging towards a change of manager. I was surprised. I urged Paul to impress upon the others the perils of a knee-jerk reaction. Given that we were just three games into the season, I thought it was a bit soon to be making that kind of decision. I recommended to Paul: 'Tell the chairman to sleep on it.'

He did. But it changed nothing. The next morning Paul called again. 'The chairman is of the same opinion,' he said. This time Paul asked me if I would be prepared to take charge again if Glenn Roeder was sacked. I was staggered by the speed of it all. And this time, of course, the circumstances were completely different. I stepped into the breach last time because Glenn was ill. This time they wanted to sack him and install me in his place.

It was a difficult decision for me but I had the impression that no matter what I decided, it would not influence Glenn's position. They thought it was time for a change. And they wanted to do it immediately. There was some logic to the timing, according to Paul. The next two games – Bradford (H) and Ipswich (A) – were in the space of four days, followed by a fortnight's break to accommodate international fixtures. England were due to play Macedonia and Liechtenstein in Euro qualifiers.

Paul stressed that the board were hopeful of conducting a search and naming a long-term successor to Glenn at some stage in that fortnight. If I agreed to take it on, it was not going to be a long commitment. At least, that's what Paul said. That day, a Sunday, a couple of hours after they had talked to me, Paul and the chairman went to see Glenn and told him that they wanted to bring in a new manager. By this time I was at a friend's Bar Mitzvah in London, unsure of the sequence of events until another guest came up to me and said: 'I've just heard on TV that West Ham have sacked the manager.'

Many people asked me in the years that followed whether it was the right decision to replace Glenn, who had worked tirelessly to make a success of his first really big job in management. I remember saying to several people at the start of that season that the seriousness of his illness dominated all other considerations. At no time did Glenn play the sympathy card but there is no doubt in my mind that no one on the West Ham board would have been comfortable had they sacked him immediately after relegation. There was a genuine desire to give him a second chance, but I must say that had it not been for his illness I suspect the board would probably have voted for a change of manager at the end of the relegation season. As it turned out, it was soon clear as a new season dawned that the patience of the club's fans was not going to last long if we made an indifferent start. We needed to start well to dispel any doubts about our ability to bounce back at the first attempt.

I agreed to take over for the games against Bradford and Ipswich, fully believing that a new manager would be installed at Upton Park during that international fortnight. My first task was to help the board sift through the potential candidates. As the director with football experience, I was going to have a big input. I knew that we were unlikely to tempt a big-name Premiership manager.

There were some high-profile names out of work, men like George Graham, but I felt that we would be better off looking for a manager who knew his way round the First Division. Our priority, after all, was to win promotion. Did we go for someone with a West Ham link, such as Stuart Pearce or Iain Dowie? Did we look for an established manager with a proven record or a young, ambitious, up-and-coming coach?

There was another suggestion: that I should do the job for a season and bring in a young coach to work alongside me. The idea was that I would groom him for the job, but I didn't really want that commitment for a year. However we packaged it for public consumption, the truth was that I would have been responsible for the success or failure of the season. It was not what I wanted.

The consensus was that we needed someone who knew the division, but also had the ability to survive in the Premiership if we were to win promotion. Among the coaches we talked about were Steve Coppell, Paul Hart, Gary Megson, Nigel Worthington and Alan Pardew. There were other names in the mix. The bookies made me 5-4 favourite for the job. Paul Goddard was 5-2, Iain Dowie 6-1, Steve Cotterill 10-1 and Joe Kinnear 12-1. Pardew and Coppell had proven records in Division One. Dowie had done well with Oldham.

We were impressed with Pardew's record. He'd got Reading into the play-offs with a lot of free-transfer players and I had him at the top of my short list of three. I liked his manner. He was confident, ambitious and said all the right things. He had a positive, logical approach to the job. He knew what he wanted to do. We both recognised that the playing squad needed an overhaul and we knew that the earlier we started doing it the better.

A window fitter by trade, Alan had played at a good amateur level for clubs like Dulwich Hamlet and Corinthian Casuals before the Crystal Palace manager, Steve Coppell, gave him a chance as a 25-year-old. He played for Palace in the 1990 FA Cup final before moving on a free transfer to Charlton Athletic and, finally, Barnet. He had a spell as reserve-team coach at Reading before they offered him the manager's job in 1999.

Getting him to Upton Park was not going to be easy. It was a sensitive subject because Reading were clearly not happy to learn of our interest in their manager. We approached the club officially and asked for permission to speak to him. They refused. We were careful to say nothing publicly but Reading, inexplicably, put the news of our approach on their website. I was travelling with the BBC team to England's European Championship qualifier against

Macedonia in Skopje in September when a reporter told me: 'My office say you're trying to get Alan Pardew.'

I can only assume that they decided to make this public because of the outcry that followed Mark McGhee's move from Reading to Leicester in 1994. The club chairman, John Madejski, was criticised by fans for not fighting harder to keep McGhee and I think this time he wanted them to know that he wasn't about to lose another manager without a fight.

We weren't happy that our request for permission to speak to Alan was now in the public domain. It wasn't in our interest to release this information. If we didn't get Alan Pardew it meant that the next in line would know that he wasn't first choice. Once the news was out, Alan said to Reading: 'Well, at least let me speak to West Ham.' Madejski said no. It was clear that he was digging in his heels. What complicated matters was the fact that West Ham's first match, once the two international fixtures were out of the way, was against, yes, Reading.

My first two games as caretaker boss had gone well – a 1-0 win over Bradford at Upton Park and a 2-1 win at Ipswich, where heroics by David James in the final minutes secured us the three points. Two games, two wins, that's where my role as interim manager should have ended. But our attempt to sign Alan Pardew was becoming more protracted. A second official approach was turned down and at that point Alan handed in his resignation.

That, too, was rejected. The Reading chairman explained: 'I believe the manager should honour his contract. While we would allow him to talk to a Premiership club, we certainly won't give him permission to talk to one of our main First Division rivals.'

Alan responded by walking out on Reading just a couple of days before they were due to play at Upton Park. Reading asked Alan's assistant, Kevin Dillon, to take charge of the team for the West Ham game. When he took his place in the Reading dugout that afternoon I was back in the West Ham dugout. Alan had decided that his best course of action was to stay away. He missed a good game. Five minutes after hitting a post, Defoe sent over a corner which Christian Dailly headed in to give me a third consecutive win.

I wondered what would happen next. It was a difficult situation for all concerned. Alan knew that we considered him the right man for the job and, in those circumstances, we could hardly turn our back on him once he'd quit his job at Reading. I was hoping that it would be settled amicably and as soon as possible. That didn't look likely when Mr Madejski decided to go to the High Court to seek an injunction for breach of contract. We had offered compensation for their loss of Alan Pardew, but the Reading chairman thought there was a point of principle at stake.

Three days after beating Reading I was back in the front seat of the team bus for the trip to Crewe. We beat them 3-0 to move into second place in the table. Fans were beginning to make complimentary noises on the radio phone-ins and some would come up to me at matches and urge me to take the job on a permanent basis. I remember saying to the media after the Crewe match: 'I do hope I'm not still talking to the press like this next April.' One or two of my supporters might have had a rethink after our match at Gillingham, where we lost 2-0 and had Jermain sent off. Had it not been for Jermain's dismissal at the Priestfield Stadium I would probably have completed my brief reign in the West Ham hot seat without losing a match. He was playing well and scoring goals, but had not withdrawn his transfer request. He'd made it quite clear that he wanted to leave.

He'd never been difficult or temperamental on or off the pitch but on this particular occasion in Gillingham it seemed to me that he allowed his frustration to get the better of him. It was a really hot day that had started badly for us when Neil Mellor was forced to withdraw from the line-up just before kick-off with a stomach upset. The first half was evenly balanced, though Jermain made a big fuss to the referee and linesman when he got clattered in front of the dugout. I was on the bench in my shirt sleeves with Paul Goddard and Roger Cross and we all urged him to cool down.

A few minutes later he got clattered again and once more berated the same linesman. On the bench we all felt that he was going to end up in the referee's notebook if he wasn't careful. As if to reinforce this, the next time the linesman came near the dugout he shouted: 'Trevor! Trevor! You've got to have a word. He's bad-mouthing me.' By this time we were already a goal down. Tomas Repka, an uncompromising Czech full-back who had little natural rapport with referees, had fouled Danny Spiller about 30 yards from goal. The referee awarded the free kick but Tomas disputed the decision and was booked.

This just happened to be the season when referees in Division One were trialling a new refinement to the Laws of the Game. If a player disputed the referee's award of a free kick, the kick was to be advanced by ten yards. The referee in this case, Paul Armstrong, moved the free kick forward the statutory ten yards. The ball was now positioned on the edge of our penalty area. Marlon King, the much-travelled Jamaica striker, curled his free kick wide of our defensive wall and past David James into the back of the net. We could still have salvaged a draw until 12 minutes from time when Jermain was fouled again. He jumped up, swearing and cursing, and took a couple of steps towards the same linesman. 'Jay's in trouble this time,' I muttered to the others on the bench. Sure enough, the linesman's flag went up, the referee came over for a consultation and then flourished the red card. So we were a goal down and a man down.

It was a bad day and it got worse when another Jamaica striker, who had played for England's Under-21 side when he was with

Leicester City, scored Gillingham's second goal. Trevor Benjamin was one of those old-style journeyman footballers who played for a total of 16 different Football League clubs before slipping down into the non-League game.

It was Jermain's first sending-off and, to me, was an indication that he was getting frustrated playing for West Ham in Division One. I was disappointed with him at the time but just eight weeks later I was chuckling when I recalled his role in my only defeat as West Ham manager. When I went to the Football Association offices in Soho Square to discuss my new job I was taken around the various departments. When I walked into the referees' department the first person I met was the linesman who Jermain had confronted at Gillingham. I couldn't believe it. I hadn't realised that Mark Ives was not only a linesman but also the disciplinary manager in the FA's Governance Division. He said: 'I didn't think you'd remember me.'

'How could I forget?' I said. We laughed about it, and still do. Mark played amateur football in the old Isthmian League, spent 27 years refereeing and was on the National List of Assistant Referees for nine years. He knows a bit about it!

Three days after the Gillingham defeat I was beginning to wonder whether I was losing my touch. We faced Cardiff at Ninian Park in the second round of the Carling Cup and within 25 minutes had conceded two goals to their Wales striker Robert Earnshaw. Defoe shot us back into contention from the penalty spot in the 45th minute and completed his hat-trick with a cracking left-footer from 20 yards two minutes from time. The reward was a third-round date with Tottenham at White Hart Lane at the end of October and I was hoping that my caretaker role would have finished by then.

Happily, the club were making progress on the Alan Pardew front. He had been given 'gardening leave' while the two clubs tried to reach some sort of compromise. In the end agreement was reached and the case was settled. West Ham agreed to pay £380,000 in compensation and costs and were told they could take no other Reading staff. Alan was told he could join West Ham on 18 October. This meant that I would be in charge of the team for a further five matches. It wasn't what I wanted but at least the end was in sight. To be honest, the pressure hadn't been quite as intense as a few months earlier when, in my first stint as manager, I'd been fighting to keep the club in the Premiership. It only became a worry for me when it was obvious that replacing Glenn would take longer than originally anticipated. The idea, as envisaged by the board, was to resolve the problem as quickly as possible and thus give the new manager the chance to settle in early and give him as long as possible to create the impetus for a promotion bid in the second half of the season.

The whole purpose of my role, really, was to prepare the ground for the new manager and present him with a situation that gave him a realistic chance of securing promotion. I felt team spirit was good and there was fierce competition for places, particularly among the main strikers, Defoe, Connolly and Mellor. I also thought that the atmosphere in the dressing room was different to that I had encountered at the end of the previous season. A few months earlier there had been a diverse mix of languages and cultures – and some big names, big earners and big egos.

Now, it was more like a dressing room I remembered from my own playing days. It was a bit more homely. It was essentially British, and English was the only language you heard. During my time as manager in Division One in 2003–04 I used a total of 20 players, but only four were from outside the UK – Tomas Repka (Czech Republic), Richard Garcia (Australia), Youssef Sofiane (France) and Niclas Alexandersson (Sweden). Many of the big egos were among the 19 players who had moved on. I was left with a group of players who, by and large, had things to prove.

My last game in charge was a 2-2 draw with Burnley at Upton

Park. A crowd of more than 31,000 turned up to see Alan Pardew introduced to the fans. I was pleased he was at the game. He could see the team's strengths – and weaknesses – and therefore had a good idea of what lay ahead of him. It wasn't a great performance on our part and my last significant act as manager was to send on Don Hutchison from the substitutes' bench. Happily for us, he volleyed an equaliser with four minutes remaining. His late goal meant that I retired from management with a record that read: played 14, won 9, drawn 4, lost 1. My record in detail was:

Premiership 2002–03 – Manchester City (A) 1-0 Kanoute; Chelsea (H) 1-0 Di Canio; Birmingham City (A) 2-2 Ferdinand, Di Canio

Division One 2003–04 – Bradford City (H) 1-0 Defoe; Ipswich (A) 2 1 Defoe, Connolly; Reading (H) 1-0 Dailly; Crewe (A) 3-0 Connolly (2), Etherington; Gillingham (A) 0-2; Millwall (H) 1-1 Connolly; Crystal Palace (H) 3-0 Defoe, Mellor (2); Derby (A) 1-0 Hutchison; Norwich (H) 1-1 Edworthy (og); Burnley (H) 2-2 Connolly, Hutchison

Carling Cup – Cardiff (A) 3-2 Defoe (3)

The team was in a good position in the table – fifth – when Alan took charge for the game against Nottingham Forest at Upton Park on 22 October. I was pleased to be able to hand over a side that was enjoying good form but realised that this in itself created a pressure for the new manager. I read somewhere that my ten First Division games had produced a total of 21 points. This was an average of 2.1 points per match. If we could maintain that rate over a 46-match season we would finish with 96 points. That would have been enough to end the season as champions, two points ahead of Norwich, who were the winners with 94 points.

Looking back, I think in one sense it would have been easier for Alan had we been struggling a bit. The expectancy level wouldn't have been quite so high. As it turned out, he had to wait until his eighth game before he could register a victory. His opening game against Forest, with his first signing, Hayden Mullins, in midfield, required a Defoe equaliser to secure a 1-1 draw. A run of four further draws followed, interrupted only by a 3-4 home defeat to West Brom. By the time he recorded his first win – 4-0 against Wigan – he had strengthened the goal-scoring department by signing Marlon Harewood for £600,000 from Nottingham Forest and Brian Deane on a free transfer from Leicester City.

Back in the boardroom, I still felt a responsibility although I knew it was important for me not to linger around the training ground or dressing room. It was now Alan's problem but I told him that I would always be available if he wanted to talk to me. Funnily enough, when I was around the players at the training ground I felt more comfortable than I had when Glenn was in charge. With Glenn I often wondered whether he felt that I was hovering around for a purpose. I was an ex-player with a profile at Upton Park. Did he ever think that I was trying to get something more significant than my non-executive director role?

I hope not. It wasn't something I wanted, but I would have understood if he felt that way. The territories were more clearly defined with Alan Pardew. I'd been partly responsible for signing him. He knew that I was his link to the boardroom and he accepted that was the limit of my involvement. My working relationship with him was a very good one. He didn't know, though, that it would be a brief one. It was at this time that the Football Association asked me to consider the newly created role of director of football development. I was happy to accept this new challenge even though it obviously meant having to relinquish my role at West Ham. Nothing, though, altered the fact that I remained, first and foremost, a fan of the club.

What my two spells in charge at West Ham taught me is that I could probably have made a career for myself as a manager had I chosen that path. I found it flattering, doing the job for the second time, when several players tried to persuade me to take it on permanently. First time round I'd had to deal with a lot of overseas players and a lot of big-name personalities. Second time round we had a lot of new faces and, in the main, the egos were smaller. They rose to the challenge. We got some good results and, I think, put in place something for Alan Pardew and the club's immediate future. I remember asking two or three players after Glenn had lost his job whether they thought I had established a rapport with the squad. They all responded positively, which I found encouraging.

It interested me because what I was doing with them on the training pitch was exactly what I used to do as a player 20 years before with Ron Greenwood and John Lyall. They were the only two managers I had in my club career. I was doing with my players exactly what they had done with their players. There was no difference at all. When I started my caretaker role I used to wonder whether the young players were thinking: 'What on earth is he on about?'

But I had no problems with them. I tried to involve the players in what I was thinking and trying to achieve. Ron and John believed in giving players responsibility. I told mine that I believed in them and that they should have confidence in what they were trying to accomplish. The response was so encouraging that, one day as I drove home from training, I remember thinking to myself, 'You must be doing something right.'

Alan Pardew arrived with his own ideas and a clearly defined set of principles, a new set of rules and a range of player fines covering everything from dress code to discipline on and off the pitch. The players responded well to him, but home defeats against Stoke, Ipswich and Preston – nine points dropped – more or less killed any realistic hope of winning automatic promotion. We finished fourth, 12 points behind second-placed West Brom, and qualified for that end-of-season nightmare for those involved – the play-offs.

We faced Ipswich in the two-leg semi-finals and lost the first match 1-0 at Portman Road. Three days later, on a euphoric night at Upton Park, 34,002 watched Matthew Etherington and Christian Dailly score the goals that gave West Ham a 2-0 win (2-1 on aggregate) and a place in the First Division play-off final against Crystal Palace at the Millennium Stadium in Cardiff. For the two managers involved, the big day in Cardiff was likely to be a once-in-a-lifetime experience. Alan Pardew, of course, had played for Palace and their manager, Iain Dowie, had played for West Ham. For the clubs themselves the most important aspect of the big day was the £20-25 million that came with Premiership football. So, for West Ham this was the most important game of a long and difficult season in which, at various times, three different managers had held the reins.

West Ham's line-up that day illustrated just how much had changed among the playing staff at Upton Park in the space of a year. Of the team that started against Palace only Repka, Lomas and Dailly had been in the line-up for the final game of the season 12 months earlier. Sadly for the fans who made the long pilgrimage to Cardiff – I was among them – the play-off final was a huge let-down. A Neil Shipperley goal gave Palace a 1-0 victory and condemned West Ham to another season in Division One.

Alan Pardew was bitterly disappointed by the result and the performance and, as a former manager myself, I knew exactly how he felt.

CHAPTER 16

OLYMPIC 'GAINS'

I WAS A SCHOOLBOY IN SHORTS when I first went to watch West Ham. A match programme cost six old pennies (2½p) and the club's record signing was Johnny Byrne, who cost £65,000 from Crystal Palace. That was many years ago now, so the prospect of abandoning the familiar and homely confines of Upton Park generates all kinds of emotions. There must be generations of West Ham fans who have mixed feelings about relocating to the Olympic Stadium in Stratford. Like many of them, I will be sad to bid farewell to Upton Park but the move to a brand-new stadium just four miles away was an opportunity that the club could not afford to ignore.

The home of the Hammers – the Boleyn Ground to be accurate – houses a million memories of promotion triumphs, relegation dramas, big European nights, great FA Cup adventures and sad goodbyes to lost heroes. It has become an integral part of the community in that part of east London and I'm sure there are old-timers who still remember the V1 flying bomb that damaged the South Bank in 1944. The Boleyn Ground takes its name from a 16th-century hunting lodge that stood on the site. When West Ham moved there in 1904 the hunting lodge, known as the Boleyn Castle, was being used by a Roman Catholic school. West Ham paid rent for the land until the Archdiocese of Westminster agreed to sell it to the club for £30,000 in 1959.

The move from the Memorial Ground in the docklands to the Boleyn Ground in Upton Park was prompted by a series of disagreements with the club's erstwhile benefactor, Arnold F. Hills, the president of Thames Ironworks. The decision to switch grounds laid the foundations for West Ham's later success as a professional football club. At the time, the club was struggling financially. The players' average weekly wage was £2.50 and they received a £10 signing-on fee, which doesn't sound much these days. But on arrival at Upton Park the club had an overdraft of £770 and assets of less than £200. What was important was the increase in revenue in that first season at the Boleyn – up from £2,900 to £4,300.

This produced a sense of optimism which was soon to be justified. The first match at the new ground in September 1904, a 3-0 win over Millwall, attracted a crowd of 10,000. When Spurs were held to a goalless draw three weeks later the crowd was 16,000. It soon became obvious that the move from the docklands benefited the club hugely. By 1911 assets exceeded liabilities for the first time and two years later they were able to invest £4,000 in a new stand.

Financial considerations may not be quite as critical for the current board of directors at West Ham, though I think the move to Stratford could be as significant a landmark for the club as the move to the Boleyn Ground 110 years ago. I think playing in the Olympic Stadium will raise the profile of the club and present opportunities that simply didn't exist at Upton Park.

It's a fabulous, brand-new stadium with great transport links and lots of potential for increasing the club's fan base. The proposed 54,000 capacity in the Olympic Stadium is about 20,000 more than the club's average attendance and that presents the promotion and marketing people with a challenge. West Ham has a very loyal fan base and there is no reason why this cannot be extended significantly in the years ahead. The transport links mean that West Ham will be one of the easiest clubs to visit in London and I suspect that we could attract a lot of new corporate clients from the City and Canary Wharf.

The Olympic Games in 2012 were a huge success for London, and West Ham are privileged to have been chosen to play a part in protecting the legacy of one of the great events in world sport. The Olympic Park in Stratford is being converted into a recreational area the size of Hyde Park, with sports facilities, wildlife habitats, woodland, landscaped gardens and play areas.

It's going to cost about £150 million to convert the Olympic venue into a soccer stadium and, although some argue that taxpayers should not have to underwrite a Premier League club's removal costs, the fact is that the stadium will be available to host other events. It is surely a more logical proposal than Tottenham's plan to demolish the stadium and rebuild it.

About 15 years ago, when I was chairman of Sport England, I was involved in the founding of the City of Manchester Stadium, which became the fifth largest ground in the Premier League. The success of this stadium is an example of what can be achieved with perseverance, patience and hard work. Manchester first proposed a new stadium nearly 30 years ago and hoped that it would be the centrepiece of their bid to host the 1996 Olympic Games. Atlanta were the eventual winners of the bidding process but Manchester were undeterred.

When they won the right to host the 2002 Commonwealth Games they built their showpiece stadium for the major events for

£112 million, with Sport England contributing £77 million and Manchester Council the rest. Many significant figures, such as Sebastian Coe and Jonathan Edwards, wanted a stadium with an athletics legacy but the feeling at Sport England was that this would become a white elephant, rarely used for athletics. It would cost £1 million a year just to maintain the stadium.

In 1998 Manchester City, then in Division One, agreed to lease the proposed new stadium from the council after the Commonwealth Games. Conversion to a football stadium would cost the council £22 million and the football club would pay a further £20 million fitting it out. City moved into the new stadium in 2003–04 and, although supporters were initially sceptical about abandoning Maine Road, their home for 80 years, the move has been a huge success. As a Championship club, City were getting attendances of around 20,000. They agreed that should they win promotion they would pay a commission once the gate figure reached 25,000, extra for 30,000, more still for 35,000 and so on.

This commission was paid to the council and invested in a sports trust which was used for the benefit of the entire city. This scheme raised a lot of money for the community and eventually the new Arab owners of the club bought out the agreement because it was costing them a small fortune in commission payments. To my way of thinking, it was a great example of what could be achieved when all parties shared a common purpose and were singing from the same song sheet. Now, of course, sponsored by Etihad, the club's current proposals include expansion plans that will increase capacity to 62,000.

The development of the Etihad Stadium was one of the most satisfying chapters of my time in sports administration. It showed that we could build a top-class facility, stage a world-class event and, at the same time, regenerate a poor part of Manchester. I think our success in Manchester convinced the government that we should bid to stage the 2012 Olympic Games. There is no reason why West Ham's move should not be just as successful in the long term even though, unlike the Etihad, the Olympic Stadium was designed to have an athletics track as part of its legacy. Lord Coe was notable among those pressing the case for track and field. But who would have used the track? And how often? I believe it would have been a real drain on the public purse.

Many of the people involved in the development of the Olympic Stadium had also played a part in the building of the City of Manchester Stadium, but the ease with which the Manchester project progressed contrasted sharply with the problems faced in Stratford. Looking back, I think it's a great shame that the same foresight wasn't applied to both projects. I was also involved in a third big government project – the rebuilding of Wembley Stadium. That was going to cost around £350 million. Then the Minister for Sport, Kate Hoey, suspended the project because it didn't have a dedicated athletics track. That put completion back by three years and doubled the cost. The FA are still paying for it.

I think sport should be an essential part of all our lives and these high-quality facilities are important, but they must be sustainable in the long term. In my 15 years in sports administration I came to realise just how difficult it was to fund sport for all. Much of my time at the Sport Council was spent trying to get funding for sport, particularly at grass-roots level. I think the experience I gained was a key factor in the FA deciding they wanted me to help with the development of football at all levels.

I had a career in professional sport. Not everyone is that lucky but sport should be available to all. As a schoolboy I seem to remember that access to sport was easier than it is now. I loved sport at school – football, cricket, tennis, anything. Nowadays it's difficult to find teachers willing to give up their time outside school hours to coach children or take them to events.

When I was at the Sports Council I began to discover that there was a major problem with the number and quality of school playing fields. Providing sports facilities should be a statutory requirement. Go to France or Germany and look at the facilities in even the smallest communities. In those countries, if you build a new housing estate you have to provide amenities for sport and leisure. That is not the case here. Sports facilities are the luck of the draw. Some councils provide them, some don't. As a result, we see increased rates of obesity and anti-social behaviour among the young due, in part at least, to a lack of the sort of amenities that can channel the energies of young people. Obesity is a growing problem and I suspect that eventually the health service will simply be unable to cope. Sport for the young could help to combat that.

But more and more local authorities, faced with budget cuts, are looking for ways to generate extra revenue. Lots of junior and local sports clubs are being asked to pay increased and unrealistic fees for using facilities. So, if they don't have the money, the kids who might be enjoying the facilities ignore them. In an FA survey of grass-roots football 84 per cent of respondents claimed that 'poor facilities' was their main concern. I remember a lively radio debate with the then Minister for Sport Richard Caborn in 2002 when I criticised the Labour government for a lack of funding for sport.

From a football viewpoint the biggest challenge involves the 16–25 age group. That's when they have to start paying. Many are unemployed or in further education and can't afford to tap into sport. The drop-out rate at that age is our biggest challenge. Even at the higher levels of the game the drop-out rate is worrying. A total of 54 players represented England at the European Under-17 Championship finals in 2005, 2007 and 2009 but four years later only ten remained active in the Premier League. There are no simple answers. We need more coaches and better coaches. At the highest level we have 203 coaches in England who hold the full

UEFA Pro Licence. Spain, for example, has more than 2,000 coaches at that level.

It is a changing game. Progress for a young player seemed so much more straightforward back in the days of Hurst, Moore and Peters but, of course, there were many who failed to make the grade even then. I think it's tough for English youngsters and likely to get tougher. On any weekend you care to name only 33 per cent of the players in action in the Premier League will be English. Just as worrying are the figures showing that many overseas players, unable to make the grade in the Premier League, are seeking consolation in the Championship. This drift into the second tier meant that at the end of 2013–14 around 50 per cent of the players in the Championship were from overseas.

More and more club owners are also from abroad. Many don't appreciate the culture within English football. The traditional fan has a set of values and ambitions, some unchanged for decades, that may not be shared by foreign owners. Some owners have a portfolio of several clubs and an agenda that comprises international rather than just domestic football. I can envisage a time in the not-too-distant future when our top three or four clubs desert the Premier League and play in an 18-club European Super League. There would be a lot of support for that among some of the blue-chip clubs in Europe.

The game must progress and evolve, but I think it's important that football continues to cater for the traditional fan. It's important that clubs understand that. Not all do. West Ham is a club with deep and rich traditions and I hope we maintain them. The club's co-chairmen, David Sullivan and David Gold, inherited debts approaching £100 million and have steered the club through difficult times. They know what West Ham United FC means to the supporters. They know that anyone who remembers the old Chicken Run will be sad when the last ball is kicked in the last match at Upton Park. But they know, too, how difficult it's going to be in the years ahead. I think it will be challenging to cope with the ups and downs of relegation in the future for middle-ranking clubs like West Ham. I believe stability will be harder to find but the Olympic Stadium gives us a better chance of doing so.

One of the most worrying recent trends is the decline in participation in the 11-a-side game even though men's football remains the number one sport in the country. On the flip side, there has been encouraging growth in five-a-side and mini football, and the girls' game is positively booming. Figures suggest that by 2017 women's football in this country will have more participants than any men's sport – apart, of course, from men's football. But the clubs, administrators and government bodies still have a lot to do, particularly if we are to halt the decreasing numbers in the men's 16–25 age group.

There are no easy answers but I believe that we need a big increase in the availability of third generation pitches. We need to invest in more high-quality artificial pitches – 40 to 50 a year to reverse the downward trend – so that people can play all the year round, regardless of the weather. In my view, this could transform participation levels as well as speed up the development of youngsters at grass-roots level.

CHAPTER 17

'MY GOOD FRIEND TREVOR BROOKLING!'

I N MANY WAYS I SHOULD thank Billy Bonds for my second career. When considering life after football at West Ham, I gave very little thought to television and radio as a means of supporting my family. I knew that football management wouldn't interest me or be welcomed by my family and, initially at least, the media wasn't an option. Thirty or forty years ago, the business of sports commentating for TV and radio was almost exclusively the pre-serve of media professionals.

This began to change as TV stations realised that viewers enjoyed watching and listening to former players such as Jimmy Hill, Jimmy Armfield and Bob Wilson. I was in the autumn of my playing career, had written occasional columns for the *Sunday Express* and London *Evening Standard*, and had emerged quite unwittingly as the unofficial after-match spokesman for the West Ham dressing room. This job was essentially the responsibility of

the club captain, but at West Ham the club captain was Billy
Bonds and he had never been comfortable talking to the media.
He had nothing against journalists but simply didn't enjoy talking into a microphone or facing a camera. He had all the
attributes that make a truly great captain, but at the end of every
match all he ever wanted to do was get home. He was always first
out of the dressing room. If we were playing at home, he was
driving out of the car park within 20 minutes of the end of the
match. If we had an away fixture, he would be first on the team
bus after the match.

The media professionals who wanted to talk to the manager,
captain or star of the match at the end gradually came to realise that
they were wasting their time trying to get Bill to answer their questions. He would always slip away unnoticed. If he were playing
today, he may not have got away with it so easily. Media access now
has a structured agenda and post-match interviews, for instance, are
obligatory for all managers.

Bill's reluctance meant that the journalists seeking after-match
comments at West Ham turned more and more to the other senior
statesman in the team – me. Bill was pleased that I was happy to
undertake interviews and would often tell me as he dashed off
home: 'Remember to talk to the press.' Then, as he wriggled past
the waiting press men outside the dressing room, he'd say: 'Trevor
will be out in a minute. He'll talk to you.'

So it was that I got to know the top men at BBC Radio – Peter
Jones, the match commentator, and Bryon Butler, the football correspondent who had previously been a highly regarded football writer
on the *Daily Telegraph*. I would speak to them regularly after matches
and, as retirement grew near, they used to ask what I planned to do
with the rest of my life. Apparently, the BBC were thinking of using
two match commentators at each game they covered. Would I, they
asked, be interested in trying out as a co-commentator? I gave it a try

and was co-commentating at midweek matches before I actually played my last games for West Ham. There was an art to it, but I enjoyed it.

Peter Jones taught me almost everything I know about radio commentary. Sadly, he died many years ago but even today people still recall his eloquent, mellifluous delivery with just a hint of his Welsh background. He covered all the World Cup tournaments from 1966 to 1986 and is particularly remembered for his moving coverage of the Heysel Stadium disaster in 1985. He was deeply affected, too, by the Hillsborough disaster in 1989 and a year later collapsed on the BBC launch while covering the Oxford–Cambridge boat race. He died the following day.

He was perhaps the last of the old-style broadcasters. Soon after his death, broadcasting in the UK underwent something of a revolution with the advent of Sky TV and BBC Radio Five Live and the introduction of their more informal, populist style.

What commentators like Peter Jones would have made of today's social media, I can't imagine. The internet and Twitter, along with more traditional media outlets, combine to set the tone for the professional game on a daily basis. Media interest is more intense and intrusive than it has ever been and clubs are becoming more aware of the dangers of social media. They are trying to introduce controls that make players aware of their responsibilities. Players who don't adhere to the regulations face disciplinary action in many cases.

One of the difficulties, of course, is that the fans do not have the same restrictions. They can say what they want. They can create problems and exert pressures that simply didn't exist 30 years ago. My old West Ham manager wouldn't have survived the kind of pressures that managers have to confront today. It was a more benign period in the sixties and seventies. Ron Greenwood would have hated the instabilities created by modern media outlets.

I don't know what it will lead to in years ahead. Nearly 40 per cent of Premier League players have Twitter accounts. I thought that was high until I learned the figure for academy players in the 16–21 age group – 98 per cent. Clubs are having to warn young players of the consequences if they post something inappropriate on Twitter. I think it's a minefield.

As my career at the BBC evolved, I was asked to sit in the studio on a Saturday night and give my opinions on *Match of the Day*. Des Lynam was the presenter and the top TV commentators at the time were Barry Davies and John Motson. They were all outstanding professionals. Guided by them, I quickly learned the different requirements of TV and radio. On radio you have to describe what is happening. But on TV the viewers have seen for themselves, so you have to explain *why* it happened. On TV you have to learn when to be silent and allow the pictures to tell the story. But there is a need to keep talking on radio, which means you need to be quicker and sharper. TV can be a bit more leisurely.

For me, Peter Jones was the master. When you were working with him he'd often put you on the spot with a pointed question. Many commentators will say: 'Don't you think that was disgraceful, Trevor?' You know what they are thinking and they lead you into the answer. Peter didn't give you a clue. You got no hint of what he thought. 'What about that, Trevor?' he'd say. 'What do you think of that?' You had to make up your own mind. I think he helped me become more authoritative because he allowed me to offer a fresh opinion uncluttered by what he thought personally about the issue.

I was sometimes accused of sitting on the fence. I could understand why some people felt that, but I didn't think I was avoiding giving my opinion. In all honesty, I found it difficult at first to personally criticise those I had played with over the years. I always tried to be fair and give the benefit of the doubt. If asked for my opinion I would always give it, but I didn't feel it was my place to embarrass people with my answers. I never wanted to be destructive or unfair with my comments. I always tried to be balanced and constructive. It's getting harder now to have middle-of-the-road views because today's world expects you to be opinionated. Football pundits on TV are inevitably going to alienate people – that's now part of the job. That's why I couldn't be a critic and work for the FA at the same time. Today's presenters ask the pundits questions that leave little room for manoeuvre: 'Should Sam Allardyce be sacked? Yes or no?'

There really is no hiding place where TV is concerned, particularly on the pitch. With so many cameras around the ground there is almost no element of a match that escapes the all-seeing eye of TV, whether it's on the pitch, in the dugouts or in the stands. Graeme Souness, a tough-guy Liverpool captain who is now a pundit for Sky among others, admits that the kind of challenges he got away with in the seventies would not escape the attention of modern TV. Graeme is just one of many former players now appearing regularly on your screens. It has become something of a cottage industry for dozens of former players – Lee Dixon, John Hartson, Alan Shearer, Danny Murphy, Jamie Carragher, Gary Neville, Jamie Redknapp and Martin Keown to name just a few.

From the modern game the doyens of the business are the former Liverpool centre-backs Alan Hansen, who worked for the BBC from 1991 to 2014, and Mark Lawrenson, who started in 1995. The presenter Gary Lineker joined the BBC in 1994 and has been the *Match of the Day* anchor since succeeding Des Lynam in 1999. Des, who succeeded Jimmy Hill in 1988, was a hard act to follow but Gary has made a really impressive job of it.

Des, who was born in Ireland but moved to Brighton with his family at the age of six, was a great professional with vast experience of TV and radio. He got on really well with Gary and had a great rapport with Alan Hansen. I think they played a bit of golf together. Des was good at bringing the best out of Alan. Initially,

Alan's answers were brief and abrupt. Des encouraged him to elaborate. I think Alan found it difficult at times but Des helped him become a comfortable and confident TV personality, and the football analyst to emulate over the last 30 years.

We all, of course, had our difficult moments and I'm sure that present-day players, going into an unfamiliar TV studio, are faced with many of the challenges that I confronted. Personally, it took me a while to get used to the ear piece. Whenever I got the chance I abandoned mine. For someone doing Gary's job, though, it is essential. While having a conversation on air with me, or Alan or Mark, he's also listening to his producer giving instructions through his ear piece. It takes a bit of getting used to.

I worked for the BBC from 1984 to 2003 and, because of a possible conflict of interests, had to leave when I joined the FA. I was fortunate enough to attend five World Cups and five European Championships in my 19 years with the BBC. I considered it a privilege to travel around the world watching the game I loved. What a way to earn a living!

The great professionals of my time included people like John Arlott, Henry Blofeld, Peter O'Sullevan, Brian Johnston, Eddie Waring, Harry Carpenter, Eamonn Andrews, David Coleman, Ken 'They think it's all over' Wolstenholme and, of course, the two great doyens of modern BBC radio, Mike Ingham and Alan Green. The sportsmen who became noted commentators included Geoff Boycott, Peter Alliss, Jonathan Agnew, Richie Benaud, Trevor Bailey and Dan 'Oh! I say!' Maskell.

In commentary terms I never came close to those people but I know I left a mark because you can find the evidence if you trawl the internet. Who was it who said during an exciting football commentary: 'It's great end-to-end stuff, but from side to side!'? I did. And who said: 'He chanced his arm, with his left foot!'? Me, again!

Most of the remarks you'd like to forget are eventually forgotten

by the rest of the nation. But not all. Long after his retirement from
the BBC, people will be reminding Alan Hansen of what he said
about Alex Ferguson's young side at Manchester United: 'You can't
win anything with kids!' They went on, as we know, to become one
of the greatest club teams of all time.

Hopefully, most people have forgotten about my TV encounter
with Pele in 1994. I'd met him once, in the company of Bobby
Moore, and played against him once when he was a 40-year-old in
the Team America side beaten 3-1 by England in the Bicentennial
game in Philadelphia. In 1994 I was working for the BBC at the
World Cup in the United States. Pele was a FIFA ambassador and
we secured a 'live' interview with him. He was facing the camera
and was told that he would be asked questions by someone in the
studio he knew well – a former playing opponent, Trevor Brooking.
'Oh! Fine!' said Pele to camera. 'It'll be nice to hear from my good
friend Trevor Brookling!'

Des Lynam couldn't stop laughing. He's been calling me Trevor
Brookling ever since.

CHAPTER 18

BATTERED IN BRAZIL

I had hoped to end my career in professional football on a high note in Brazil. It didn't work out that way. England's failure to progress from the World Cup's Group D was the most disappointing episode in all the years I spent with England either as a player or administrator.

It was a wake-up call, if one was needed. There were clear warning signs with England's failure to qualify for Euro 2008, followed by the woeful World Cup performance in South Africa two years later. The message was simple and brutally confirmed in Brazil: we are just not good enough at the moment.

As is usually the case in these circumstances, fingers were pointed in the aftermath of England's humiliation, all kinds of 'reasons' for failure were put forward and far-reaching solutions were explored. This time, though, there also seemed to be a reluctant acceptance that our early exit was not entirely surprising. There were calls for the inevitable enquiry into the state of the game, for reform at the Football Association and ludicrous suggestions that the failure was due to the fact that the players didn't try hard enough.

This simply wasn't the case. The players wanted to win just as much as the thousands of loyal England fans who spent fortunes following them across the world. The training and preparation programmes, organised by manager Roy Hodgson, were top class. His tactics were relevant and appropriate for the conditions and the opposition.

So, were the players up to the task facing them in Brazil? Some were clearly not comfortable at that level of competition. It *is* demanding and sometimes I wonder whether we are tough enough these days. I remember from my own playing career with England just how taxing, both physically and mentally, it can be to play against the best in the world.

Sadly, injury restricted my playing time at the 1982 World Cup to just a few minutes against Spain, but it was a real privilege to be part of an England squad that returned home from the tournament unbeaten in five matches. We conceded only one goal in those five matches and were generally considered to be one of the hardest teams to beat.

Remember, the England manager in those far-off days was Ron Greenwood, an advocate of open, attacking football. Yet he had put together a team with a resilient core, a team that would not yield to anyone. We had players like Terry Butcher, Phil Thompson, Mick Mills and Bryan Robson, all of whom could put the fear of God into the opposition.

In many ways they represented the traditional strengths of the English game. Foreign teams rarely enjoyed facing England because they knew they would have to overcome the physical challenge if they were to have any chance of winning the match.

Times change. The hard, unforgiving qualities of generations of England players, from Nobby Stiles and Norman Hunter to

Tony Adams and Stuart Pearce, have largely been eclipsed in the search for improved technical ability and enhanced attacking options. As an attacking player myself, I have supported the drive to improve technique, but England's woeful showing in Brazil brought home to me the consequences of abandoning our traditional strengths.

Yes, we are improving as an attacking team, but the fact that we are focusing more on going forward should not be allowed to undermine our defensive stability. There were times in Brazil when senior players like Steve Gerrard and Frank Lampard voiced the opinion that we were allowing opponents to get in our faces and intimidate us. This is what we used to do to opponents. There were certainly occasions in the defeats against Italy and Uruguay when we were simply unable to compete on a one-against-one basis with opposing attackers. We have to be able to do this if we hope to be successful in the modern game.

After the disappointments under Fabio Capello in South Africa in 2010, when the 1-0 defeat of Slovenia was our only win in four games, we had justifiable hopes of making better progress this time. Our form in the qualifying competition had been encouraging. We recognised that we were in one of the toughest groups in the finals and, like most other people, thought the two nations to qualify for the last 16 would come from the three obvious teams – England, Italy and Uruguay. How many people would have tipped Costa Rica to top the group?

When we faced Italy in our opening game, I remember thinking to myself that the England team could not have been better prepared. I think Roy Hodgson did a comprehensive job. His training schedules in Portugal, St George's Park and Miami were perfectly tailored to England's needs and the three warm-up matches against Peru, Ecuador and Honduras created a great atmosphere in the dressing room and good interaction between the players. The squad was as relaxed, focused and positive as I'd seen during my association with the England international set-up.

I travelled with the squad throughout the build-up period and, although not part of Roy Hodgson's coaching staff, would offer opinions if asked. As the FA's Director of Football Development I had been involved in identifying Fabio Capello's successor and believed that Roy was the right man for the job. I still do believe that.

We all thought that the opening game against Italy in the sultry heat of Manaus would be critical and we believed that we were good enough to beat the Italians. They had some senior statesmen in their team – none more stately than the 35-year-old Andrea Pirlo – but, to be fair, their fitness stood up well in the conditions. We had our chances, but conceded two soft goals and lost 2-1.

From that moment we were under pressure. Uruguay, our next opponents, had their goalscoring hero Luis Suarez returning from injury to face us. They were in our faces from the kick-off, but when Wayne Rooney equalised I thought we might go on to win. Instead, an unlikely series of events, culminating with Steve Gerrard's touch inadvertently playing Suarez onside, conspired to produce Uruguay's winning goal for Steve's Liverpool team-mate.

After just seven days of competition, with many teams still to play their second qualifying game, we knew we would be returning home whatever the result of our final match with Costa Rica. Daniel Sturridge could have scored a hat-trick against them, but didn't. We drew 0-0, ended up bottom of the group and went home with our tail between our legs. One point from nine was an awful return. We were bitterly disappointed. But it's a results business and our results weren't good enough.

So where do England go from here? There are issues still to address but I think we now have a structure in place that could produce significant results within a decade. I think the European

298 | TREVOR BROOKING

Championship of 2016 is going to be too early for us, but I firmly believe that we will be serious challengers at the 2018 World Cup or the 2020 European Championship.

I think our grass-roots structure is now as good as any in Europe and our emphasis on youth development is already beginning to pay dividends. For instance, Roy's invitation to Jon Flanagan and John Stones to join England's World Cup preparations in Miami meant that ten of the 25 players training there were 22 or under. Roy is leading us in the right direction and to my way of thinking youngsters like Jack Wilshere, Alex Oxlade-Chamberlain, Luke Shaw, Ross Barkley and Raheem Sterling are among those who could look forward to playing in several major tournaments in the years ahead.

Certainly, from an attacking point of view, the England manager is going to have a greater depth of talent to choose from in a few years. This should be just one of the benefits to emerge from the overhaul of the coaching programme. We have new structures in place, with more staff and an emphasis on technical development. The Premier League academies are investing in upgrading their coaching programmes and hopefully we will see long-term benefits in terms of quality English graduates coming through the system.

I think in the last two or three years we've made as much progress as we did in the previous seven or eight. In coaching terms it's been a bit of a political roller coaster, but the big turning points came in 2008 when we failed to qualify for the European Championship and 2010 when we had a poor World Cup campaign in South Africa. We revamped the youth coaching modules – the three age groups are 5-11, 12-16 and 17-21 – and started making changes at grass-roots level.

The lack of progress at 5-11 was evident to me, so that became the initial priority. We developed a skills programme and the support of Tesco allowed us to employ 150 full-time junior coaches nationwide. In time the success of this programme encouraged professional academy clubs to adopt similar schemes, and now we are starting to see an improvement in the quality of young players emerging from this age group.

The most significant problem now is in the 12-16 age group, where the challenge involves transferring the ball skills developed in small-sided games to adult pitches. What we don't want are youngsters, who've learned good technique on small pitches, suddenly hitting long passes simply because they are playing on bigger pitches. Even though England's Under-17s have been successful, the real problem for me is still in this middle age group when the kids reach their teens. At 16, when they get their scholarship at a club, so many are simply not advanced enough to be challenging for a first-team place at 18 or 19. More are coming through now, but sadly the depth is still not there among English youngsters.

I believe those in the 17-21 age group should be good enough to play first-team football. If we bring them through the first two phases properly there is no reason why they should be overlooked. One of the key problems was that the two younger age groups were usually coached on a part-time basis. With that in mind, we managed to include, as part of the Elite Player Performance Plan, the ruling that each club should employ an additional four full-time coaches – two for each of the younger age group levels. The result of this is that full-time coaches now have the time to assess and observe older age groups and therefore recognise the standards required for successful graduates.

We are still not stretching youngsters enough in the two younger age groups. To do this we need top-quality coaches but to attract the best we have to offer salaries of around £40,000 a year. Presently, those working with the younger age groups earn £15-20,000 a year. We are losing the better ones because they want to work with the oldest age group where they can earn £40-50,000. If we have a concentration of the best coaches in the 17-21 group, it follows that a lot of their teaching talent will be wasted because the players they are working with will not be of the required standard. You can be the best coach in Europe but if the quality of the players you are coaching is not high you haven't got much chance, have you?

The fact is that we can produce players good enough to win trophies. For all the problems, the Under-17 age group was a beacon of optimism during my 11 years at the FA. In 2010 they went through the season unbeaten and won the UEFA Under-17 title for the first time. They won it again in 2014. John Peacock, the FA's head of coaching and a specialist in youth development, was the coach on both occasions.

England had never won the Under-17 title, or its Under-16 predecessor, when John took them to Liechtenstein for the final tournament in 2010. They were crowned champions with a 2-1 win against Spain, completing a run of 11 straight victories that season, including five in the final tournament. Spain were highly fancied to win and their senior squad travelled from their 2010 World Cup warm-up base in Austria to support the youngsters.

A fine individual goal from Connor Wickham clinched the title for England and secured him UEFA's Golden Player of the Tournament award. The last England youngster to win this was Wayne Rooney back in 2002. The success in 2010 was a sign that we were moving in the right direction. It was England's first European title since the Under-18 triumph of 1993 – the year most of the 2010 squad were born – with a group of young hopefuls that included five future stars: Sol Campbell, Gary Neville, Paul Scholes, Robbie Fowler and Nicky Butt.

All five played for England at senior level, winning nearly 300 caps between them. Hopefully, graduates from the 2010 squad will make similar progress. Certainly, the Everton midfield player Ross Barkley has made an outstanding start to his career and there were others, like Birmingham goalkeeper Jack Butland, Chelsea's Josh McEachran and West Brom's Saido Berahino, who all caught my eye in Liechtenstein.

Four years after that success the Under-17s did it again. This time the venue was Malta. Fifty-three nations participated in a two-round qualification stage to determine which seven teams would join Malta in the final tournament. Having safely reached the last eight, England then beat Malta 3-0 and Turkey 4-1. We lost 2-0 to the Netherlands but still qualified for the semi-final, where goals from Chelsea's Dominic Solanke and Fulham's Patrick Roberts gave us a 2-0 victory over Portugal.

In the final we met the Netherlands again. We drew 1-1 – Solanke scoring his fourth goal of the tournament – and then finally overcame England's penalty curse by winning the shoot-out 4-1. It was a tremendous performance by our lads and underlined the improvements being made at youth level. Apart from Solanke and Roberts, others who impressed included Isaiah Brown of Chelsea and Josh Onomah of Tottenham.

With a bit of good fortune, Roy Hodgson should be able to call upon these emerging youngsters and in the future his successors should be able to reap the benefits of a coaching and development structure that is as good as you could find anywhere. I took a lot of satisfaction from the opening of the FA national training centre at St George's Park on 330 acres near Burton upon Trent. The idea for such a facility had been around for years and it came to fruition when the professional game finally recognised the decline in the numbers and quality of young English players. The centre was officially opened by the Duke and Duchess of Cambridge in October 2012 and is now the base for all coaching and development work undertaken by the FA, and is the training and preparation ground for the England national teams. We have received lots of plaudits for the quality of the facilities at St George's Park.

David Bernstein, who began his brief reign as FA chairman in January 2011, was an influential figure in establishing the development programmes. He understood what we needed to do and was a source of great encouragement. He also gave me the opportunity to recruit key members of the coaching team. I brought Gareth Southgate back as Under-21 coach and appointed West Brom's Dan Ashworth as the FA's director of elite development. I believe both men can make significant long-term contributions. We now have really top-class professionals on the coaching staff to face the challenges ahead and I think that in the coming years we will have the opportunity to enhance the quality and quantity of young English players.

The coaching of footballers during my time as a player was much more straightforward than it is today. Many players from my era hung up their boots, studied the coaching manuals, took the courses, qualified for the badge and were ready to work. Twenty or thirty years ago a retired top player would walk into a dressing room and have instant credibility because of his playing reputation. It's not as simple as that today. Dealing with players can be a minefield. Most of them are multi-millionaires who are taking advice from battalions of agents, lawyers, accountants and other advisors. Those not already millionaires are intent on achieving that status as quickly as possible.

For the coach, trying to establish a relevant working relationship with a large group of players has become a complex business; far too complex for one man. Most Premier League clubs now have teams of coaching assistants fulfilling different roles. It's no different with the FA and England. That's why Roy Hodgson strengthened his coaching staff with people like Dave Reddin and Steve Peters. Dave is the new head of performance services at the

FA. He is an expert in strengthening the mindset of sportsmen. He helped British Olympians and England's 2003 Rugby World Cup winners. He looks after sports science and performance analysis. Psychology is also an important part of his remit. Remember, England went out of tournaments in penalty shoot-outs in 1990, 1996, 1998, 2004, 2006 and 2012.

That was why Roy brought in Steve Peters, a specialist sports psychologist. Twenty-five years ago a coach would have thought he was undermining his own position by bringing a sports psychologist into the dressing room. Steve has carried out consultancy work in a wide range of sports, but it was his involvement in British cycling that propelled him into the public eye. Before joining the FA he had already worked closely with Steve Gerrard and snooker champion Ronnie O'Sullivan.

Compared to the days when I played, the back-room staff is now vast. Apart from coaches, there are physiotherapists, masseurs, doctors, security teams and video experts. Every England player in Brazil watched video analysis of everything he'd done in each game. That was the individual analysis, player by player. Each grouping was also analysed, so that the back four, for instance, saw video clips of them working together as a unit. That is something in the modern game as valuable to the coach as the work done by physios and masseurs.

All these people are part of the team and the team has to function as a cohesive unit. Before the England party left for Brazil, all the staff met with Roy to address the importance of maintaining confidence and optimism throughout the tournament. It's often the masseurs and physios who unwittingly become the 'agony aunts' to some of the players. Unhappy players often share their grumbles with the staff in the treatment room. Steve Peters stressed how crucial it was for the staff to react in a positive, optimistic and united fashion if any of the players started complaining. Players love to moan – about food, boredom, training, being left out of the team, anything. I know because I was a player! The only complaint voiced in Brazil as far as I know was about the time it took to travel from the team hotel to the training ground. It was about 40 minutes with a police escort. To be honest, there was little to complain about – apart from the results!

I think Roy, his staff and the players worked well as a unit. Most days I watched Roy working on the training ground and there is no doubt that he is a coach of huge experience and knowledge, with a deep interest in coach education. He always attends the major UEFA coaching seminars. A highly respected figure in the top echelons of the game, he is able to put his ideas across to players in a challenging and stimulating fashion.

I was involved in the process of appointing him. He was the only candidate we interviewed. He was the right man for the job. When it was obvious that we were not going to progress from the group stage in Brazil, the FA immediately voiced their support for him. I think it was important that we did that because it quickly rendered irrelevant any 'Roy must go' campaign. The FA chairman Greg Dyke made it clear that Roy would remain with the FA for at least the next two years.

I think Roy did his best with the players available to him. Some argued a case for the inclusion in the squad of Chelsea's John Terry and Ashley Cole. Their experience might have improved us in some areas of the field. But my own view is that the advantages of introducing a youngster like Luke Shaw to the World Cup and tournament football outweighed in the long term any benefit that might have accrued had John and Ashley been included. This is a transitional period for the England team and the progression will only come about if you bring in fresh blood. Our youngsters had the appetite and attitude in Brazil, but couldn't quite deliver. Their time will come.

What so pleased me was the way Roy embraced the youth policy. Hopefully he and his youngsters will enjoy some reward at the 2016 Euros in France but, if not, I'm sure future England managers will benefit. It's a long time since the late Bobby Robson steered England to the 1990 World Cup semi-finals and even longer since Alf Ramsey's team won the Jules Rimet trophy for the only time in 1966.

To be fair, the senior team hasn't got close to winning anything during my 11 years at the FA. Sven-Goran Eriksson was probably the closest, in the 2004 Euros in Portugal. A young Wayne Rooney scored two goals against Switzerland and, another two against Croatia before breaking a metatarsal in the quarter-final with Portugal. Sol Campbell had a goal disallowed and when the match ended 2-2 after extra time, David Beckham and Darius Vassell missed their shots in the penalty shoot-out. We played really well that day and I thought we should have won.

Sven's best result was the 5-1 victory over Germany in a World Cup qualifier in Munich in September 2001. It was a stunning result and Michael Owen claimed a hat-trick. Sven was a 4-4-2 man. He favoured two front runners, like Owen and Emile Heskey, who played together that day. I liked Sven. He had a good sense of humour, was very easy-going and created a relaxed environment when the players gathered. There were few rules, but no one took advantage. I don't think I ever saw him lose his temper but beneath that calm exterior he was desperate to win. In the context of England coaches of the modern era, I think he was pretty successful.

Steve McClaren was on the payroll as Sven's assistant and was one of the five candidates for the big job when Sven left the FA. Sven had been England's first foreign manager and there was a long debate about the qualities of the available English coaches. The selection panel asked me for my choice. I favoured a British coach and selected Northern Ireland's Martin O'Neill, who was between jobs. He had been manager of Celtic and was about to join Aston Villa.

The other candidates were the Portugal manager, 'Big Phil' – Luiz Felipe – Scolari, and three English coaches: Alan Curbishley, Sam Allardyce and Steve McClaren. Scolari was at the bottom of my list. I thought it was a bit early in his career for Steve McClaren, so Alan Curbishley was my choice of the English coaches. The Premier League representatives on the selection panel – Dave Richards, David Dein and Noel White – were keen on Scolari, so I stepped away from the process.

Brian Barwick, the FA's chief executive, went out to Portugal to interview Scolari. The media found out and in the frenzy that followed Scolari decided to withdraw his name. The selection panel then decided to go for Steve. I didn't think it was the right time for him. He appointed Terry Venables as his assistant. It was a brave move but I didn't think it was an ideal mix. The two years with Steve in charge didn't really work. I think he would admit now that it was a little too early for him, but he's a talented coach and has proved that with Middlesbrough, FC Twente and, most recently, Derby County.

Failure to qualify for Euro 2008 cost him his job. I was again involved in the process to find his successor. Brian Barwick headed a tight selection panel of just four people. There were few top-class coaches available at the time and we didn't want to be accused of 'poaching'. We considered Arsene Wenger at Arsenal. We liked Jose Mourinho at Chelsea, but he stepped away from the process. Fabio Capello was another with a huge reputation. We thought we should hear what he had to say. He came over to London and we met at Wembley. No one knew about it. He had lost his job at Real Madrid a few months earlier. We liked him and thought he would do a good job. He had an outstanding record and we were happy when he agreed to take over.

He was more of a disciplinarian than Sven. He had rules about diet, time-keeping and mobile phones. It was different to the Sven regime but the players respected him for his track record. Early results were good and as the momentum gathered everyone wanted to be involved. But the early promise faded. England performed poorly in the 2010 World Cup in South Africa, but bounced back with a good run of results in the qualifying campaign for the Euros in 2012.

England were unbeaten in nine matches in 2011 but, sadly, events over which he had little control led him to consider a future elsewhere. He was very much his own man and he resigned as manager when the FA removed the England captaincy from John Terry following allegations made against him of racial abuse.

I liked Fabio very much. He was good to socialise with. He liked a glass of wine and was knowledgeable on a range of subjects from football to art and culture. He had a good sense of humour that few outside his circle of friends would have seen. Ray Clemence and I introduced him to golf, which he grew to enjoy. If he trusted you, he was a good friend.

Like all England managers he was desperate to do well. But he recognised that the pool of English talent was getting smaller each season. I used to tell him that it will improve. I am convinced that it will. If we can maintain our progress in the development of young English players I believe we could win the World Cup again in my lifetime. I wouldn't have said that a decade ago. I've had a full and satisfying 50-year career in football and I'm particularly pleased that I had the opportunity to devote the last decade to the development of young players. The kids are the future. The game goes on and, although I have retired, I'll still feel part of it. Football has been my life but the priority now for Hilkka and me is to enjoy our retirement with our children, Collette and Warren, and our two lovely grandchildren, Harry and Amy.

CAREER STATISTICS

SIR TREVOR DAVID
BROOKING CBE

Born Barking 2 October 1948. MBE 1981 upgraded to CBE 1999, knighted 2004.

Ilford, London, Essex Boys. England Boys v West Germany 1964. West Ham United apprentice 24 July 1965, professional 2 May 1966. England Youth 1966-67 v West Germany, Scotland (twice), Italy, Spain and Yugoslavia. England Under-23 v Switzerland 1971. Football League XI v Scottish League 1974 (one goal). Full England: 47 caps, 5 goals.

Other honours: FA Cup winner's medals 1975, 1980. Cup Winners' Cup (runners-up) 1976. Football League Cup (runners-up) 1981. Second Division Championship 1981.

Season	League app gls	FA Cup app gls	Lge Cup app gls	Europe app gls	Others app gls

West Ham United

Season	League app	League gls	FA Cup app	FA Cup gls	Lge Cup app	Lge Cup gls	Europe app	Europe gls	Others app	Others gls
1967–68	25	9	3	–	–	–	–	–	–	–
1968–69	32	7	2	–	3	1	–	–	–	–
1969–70	21	4	–	–	2	–	–	–	–	–
1970–71	19	2	–	–	1	–	–	–	–	–
1971–72	40	6	4	–	10	1	–	–	–	–
1972–73	40	11	2	–	2	–	–	–	–	–
1973–74	38	6	–	–	2	–	–	–	1*	–
1974–75	36	3	8	1	3	1	–	–	3+	–
1975–76	34	5	1	–	4	1	7	3	3ˣ⁼	–
1976–77	42	4	2	–	3	–	–	–	–	–
1977–78	37	4	2	–	–	–	–	–	–	–
1978–79	21	2	1	–	–	–	–	–	–	–
1979–80	37	3	7	2	8	1	–	–	2^	–
1980–81	36	10	3	–	7	–	5	–	1ˣ	–
1981–82	34	8	2	–	5		–	–	2#	–
1982–83	1	–	–	–	–	–	–	–	–	–
1983–84	35	4	3		5	2				
Totals	528	88	40	3	55	8	12	3	12	–

Europe: Cup Winners' Cup
Others: *Watney Cup; +Texaco Cup; xCharity Shield (one game);
=Anglo–Italian Cup Winner's Cup (2 games); ^Tennent–Caledonian Cup;
#Aberdeen Tournament

England Internationals

1974 v Portugal, Argentina, East Germany, Bulgaria, Yugoslavia, Czechoslovakia (sub), Portugal.
1975 v Portugal.
1976 v Wales, Brazil, Italy, Finland, Republic of Ireland, Finland, Italy.
1977 v Holland, Northern Ireland, Wales, Italy (1 goal).
1978 v West Germany, Wales, Scotland (sub), Hungary, Denmark, Republic of Ireland.
1979 v Northern Ireland, Wales (sub), Scotland, Bulgaria, Sweden (sub), Austria, Denmark, Northern Ireland.
1980 v Argentina (sub), Wales, Northern Ireland, Scotland (1), Belgium, Spain (1), Sweden.
1981 v Spain, Romania, Hungary (2), Hungary.
1982 v Scotland, Finland, Spain (sub).
Total: 47 caps, 5 goals

Subsequent career: Newcastle Blue Star 1984-85 (1 game), Cork City 1985-86 (2 games), in Australia, Manurewa (New Zealand) (6 games), Havering Nalgo (Brentwood Sunday League).

ACKNOWLEDGEMENTS

I would like to express my sincere thanks and gratitude to the following:

My mum and dad, my brother Tony, my wife Hilkka and our children Collette and Warren;

Ron Greenwood, John Lyall and all my team-mates with West Ham and England;

Michael Hart, a loyal friend for many years, who collaborated in the writing of my autobiography;

Ian Marshall, Lorraine Jerram, Jack Rollin and all the team at Simon & Schuster UK.

I would also like to acknowledge the following publications:
Yours Sincerely by Ron Greenwood (Collins Willow); *Nearly Reached the Sky* by Steve Blowers (Football World); *Just Like My Dreams* by

John Lyall (Viking); *1966 and All That* by Geoff Hurst (Headline); *Trevor Brooking: An Autobiography* by Trevor Brooking (Pelham); *West Ham: The Elite Era* by John Helliar (Desert Island Books); *West Ham United: The Making of a Football Club* by Charles Korr (Duckworth); *Rothmans/Sky Sports Football Yearbook* – various editions (Queen Anne Press/Headline).

INDEX